BUTTERFLIES

OF THE FLORIDA KEYS

BUTTERFLIES
OF THE
FLORIDA KEYS

MARC C. MINNO and THOMAS C. EMMEL

Department of Zoology, University of Florida
Gainesville, Florida

A Mariposa Press Edition

SCIENTIFIC PUBLISHERS
Gainesville · Washington · Hamburg · Lima · Taipei · Tokyo

1993

A Mariposa Press Edition

Published by Scientific Publishers, Inc.
P. O. Box 15718
Gainesville, Florida 32604

FRONT COVER

BACK COVER

FRONT COVER
1 Atala hairstreak
2 Schaus swallowtail
3 Julia butterfly
4 Tropical hammock

BACK COVER
5 Dainty sulphur
6 Gulf fritillary
7 Giant swallowtail
8 Common Buckeye

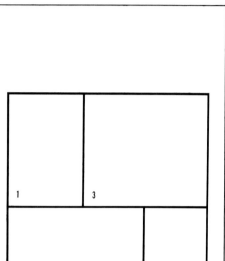

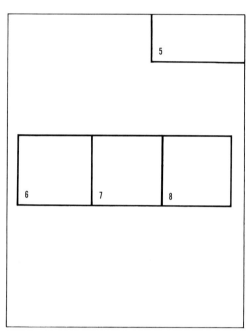

Library of Congress Cataloging-in-Publication Data
Minno, Marc C.
    Butterflies of the Florida Keys / Marc C. Minno and Thomas C. Emmel. -- Scientific Publishers
    168 p. 23 cm.
    Includes bibliographical references and index.

    1. Butterflies--Florida--Florida Keys. 2. Butterflies--Florida--Florida Keys--Identification. I. Emmel, Thomas C. II. Title.
    QL551.F6M55 1993
    595.78'9'0975941--dc20   92-9759
                                                                                      CIP

ISBN 0-945417-87-X (paper)   0-945417-88-8 (cloth)

10 9 8 7 6 5 4 3 2 1

PRINTED IN THE UNITED STATES OF AMERICA

PREFACE

Of the endless diversity of landscapes across the United States, the Florida Keys have long enjoyed a unique reputation among naturalists for their rich tropical natural history. Here, exotic butterflies such as the rare Schaus Swallowtail and long-winged heliconians, strange tropical birds, colorful land snails, miniature deer, and a wealth of offshore marine life have found a foothold next to a largely temperate continental mass. This plethora of unusual wildlife species attracts visitors from all over the world, and is a natural legacy worthy of continued preservation for future generations to enjoy.

To the butterfly enthusiast, whether his or her interests are avocational or professional, we have tried to include a full treatment of all 106 butterflies reported from the Keys. This number represents 65% of the butterflies known from the entire state of Florida, so our species accounts and illustrations will be quite useful for the south Florida area as well. Each species entry gives the full scientific name (with the author who originally described it), the common English name, the adult characteristics useful in identification, the distribution of the butterfly in the Keys and elsewhere, natural history information on behavior, host plants, immature stages, known adult flight period, flowers visited by adults, and relative abundance of the species in the Keys.

However, we have written this guide to the butterflies of the Florida Keys with a broader view in mind than just identification of the fascinating 106 recorded species. The reader will find highly readable summaries of the history of the Florida Keys, their climate, geology, biogeography, and even plant communities to be found here. Suitable precautions to take while enjoying the Keys are covered, and the themes of conservation and responsible enjoyment of the Keys' natural treasures are emphasized. A full bibliography of all literature cited in the text is given for those readers who wish further details on any point. Finally, a comprehensive check list of the butterflies of the Florida Keys will help the naturalist keep track of the species seen on each trip to this tropical island group — certainly, the only tropical islands in the western hemisphere that one can conveniently drive to and through directly from the mainland!

We hope that you will enjoy this book and will take it with you in the field every time you have the opportunity to visit south Florida and the Florida Keys. It is meant to be used; read it before you travel in the Keys, and use it to learn more about the natural environments to be found there as well as the butterflies themselves. Let us know if you find new species of butterflies, or discover new host plants or nectar sources, or even new seasonal records and distributional records on new Keys. We will gratefully acknowledge such contributions in the next edition of this book.

Gainesville, Florida   Marc C. Minno
September, 1992   Thomas C. Emmel

ACKNOWLEDGEMENTS

We gratefully acknowledge the following people and agencies for supporting our research on butterflies in the Florida Keys: James A. Sanders and Richard W. Curry of the National Park Service; David J. Wesley, Michael M. Bentzien, and Deborah Holle of the U. S. Fish and Wildlife Service; James A. Stevenson, Dana Bryan, Renate Skinner, and Jeanne M. Parks of the Florida Department of Natural Resources; and Robert M. Brantley, Don A. Wood, Brad Gruver, David A. Cook, Larry Lawrence, and Susan Cerulean of the Florida Game and Fresh Water Fish Commission. Funding was provided, in part, by the U. S. Fish and Wildlife Service, Florida Game and Fresh Water Fish Commission (Nongame Wildlife Section), the Elizabeth Ordway Dunn Foundation, and the duPont Fund. The Allyn Museum of Entomology (Florida Museum of Natural History), American Museum of Natural History, Florida State Collection of Arthropods, Snow Entomological Museum, and U. S. National Museum (Smithsonian Institution), kindly allowed access to their collections or loaned specimens for study and photography.

James K. Adams, Christa L. Anderson, Richard A. Anderson, H. David Baggett, Robert W. Brooks, John V. Calhoun, Charles V. Covell, Jr., Terhune S. Dickel, Richard Gillmore, Dale H. Habeck, Roger Hammer, Michael K. Hennessey, John B. Heppner, Michael L. Israel, Lancelot Jones, Leroy Koehn, Jacqueline Y. Miller, Lee D. Miller, Frederick H. Rindge, and Jeffrey R. Slotten kindly supplied specimens, records, or information on the Florida Keys and their butterflies. David W. Hall and Kenneth R. Langdon identified some of our plant specimens. Peter J. Eliazar, Christine Eliazar, Daryl Harrison, John B. Heppner, and Maria F. Minno were very helpful in the preparation and editing of the text and illustrations. Steve Linda provided statistical advice.

CONTENTS

INTRODUCTION

The Florida Keys are a chain of long, narrow islands that lie in an arc across the submerged tip of the Florida peninsula. These barrier islands form the outer boundary of Biscayne Bay to the north and Florida Bay to the south. White (1970) divided the Florida Keys into three groups, the High Coral Keys, the Low Coral Keys, and the Oolite Keys, based on their geology and elevation. We will refer to White's divisions as the Upper, Middle, and Lower Keys since these names seem to be more commonly used.

The upper to middle Keys are composed of a Pleistocene coral reef formation unique to this region, known as Key Largo limestone. The surface of the Lower Keys is of a different limestone, Miami oolite. The oolite was derived from deposits of precipitated calcium carbonate and bears few marine fossils. Key Largo limestone, however, contains numerous fossil corals, and was at one time quarried on Windley Key and other sites as a building stone. In the Lower Keys, Miami oolite lies on top of the Key Largo limestone (Hoffmeister and Multer, 1968). Snyder et al. (1990) note that both of these limestones can be found on the surface of Big Pine Key. Key Largo limestone forms the southern part of the island in the area around Cactus Hammock, while the rest of Big Pine Key is oolite.

On the mainland, Miami oolite (also known as rimrock or rockland) forms the Miami Rock Ridge which runs from near the northern shore of Biscayne Bay southwest into Everglades National Park. The southernmost tip of this low ridge is called Long Pine Key, because it is a pine island surrounded by everglades marshes. The oolite is often pockmarked with solution holes on the mainland. The Miami Rock ridge has a fauna and flora similar to the pine islands of the Lower Keys.

The surface of the Keys is rocky and relatively flat due to erosion by waves when these reefs were first exposed. Most land surfaces are five feet or less above sea level. On Elliott Key, the largest island within Biscayne National Park, the highest recorded elevation is 8 feet (U.S.G.S., Elliott Key Quadrangle). Maximum elevations on Key Largo range from 8 to 10 feet near the Ocean Reef Club (U.S.G.S., Card Sound Quadrangle) to 15 feet near John Pennekamp State Park (U.S.G.S., Blackwater Sound Quadrangle). Elevations in the Middle and Lower Keys are usually only about half that of the Upper Keys (White, 1970). Small areas between 12-15 feet above sea level also occur on Lignumvitae Key and Key West (Snyder et al., 1990). Slight changes in elevation are a major factor influencing the type of vegetation present.

The coral rock that forms Key Largo is estimated to be between 130,000 and 100,000 years old (Snyder, et al., 1990; White, 1970). Sea level has fluctuated greatly since this time such that much more of the Florida peninsula was exposed during glacial periods, only to become submerged when the glaciers melted. Much of south Florida and most of the Florida Keys were submersed as little as 6,000 to 4,700 years ago when sea level is thought to have been about four meters above present (Fairbridge, 1984). Smaller sea level advances also occurred 4,300 to 3,400 years before present (y.b.p.) (+3 m), 2,800 to 2,000 y.b.p. (+2 m), 1,600 to 1,200 y.b.p. (+0.6 m) and 1,000 to 600 y.b.p. (+0.3 m) (Fairbridge, 1984). Thus the flora and fauna of the Florida Keys has only been established relatively recently.

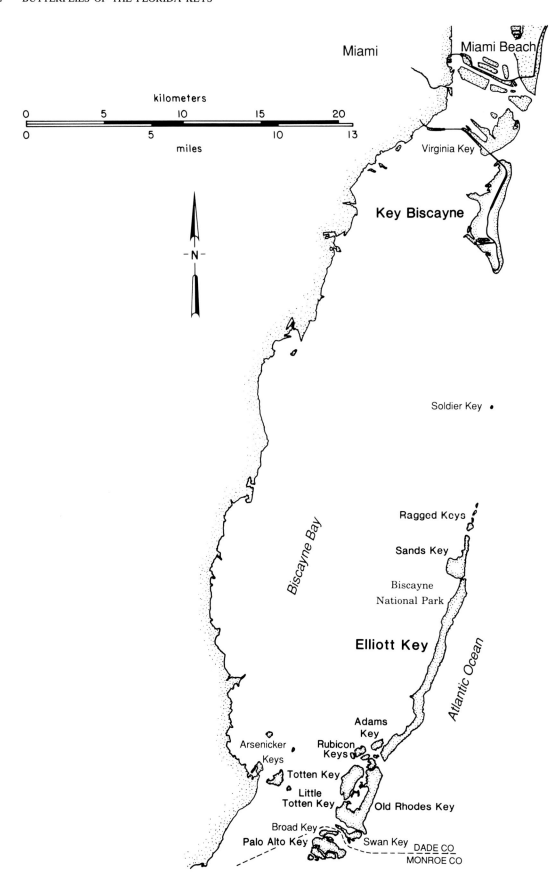

Fig. 1. The northernmost islands of the Upper Keys: the keys at Biscayne Bay, south of Miami, with adjacent Florida mainland at upper to lower left.

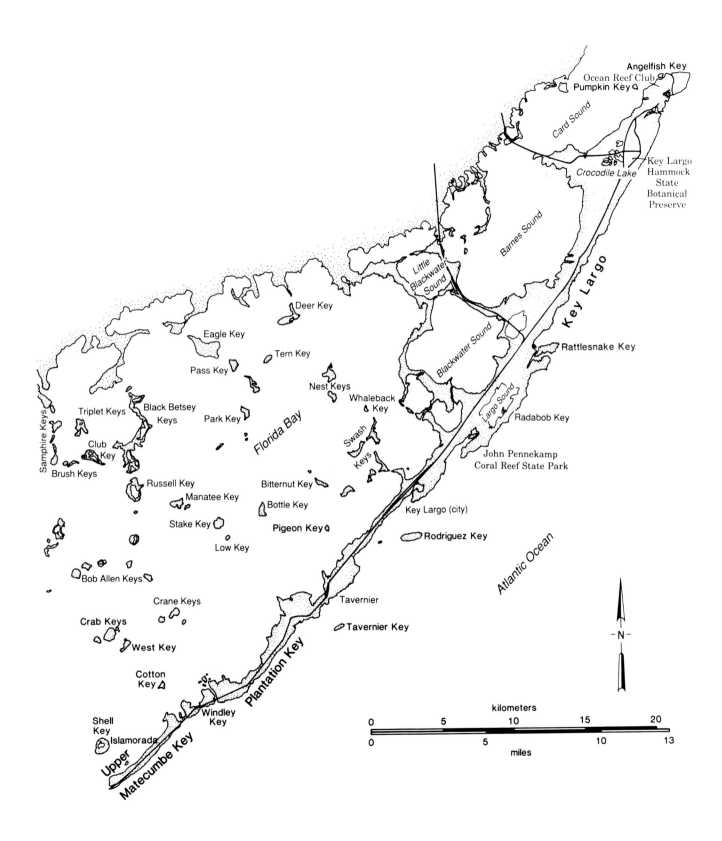

Fig. 2. The principal islands of the Upper Keys in southern Florida, and the adjacent mainland (upper left).

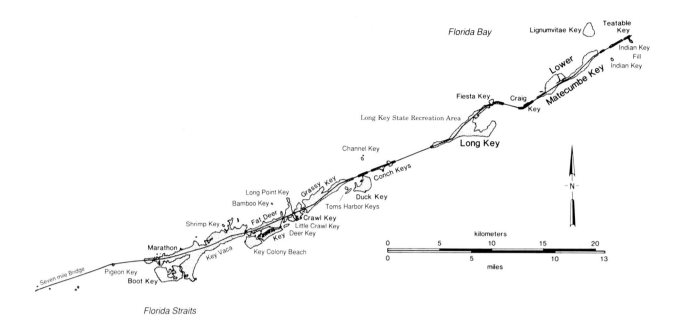

Fig. 3. Map of the Middle Florida Keys.

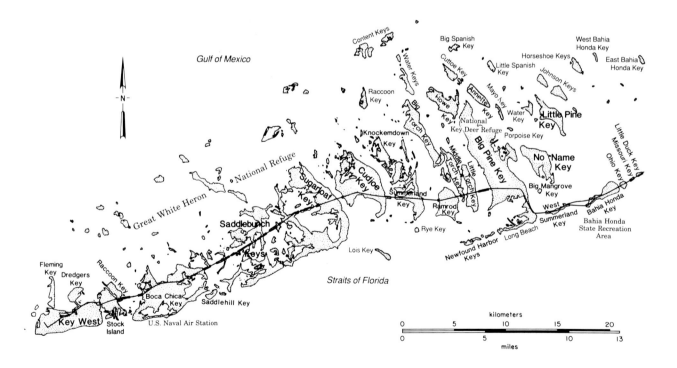

Fig. 4. The Lower Keys of southern Florida.

Soils of the Keys vary from calcareous clays (marls) to sands and organic soils. Marls are often found in low-lying, seasonally-flooded areas that support salt marshes and mangroves. Sandy soils of beaches and dunes occur along the shorelines of some Keys. The higher and drier interior areas are covered by shallow, black organic soils directly overlying limestone.

The major islands of the Upper Keys (Fig. 1 and 2) are Sands Key, Elliott Key, Totten Key, Old Rhodes Key, Key Largo, Plantation Key, Windley Key, Upper Matecumbe Key, and Lignumvitae Key. Of these, Sands Key, Elliott Key, Totten Key, and Old Rhodes Key lie within Biscayne National Park. Lignumvitae Key is a State Botanical Site administered by the Florida Department of Natural Resources. These islands are accessible only by boat. Key Largo is the largest island of the Florida Keys and is the only key connected to the mainland by roads. The major islands of the Florida Keys, from Key Largo to Key West, have been linked by bridges since about 1912.

The Middle Keys (Fig. 3) include Lower Matecumbe Key, Fiesta Key, Long Key, Conch Key, Duck Key, Grassy Key, Crawl Key, Key Vaca, Knight Key, Pigeon Key, Little Duck Key, Missouri Key, Ohio Key, and Bahia Honda Key. Most of the Middle Keys have been highly disturbed. Small parts of Long and Bahia Honda Keys are currently protected as State Parks.

The Lower Keys (Fig. 4) form a cluster of islands that are oriented more or less perpendicular to the axes of the Upper and Middle Keys. Many of the Lower Keys are accessible only by boat. Those connected by the Overseas Highway are Big Pine Key, Torch Key, Ramrod Key, Summerland Key, Cudjoe Key, Sugarloaf Key, Saddlebunch Keys, Big Coppitt Key, Boca Chica Key, Stock Island, and Key West. Big Pine Key is a particularly sensitive area, as a high number of endemics occur there. The Key Deer National Wildlife Refuge protects a variety of habitats on Big Pine Key and other islands of the Lower Keys. However, much of Big Pine Key and many other islands in the Lower Keys are also highly disturbed.

CLIMATE

Rainfall and temperatures in the Florida Keys vary seasonally (Fig. 5 and 6). The wet season typically begins in May and extends through October. The change from dry to wet or wet to dry corresponds to the change in the declination of the sun (Richards, 1952, p. 139). As the sun's insolation becomes more direct, temperatures and humidity increase and weather patterns change. June, July, and August are the warmest months.

During the wet season, most precipitation is from local thunderstorms, and on a grander scale, hurricanes. Historically, most hurricanes and tropical storms hit the Keys in August, September, and October (Fig. 7). Although thunderstorms may form nearly every afternoon on the mainland, rainfall on the Keys is much more patchily distributed, due in part to the long and narrow shapes of the islands. Generally, the Upper Keys receive slightly more rain and are a bit cooler than the Lower Keys. Average annual rainfall is 116 cm at Tavernier, and 98.6 cm at Key West (National Oceanic and Atmospheric Administration, 1988).

The dry season in south Florida usually begins in November and lasts through April. Only about one-third as much rain falls during this period. Much of the precipitation comes from storms generated by cold fronts which deposit rain over broad areas. Temperatures and humidity are lower in the dry season, with December, January, and February being the coolest months. Brief periods of below-freezing temperatures greatly affect the distribution of tropical species in south Florida. The Keys are somewhat buffered against cold temperatures by the relatively warm surrounding waters, but Charlotte Niedhauk (1973, p. 134) describes a cold wave in the mid 1930's that stunned fish in Biscayne Bay.

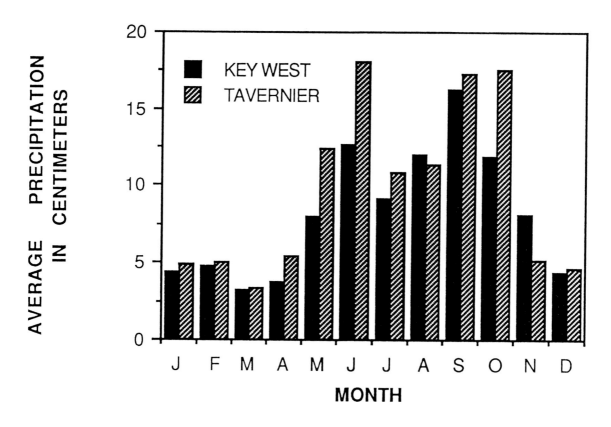

Fig. 5. Rainfall distribution in the Florida Keys.

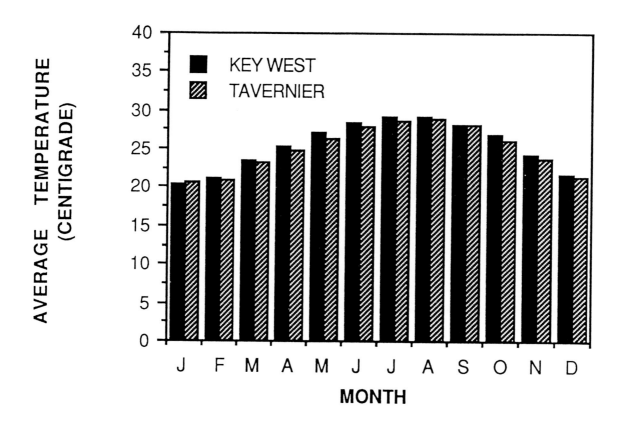

Fig. 6. Average temperatures for each month in the Florida Keys.

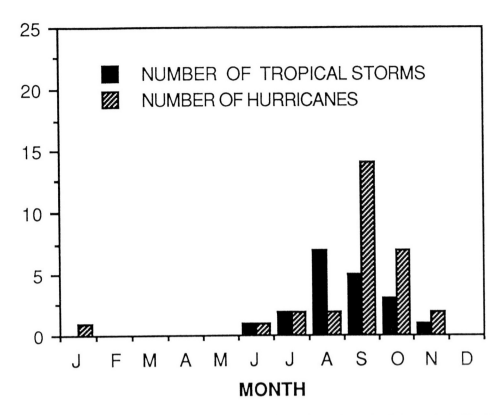

Fig. 7. The historic occurrence of major tropical storms and hurricanes for each month of the year in the Florida Keys (data from Harlen, 1979)

HISTORICAL PERSPECTIVE

The Keys have long known human occupation. The Calusa Indians who farmed, hunted, fished, built villages, and left mounds in the Keys, had dominion over this area at the time of Columbus' arrival in the New World. Juan Ponce de León claimed Florida as a territory of Spain in 1513. However, the Spanish left little of their presence in the Keys, except for shipwrecks on the reefs. The Straits of Florida were an important sea route and shipwrecks occurred with some frequency. Pirating and salvaging shipwrecks or wrecking comprised the economy of the Keys for hundreds of years (Hathway, undated). One of the more well-known pirates was Black Caesar, who gave his name to Caesar's Rock and Caesar's Creek in Biscayne National Park (Carey, 1986)

The British captured Havana in 1762, near the end of the Seven Years' War. In exchange for Cuba, Florida was given to England by the Spanish in 1763 (Ackerman, 1957). Spanish soldiers, slaves, and loyal Indians, including most of the Calusas, then left Florida for Havana and other Spanish colonies. However, British rule in Florida was to be short-lived. At the end of the American Revolution, the Treaty of Paris again returned Florida to Spain in 1783 (Tebeau, 1971). Faced with growing United States power and the decline of the Spanish empire, Florida was sold to the United States in 1818 for five million dollars. Key West was soon established as the first permanent settlement in the Keys, and by 1870 was the most populated city in Florida (Ackerman, 1957). Settlement of the Upper Keys lagged a bit, especially after the Seminoles killed the Carysfort lighthouse keeper in 1838 and massacred Dr. Henry Perrine and six others on Indian Key in 1840.

After the Seminoles retreated to the Everglades due to the efforts of the United States army to subjugate them, most of the Upper Keys were unoccupied. The U. S. Congress passed the Homestead Act in 1862 and settlers turned to farming in order to receive title to a quarter section of land. Pineapples were a major cash crop until the early 1900's when competition from Cuba and hurricanes wiped out the industry (Lancelot Jones, personal communication). Key West declined after 1886 when half of the city burned. The cigar manufacturers moved to Tampa, and a blight wiped out the sponging (Ackerman, 1957).

The Overseas Extension of the Florida East Coast Railroad linked Key West to the mainland in 1912 and revived settlement of the islands. The fertile upland areas of the Keys were planted with groves of key limes (a native of the Old World) and fields of vegetables such as peppers and tomatoes (Gentry, 1974; Lancelot Jones, personal communcation). Settlement was again hampered by disaster, however, when the Labor Day hurricane of 1935 washed out the railroad and killed hundreds of people. Competition from mainland farms then made the Keys plantations obsolete. Most of the groves and fields were abandoned and the natural vegetation regrew. Naturalized key limes (Fig. 27) and remnants of homesteads can still be found in hammocks on the Upper Keys today. The railroad line was eventually converted into the Overseas Highway.

Water was a major limitation in the Keys, as wells were difficult to dig and were often brackish. Most residents collected rainwater in cisterns. In the late 1930's a pipeline from Homestead to Key West was laid, providing a constant supply of fresh water (Ackerman, 1957). After agriculture in the Keys declined, tourism gradually evolved into the main economic base, and with it came urban growth.

Today, much of the natural communities of the Keys has been changed into habitat for humanity, and many of the areas that appear "natural" may have been a pineapple field a hundred years ago! Prior to the earliest settlers the larger Keys, such as Key Largo and Key West, evidently had a high canopy of tropical forest, up to 80 feet in height from early reports (Tomlinson, 1980), what now at most is only 40 feet in height for a few of the oldest trees remaining.

VEGETATION AND
PLANT COMMUNITIES

About 1,650 species of vascular plants, representing 177 families, occur in South Florida (Long, 1984). These include temperate species which have invaded Florida from the north, Caribbean species which have colonized the Keys and coastal mainland areas, and a small number of endemics which have evolved in Florida. Many of the vascular plants found in the Keys are widely distributed throughout the Caribbean, and in some cases, throughout tropical areas of the world. The Upper Keys seem to have fewer species of vascular plants than the Lower Keys, probably due to the lack of pineland habitats in the Upper Keys. About 300 species of vascular plants of 77 families occur naturally, or have become naturalized, in Biscayne National Park (Emmel and Minno, 1988). Dickson *et al.* (1953) record 415 species of vascular plants of 102 families from 25 of the Lower Keys. Howard (1950) found only 228 noncultivated plants on the Bimini Islands, Bahamas, which are geologically and climatologically similar to the Florida Keys, yet lie approximately 80 km east of Miami. The vegetation of the Keys may be broadly grouped into five categories as discussed below.

Fig. 8. Open sand beaches are rarely found in the Florida Keys. Eroded limestone, as here on the Atlantic coast of Elliott Key, is a more common shoreline habitat.

BEACHES: Sand beaches are uncommon in the Keys, but occur in small patches, usually on the ocean side of the islands, all the way to Key West. A few of these sites have sea oats (*Uniola paniculata*), the characteristic grass of dunes along the Florida coast, but more often they are vegetated with weedy plants such as *Bidens alba*, *Cenchrus* spp., and other grasses and herbs. Limestone forms some beaches in areas exposed to the eroding influence of waves and high winds (Fig. 8). During low tides, pools on these outcrops lend a glimpse of the rich marine life in the surrounding water. Above the tide line, rocky beaches are often vegetated with small mangroves and salt marsh species. Beach habitats provide larval host plants and adult nectar sources for a variety of butterflies, including *Strymon martialis*, *Eresia frisia*, and *Panoquina panoquinoides*. In addition, *Ascia monuste*, *Phoebis sennae*, and other migratory species often use open coastal areas as dispersal routes.

Fig. 9. Seashore Dropseed (*Sporobolus virginicus*) grows adjacent to salt marshes on northern Key Largo.

Fig. 10. Salt marsh habitats are frequently flooded at high tide or after storms, and are richly populated by mosquitoes as well as a half dozen butterfly species.

Fig. 11. A lush growth of saline-adapted plants in the salt marsh habitat. Insets show (a) saltwort (*Batis maritima*, Bataceae), a typical salt marsh inhabitant and food plant of the Eastern Pigmy Blue, and (b) glasswort (*Salicornia virginica*, Chenopodiaceae) in the salt marsh.

Fig. 12. Mangroves are commonly encountered along the shoreline in the Florida Keys. These are Red Mangroves (*Rhizophora mangle*, Rhizophoraceae) on Elliott Key in Biscayne National Park.

Fig. 13. Inside a mangrove thicket at the edge of Watson Hammock on Big Pine Key. The Black Mangrove Buckeye (*Junonia evarete*) uses Black Mangrove (*Avicennia germinans*) as a larval foodplant.

Fig. 14. The leaves and fruit of a Red Mangrove. Like most mangroves, this species has viviparous seedlings: the seed develops into a miniature plant while still attached to the parental tree. When mature, the seedlings drop off the fruit to float on the water to another site, where they implant thenselves and grow.

WETLANDS: Mangroves and salt marshes (Fig. 10) are the principal wetland habitats of the Florida Keys. Red mangrove (*Rhizophora mangle*, Fig. 12, 14), black mangrove (*Avicennia germinans*, Fig. 13), white mangrove (*Laguncularia racemosa*), and buttonwood (*Conocarpus erecta*) grow in salty soils throughout the Keys and along the southern mainland coast. Red mangrove usually grows on mud flats and sheltered tidal zones. The other mangrove species occur in slightly more elevated areas of the shoreline or in seasonally-flooded portions of the islands. All four mangroves may form either relatively pure stands or occur in mixed forests. Where mangroves are dense, little light penetrates through the canopy, and no shrub or herb layers occur. However, in more open stands, shrubs and herbs may be abundant.

Typical salt marsh shrubs include saltbush (*Baccharis* spp.), bay cedar (*Suriana maritima*), and Christmas berry (*Lycium carolinianum*). The herbs, sea oxeye (*Borrichia* spp.), saltwort (*Batis maritima*, Fig. 11), and glasswort (*Salicornia* spp.) tend to dominate salt marsh areas not covered by mangroves. Vines such as rubber vine (*Rhabdadenia biflora*), wild allamanda (*Urechites lutea*), whitevine (*Sarcostemma clausum*), and coin vine (*Dalbergia* spp.) may also be abundant in salt marshes. Salt marsh plants tend to be evergreen perennials, possibly because the specialized physiology necessary for survival in a saline environment makes vegetative growth too metabolically expensive to shed leaves annually. Loope (1980) found more species in flower in mangrove habitats during the wet season (May - October) than during the winter on Elliott Key. *Phocides pigmalion, Ascia monuste, Junonia evarete, Brephidium pseudofea, Panoquina panoquinoides,* and *Strymon martialis* are among the butterflies that typically occur in salt marshes.

HAMMOCKS: Upland areas of the Florida Keys are vegetated with forests of tropical trees and shrubs. These tropical hardwood forests or hammocks (Fig. 15, 16, 19) usually grow in thin organic soil that overlays limestone rock. Tropical hammocks have a dense canopy which moderates temperatures and humidity. Trees such as poisonwood (*Metopium toxiferum*, Fig. 26), mahogany (*Swietenia mahagoni*), gumbo limbo (*Bursera simaruba*, Fig. 17), and wild tamarind (*Lysiloma latisiliquum*, Fig. 31) often form the upper canopy. Numerous shrubs and smaller trees such as crabwood (*Gymnanthes lucidus*), torchwood (*Amyris elemifera*), pigeon plum (*Coccoloba diversifolia*), wild coffee (*Psychotria nervosa*, Fig. 34), and stoppers (*Eugenia* spp.) make up the understory. Few herbs grow in the understory of tropical hammocks except for some cactus (*Cereus* spp.) and the naturalized exotic *Agave decipiens*. Species of *Smilax, Passiflora,* and *Chiococca* are common vines in tropical hammocks. Epiphytic orchids and bromeliads (Fig. 18) are sometimes abundant in tropical hammocks, especially near ecotones with mangrove forests and saltmarshes.

Loope (1980) found that most hammock species flower between March and July on Elliott Key. Late in the dry season, many of the canopy trees shed their leaves and the hammocks appear to be rather open and sunny. However, during the wet season, when the trees and shrubs

---

Fig. 15. Tropical hardwood hammocks are composed of tropical tree species growing in higher areas of the Keys. The canopy overhead may be quite dense, as in this hammock on Totten Key. **Fig. 16.** Along the edge of the tropical hardwood hammock bordering Highway 905 on northern Key Largo, one can see the fullest development of this forest, with some trees over 50 feet high. **Fig. 17.** Gumbo Limbo (*Bursera simaruba*), a typical tree species in tropical hardwood hammocks, has flaking, thin, red bark on its trunks, as in these large individuals on Big Pine Key. **Fig. 18.** Spanish Moss hangs from the oldest tropical hammock trees on Old Rhodes Key in Biscayne National Park. **Fig. 19.** One of the finest remaining stands of tropical hardwood hammock is on Lignumvitae Key. **Fig. 20.** The reddish-flushed underside of the Schaus Swallowtail (*Papilio aristodemus ponceanus*) is quite distinctive from that of its nearest relatives in the Keys. **Fig. 21.** The Zebra (*Heliconius charitonius*) is found everywhere in the tropical hardwood hammocks of south Florida and the Keys. **Fig. 22.** Strangler Fig (*Ficus aurea*) is found in tropical hardwood hammocks and is a larval host of the Ruddy Daggerwing (*Marpesia petreus petreus*) in south Florida and the Keys.

are actively growing, these forests appear to be dense and dark. Understory trees and shrubs tend to be evergreen. Under very dry conditions, as frequently occurs during March, April and early May, the leaves and new growth of understory shrubs may wilt and droop, but most recover when the rains commence. *Papilio aristodemus ponceanus, Papilio andraemon bonhotei, Papilio cresphontes, Hemiargus thomasi, Eunica tatila, Appias drusilla, Polygonus leo* and many other butterflies are associated with tropical hardwood forests.

TROPICAL PINELANDS: Some islands of the Lower Keys support pinelands similar to those found in the rimrock areas of the mainland. This community consists of open stands of *Pinus elliottii* with a rich variety of grasses and herbs below (Fig. 35). Characteristic shrubs include locust berry (*Byrsonima lucida*), sweet acacia (*Acacia farnesiana*), *Croton linearis* (Fig. 42), and small palms (*Serenoa repens, Coccothrinax argentata*, and *Thrinax* spp., Fig. 38 and 45). Sawgrass (*Cladium jamaicense*) frequently grows in wet areas within the pinelands. Pinelands that are not burned every few years quickly become overgrown with broadleaved trees and shrubs, and gradually grow into hardwood hammocks (Alexander, 1967). Pineland habitat does not currently exist in the Upper Keys, although pine logs and stumps were found in an area of northern Key Largo (25°17'25" latitude, 80°17'40" west longitude) as recently as the year 1953

Fig. 35. Pineland community scene on Big Pine Key.
Fig. 36. *Cassia chapmanii* (Fabaceae), a larval foodplant for *Phoebis* sulphur butterflies in the pineland habitat.

Fig. 23. The Florida Purple Wing (*Eunica tatila tatilista*) rests on a tree trunk in the hammocks on Old Rhodes Key. **Fig. 24.** The Bahama Swallowtail (*Papilio andraemon bonhotei*) basks on a leaf in the tropical hammock on Elliott Key. **Fig. 25.** Morning Glory (*Ipomoea indica*) vines in the family Convolvulaceae attract the larger skipper species to nectar along the edge of the hammock on northern Key Largo. **Fig. 26.** Poisonwood (*Metopium toxiferum*) is in the same family (Anacardiaceae) as poison ivy, and is one of the hazards to watch for in tropical hardwood hammocks. **Fig. 27.** Key Lime (*Citrus aurantifolia*, family Rutaceae), naturalized on Totten Key, is a host plant to the Giant Swallowtail (*Papilio cresphontes*), and produces limes useful in making pies. **Fig. 28.** Wild Lime (*Zanthoxylem fagara*, family Rutaceae) looks quite different from *Citrus*, but has the same aromatic oils and is an important host plant for the Schaus Swallowtail, Bahama Swallowtail, and Giant Swallowtail. **Fig. 29.** Torchwood (*Amyris elemifera*) is the main host plant of the Schaus and Bahama Swallowtails in the hammocks of the Florida Keys. **Fig. 30.** Manchineel (*Hippomane mancinella*, family Euphorbiaceae) has poisonous milky sap which can cause severe skin irritation: it grows on shell mounds near the coastline. **Fig. 31.** Wild Tamarind (*Lysiloma latisiliquum*) grows in hammocks on the Keys and in the Everglades. **Fig. 32.** The Gulf Fritillary *(Agraulis vanillae)* flies abundantly in tropical hardwood hammocks; its larvae feed on passionvines. **Fig. 33.** The Long-tailed Skipper (*Urbanus proteus proteus*) perches in hammock clearings. **Fig. 34.** Wild Coffee (*Psychotria nervosa*) has small white flowers visited by both Schaus and Bahama swallowtails in hammock habitats.

Fig. 44. Habitat destruction, here on Key Largo, has greatly altered the habitats of most of the land area of the Florida Keys.
Fig. 45. Thatch palms (*Thrinax* species), on Lignumvitae Key, occur in hammocks and along shorelines throughout the Florida Keys.

(Alexander, 1953). Pineland plants such as locust berry, silver palm, sweet acacia, bracken fern, and sawgrass can still be found in this same part of Key Largo today. *Anaea troglodyta floridalis, Strymon acis bartrami, Hesperia meskei,* and *Euphyes pilatka klotsi* are a few of the butterflies found chiefly in the pinelands of the Lower Keys.

URBAN LANDS AND DISTURBED SITES: The plant and animal communities of the Florida Keys are continually subjected to disturbance and degradation by both natural and anthropogenic means. Hurricanes and tropical storms are powerful forces that cause temporary local destruction. Ultimately, however, such storms create a greater diversity of habitats and species in the Keys. During a hurricane, high winds and flying debris strip off leaves, break branches, and uproot trees (Visher, 1925). Animals such as insects may be killed or blown or washed away. Alexander (1968) reported that after Hurricane Betsy (September 7-8, 1965) passed through Everglades National Park, a high percentage of hammock trees were severely damaged or killed from high winds and exposure to salt water. Mangrove vegetation was less affected by the storm. Large changes in the abundance of many plants were noted several months after Hurricane Betsy. Hurricanes and tropical storms are important factors in the dynamics of the terrestrial communities of the Florida Keys. It will be interesting to follow Upper Keys succession and butterfly recovery in the years following Hurricane Andrew (August 24, 1992).

Fig. 37. The tiny Key Deer still survives in the pineland on Big Pine Key. **Fig. 38.** The Silver Palm (*Coccothrinax argentata*) grows in pineland on Big Pine Key. **Fig. 39.** A male Cloudless Sulphur (*Phoebis sennae*), feeding on Lantana in a disturbed area of Big Pine Key. **Fig. 40.** The Dainty Sulphur (*Nathalis iole*) is the smallest pierid butterfly in the Americas, and flies in open disturbed habitats, including pineland. **Fig. 41.** The Fiery Skipper (*Hylephila phyleus*) is widely distributed in the Florida Keys and throughout the warmer parts of the western hemisphere. **Fig. 42.** Pineland Croton (*Croton linearis*) grows on Big Pine Key and serves as the larval foodplant for Bartram's Hairstreak (*Strymon acis bartrami*) and the Florida Leaf Wing (*Anaea troglodyta floridalis*). **Fig. 43.** The Ceraunus Blue (*Hemiargus ceraunus antibubastus*) flies in pinelands and open disturbed sites in the Keys.

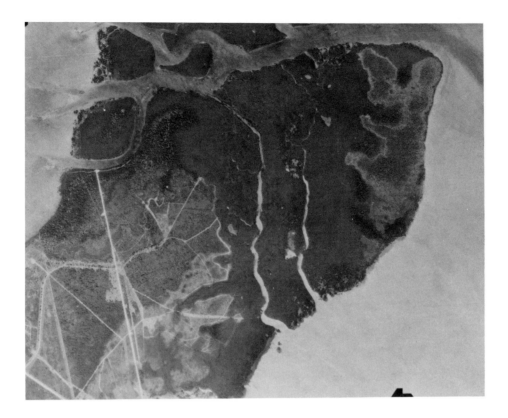

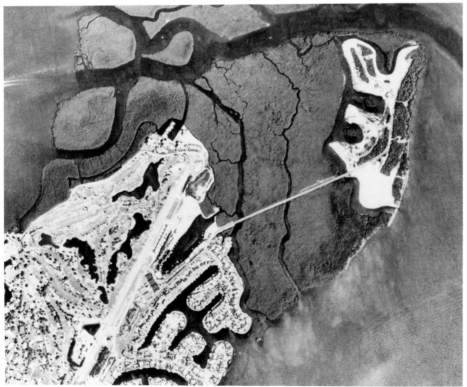

Fig. 46. An aerial photograph of northern Key Largo in 1952. Note the network of roads and trails through the tropical hardwood hammock (lower left quadrant). The hammock on Angelfish Key (upper right) was still pristine at the time this photo was taken.

Fig. 47. The same aerial view of northern Key Largo in 1984, showing the replacement of nearly all of the hammock by the Ocean Reef Club development.

In historic times, the natural communities of the Keys have been greatly changed by anthropogenic forces such as the cutting of trees for lumber and charcoal, clearing for agriculture, and replacement by residential and urban communities. Even islands currently protected from development such as Lignumvitae Key and Elliott Key have had a long history of anthropogenic disturbance. Charlotte Niedhauk (1969) writes as follows:

"At one time a colony of about 25 people farmed quite a few acres of Elliott Key, growing pineapples, rock melons, tomatoes, and key limes. Ship builders from the mainland cut madeira and Jamaica dogwood timbers and 'natural knees' there. At one time hogs that had been abandoned by the early settlers became wild and dangerous but they did kill all of the rattlesnakes on the key. When the Overseas Extension of Flagler's East Coast Railroad opened up the chain of islands to Key West, Elliott Key was abandoned except for a few fishermen and passing smugglers, rumrunners, and other lawless characters."

It seems likely that few if any of the major islands of the Florida Keys are still in a pristine state, and most have been greatly altered (Fig. 44, 46, 47). Anthropogenic disturbance has had a negative effect on species native to the Florida Keys and has allowed many exotic species to become established (Peck and Howden, 1985).

Many hammock trees have tremendous regenerative powers and quickly resprout after cutting. Some, such as gumbo limbo, may be propagated by cutting limbs and planting the cut ends in soil. Thus sections of tropical hammock which have simply been cut are likely to regrow and appear much the same in a short period of time. Burning or bulldozing of tropical hammock has much more devastating and long-lasting effects. Not only are the trees killed, but much of the soil is burned or scraped or eroded away. These areas first become covered with weedy herbs such as Spanish needles *(Bidens alba)*, blue porterweed (*Stachytarpheta jamaicensis)*, goosegrass *(Eleusine indica)*, sandspurs (*Cenchrus* spp.), and spurges (*Chamaesyce* spp.). Woody shrubs, especially cheese shrub *(Morinda royoc)* and wild sage *(Lantana involucrata)*, vines (*Ipomoea indica*, Fig. 25; *Cardiospermum halicacabum*, Plate 28), and young hammock trees such as poisonwood (*Metopium toxiferum*, Fig. 26), mahogany (*Swietenia mahogani*), wild tamarind (*Lysiloma latisiliquum*, Fig. 31), and black bead (*Pithecellobium keyense*) gradually come to dominate. Eventually, the tropical hammock regrows, but species composition is most likely to be somewhat different from the original forest. Butterflies associated with open, weedy habitats include *Eresia frisia, Junonia genoveva, Phoebis philea, Tmolus azia, Strymon melinus, Siproeta stelenes, Leptotes cassius, Agraulis vanillae, Phyciodes phaon, Eurema daira, Nathalis iole, Cymaenes tripunctus, Hylephila phyleus, Lerema accius, Pyrgus oileus,* and *Urbanus* spp.

THE KEYS BUTTERFLY COMMUNITY

ORIGIN OF THE WEST INDIAN BUTTERFLIES

Since many modern butterfly and moth families are worldwide in distribution, it is thought that the Lepidoptera arose in Mesozoic times before the break up of the supercontinent Pangaea (Shields and Dvorak, 1979; Miller and Miller, 1989). The Mesozoic Era (Age of Dinosaurs) ended rather abruptly (in geological terms) approximately 65 million years ago. Alvarez *et al.* (1980) proposed that the mass extinction of dinosaurs and other groups at the end of the

Cretaceus Period (144 to 65 million years ago) was caused by the collision of a comet or large asteroid with the earth. This theory, based on elevated levels of iridium (a rare element on earth) in a worldwide clay layer some 65 million years old, has gained considerable acceptance. New studies aimed at determining the site of the collision indicate that the impact probably took place in the Caribbean region, perhaps on the present-day Yucatan peninsula or just north of Venezuela (Hildebrand and Boynton, 1991). Such a catastrophic event would certainly have wiped out most living organisms in the region and may help to explain current patterns of biogeography.

The Caribbean region is geologically complex (Perfit and Williams, 1989). The islands of the West Indies have not always been located where they are today, but are slowly moving in relation to themselves and to the continents due to the dynamics of the earth's crust. Some islands such as Cuba and Hispaniola are actually composed of several smaller land masses that have collided and joined together.

Two competing theories attempt to explain current patterns of biogeography in the West Indies (Williams, 1989). Dispersalists argue that the butterfly faunas of the West Indies were derived by chance dispersal over water of mainland species (Scott, 1972; Brown, 1978). On the other hand, supporters of vicariance (Rosen, 1976; Shields and Dvorak, 1979) hold that the major islands of the West Indies were once connected to the mainland, but have since split off and moved to their present positions through plate tectonics. After millions of years of isolation, the islands have lost some species by natural extinction, while new taxa have arisen. As Perfit and Williams (1989) point out, we may never be able to reconstruct the geological history of the Caribbean region in sufficient detail to determine which theory is more correct. Miller and Miller (1989) proposed a combination of vicariance and dispersal to explain butterfly distributions

---

Table 1. Butterflies endemic to tropical Florida.

FAMILY	SPECIES
Hesperiidae	*Ephyriades brunnea floridensis* Bell and Comstock *Euphyes pilatka klotsi* Miller, Harvey, and Miller *Hesperia meskei* (Edwards) (un-named subspecies) *Phocides pigmalion okeechobee* (Worthington)
Lycaenidae	*Eumaeus atala florida* Röber? *Hemiargus thomasi bethunebakeri* Comstock and Huntington *Strymon acis bartrami* (Comstock and Huntington) *Strymon columella modestus* (Maynard)
Nymphalidae	*Anaea troglodyta floridalis* Johnson and Comstock *Dryas iulia largo* Clench *Heliconius charitonius tuckeri* Comstock and Brown
Papilionidae	*Papilio aristodemus ponceanus* Schaus
Pieridae	*Aphrissa statira floridensis* (Neumoegen) *Appias drusilla neumoegenii* (Skinner) *Ascia monuste phileta* (Fabricius) *Phoebis agarithe maxima* (Neumoegen)

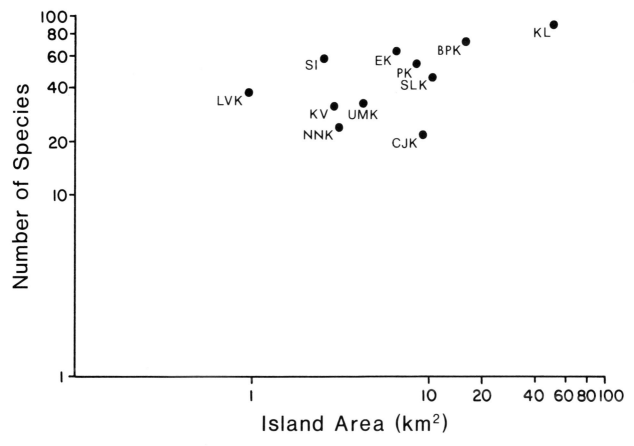

Fig. 48. The log number of species-log area relationships of butterflies recorded from 11 of the most intensively collected Florida Keys. A least square regression analysis did not find a significant linear relationship. Abbreviations are Big Pine Key (BPK), Cudjoe Key (CJK), Elliott Key (EK), Key Largo (KL), Key Vaca (KV), Lignumvitae Key (LVK), No Name Key (NNK), Plantation Key (PK), Stock Island (SI), Sugarloaf Key (SLK), Upper Matecumbe Key (UMK).

in the West Indies. The West Indian flora and fauna of Florida has certainly become established by dispersal over water from Cuba and the Bahamas, adding a twist to the dispersalist's viewpoint in that island species have colonized the mainland (Scott, 1972).

DIVERSITY

Neotropical forests, especially those of Amazonian Peru and western Brazil, house the greatest diversity of butterflies on earth (Lamas, 1983; Emmel and Austin, 1990). The West Indies are part of the Neotropical Region, but they support a relatively low number of species (Scott, 1972; Shields and Dvorak, 1979). Scott (1986b) lists 102 butterflies from tropical Florida, 171 from Cuba, 60 from Andros, 23 from Grand Bahama, 126 from Jamaica, 177 from Hispaniola, and a total of 279 species from the West Indies. After exhaustive field work in Haiti and the Dominican Republic, Schwartz (1989) lists 193 species from Hispaniola, the highest number known for any of the West Indian islands. In contrast, Trinidad, which is about the same size as Andros but lies only about 15 km off the coast of Venezuela, has over 650 species (Scott, 1972).

Although the fauna of the West Indies is depauperate, many butterflies occur nowhere else. Perhaps 45% of the species and 12% of the genera are endemic to the West Indies (Scott, 1972; Miller and Miller, 1989). Endemism of butterflies in Florida is at a finer scale. There are no species restricted only to the state, but unique races of at least 15 tropical butterflies are confined mostly to Florida (Table 1).

Table 2. Species-area relationships for butterflies in the Florida Keys. Area estimates are from Peck and Howden (1985), except that of Elliott Key which is from Emmel and Minno (1988).

LOCATION	AREA IN Km²	NUMBER OF SPECIES	NUMBER OF SPECIES PER Km²
Lignumvitae Key	0.98	41	41.84
Stock Island	2.54	57	22.44
Key Vaca	2.93	31	10.58
No Name Key	3.13	24	7.67
Upper Matecumbe	4.30	33	7.67
Elliott Key	6.45	62	9.61
Plantation Key	8.60	52	6.05
Cudjoe Key	9.19	21	2.29
Sugarloaf Key	10.17	44	4.33
Big Pine Key	17.19	68	3.96
Key Largo	55.13	84	1.52

The West Indian fauna may be impoverished due to the limited resources of island habitats and the distance from the mainland. According to the model of island biogeography proposed by MacArthur and Wilson (1963, 1967), the number of species present on an island is balanced between the rate of immigration and the rate of extinction. Larger islands, closer to the mainland, should have more species than those that are smaller and farther away.

Correlations between the size of certain Caribbean islands and the number of butterfly species present were found by Munroe (see Gilbert, 1984, p. 42) and Scott (1972, 1986b). Peck and Howden (1985) found significant species-area relationships for scavenging scarab beetles in the Florida Keys. However, we have not found this to be true for the Keys butterflies (Figure 48). When our data for the eleven most intensively-collected keys (Table 2) were analyzed using a least squares linear regression of the natural log numbers of species of butterflies against the natural log island areas, we found no relationship (log y = 3.4087 + 0.1958 logX; r^2 = 0.23; p < 0.1330) using the Proc Reg proceedure of PC-SAS version 6.03 (Ray, 1982). Scott's (1986b) equation for estimating the number of species present on islands of the West Indies (Species = 7.955 Area$^{.258}$) yields values that are about 3.5 times too low for the Florida Keys. Island size is probably less of a factor determining butterfly distributions in the Keys, due to the close proximity of other islands and the mainland. Should a butterfly become locally extinct, nearby sources of new stock allow for rapid recolonization. Many of the butterflies of the Keys are good dispersers, and fly over short expanses of ocean with ease.

Table 2 presents a list of the better-known Keys, their area, the number of butterfly species recorded, and the number of species per square kilometer. One of the smaller islands, Lignum-vitae Key, has fewer species than Key Largo, the largest island. However, if numbers of species are compared on a per square kilometer basis, Lignumvitae Key has a tremendous fauna relative to the other Keys. Thus, even small islands in the Florida Keys may be relatively species-rich, if sampled over a long period of time. Simply adding more area of habitats already present seems to contribute little toward increasing species richness. When Scott's (1986) data are converted into species per square kilometer, it is apparent that the Florida Keys have the richest fauna in the West Indian region. Only Bimini with 1.11 species/km^2 and Little Cayman Island, Saba, and Isle des Saintes, each with 1 species/km^2, even come close to the diversity of the Keys. Gerberg and Arnett (1989) listed 164 species of butterflies for Florida. We report in this work 106 species from the Florida Keys or 65% of the butterflies known for the entire state. From this point of view, the Keys have a remarkably diverse fauna for so small an area.

Our knowledge of the butterflies of the Florida Keys has been accumulating since the first lepidopterists visited this region during the 1800's. Even though over one hundred species have been reported from the Keys, the number of different butterflies that one is likely to encounter during a single visit is much lower. On some of our trips, we have found the Keys to be practically barren of butterflies. For instance on 22 September 1991, MCM visited Big Pine Key and saw a single butterfly, *Phoebis agarithe*, in one hour of searching. In northern Florida one week later (28 September 1991), MCM found 31 species behind a shopping plaza in the city of Gainesville in the same amount of time! Much effort and luck are needed in order to develop a Keys butterfly list of any great length, and yet there is always the possibility that one may encounter some splendid tropical butterfly that has never before been seen in Florida. That is the excitement of studying butterflies in the Keys.

DYNAMICS

Several authors (Leston *et al.*, 1982; Schwartz, 1987) have attempted to analyze the dynamics of the Keys butterfly community by categorizing the species as residents or immigrants. Although the extremes of the residency spectrum may be well-defined (endemics vs. strays), classifying the status of species that are not always present, but occur more than a few times, becomes highly subjective.

It is clear from our observations that there is a tremendous turnover in butterfly species in the Florida Keys. On Elliott Key, species such as *Phyciodes tharos, Anartia jatrophae, Nathalis iole, Eurema daira, Eurema nise, Eurema lisa, Kricogonia lyside, Danaus gilippus, Danaus plexippus, Battus polydamas, Urbanus dorantes, Urbanus proteus, Hemiargus ceraunus,* and others will suddenly appear in abundance after being absent for months or years at a time. These butterflies will often lay eggs and produce one or two generations before dying out. Equally remarkable, some species such as *Eurema daira* are resident on Key Largo, but transient on nearby Elliott Key, even though apparently suitable habitat and host plants are available.

Some species well-adapted to the Keys such as *Appias drusilla, Ascia monuste, Papilio aristodemus ponceanus,* and *Eunica tatila tatilista,* exhibit boom and bust population cycles, where there are good years of high abundance (coupled with migratory tendencies in some) followed by intervals of low abundance. The Keys seem to be a harsh environment to colonize, perhaps due to salt spray, high winds, unpredictable rainfall, high temperatures, seasonal influx

Table 3. The monthly occurrence of butterflies in the Florida Keys. (An "X" indicates adults of the species have been found in the Keys during that particular month; dashes denote absence or that no data are available. Species are listed in alphabetical order (by genus name) to facilitate reference.)

SPECIES	J	F	M	A	M	J	J	A	S	O	N	D
HESPERIIDAE: HESPERIINAE												
Asbolis capucinus	X	X	X	X	X	X	X	X	X	X	X	X
Atalopedes campestris	X	X	X	X	X	X	--	X	X	X	X	X
Calpodes ethlius	X	--	--	--	--	--	--	--	X	X	X	X
Copaeodes minima	--	--	--	--	X	--	--	--	--	--	X	X
Cymaenes tripunctus	X	X	X	X	X	X	X	X	X	X	X	X
Euphyes arpa	X	--	X	X	X	--	--	--	--	X	--	X
Euphyes pilatka	X	X	X	X	X	--	--	--	X	X	--	X
Hesperia meskei	X	--	X	X	X	X	--	--	X	X	X	X
Hylephila phyleus	X	X	X	X	X	X	X	X	X	X	X	X
Lerema accius	X	X	X	X	--	--	X	X	X	X	X	--
Lerodea eufala	X	X	X	X	--	--	X	X	X	X	X	X
Nastra neamathla	--	--	--	--	--	--	--	--	X	X	--	--
Nyctelius nyctelius	--	--	--	X	--	--	--	--	--	--	--	--
Oligoria maculata	X	X	X	X	X	X	X	--	X	X	X	X
Panoquina ocola	--	--	--	--	--	X	--	--	X	X	--	X
Panoquina panoquin	--	--	--	--	--	--	--	--	--	X	--	X
Panoquina panoquinoides	X	X	X	X	X	X	X	--	X	X	X	X
Polites vibex	--	--	--	--	--	X	--	--	--	--	--	--
Wallengrenia otho	X	X	X	X	X	X	X	X	X	X	X	X
HESPERIIDAE: PYRGINAE												
Epargyreus zestos	--	X	X	X	X	X	X	X	X	X	X	X
Ephyriades brunnea	X	X	X	X	X	X	X	X	X	X	X	X
Erynnis zarucco	X	X	X	X	X	X	X	X	X	X	X	X
Gorgythion begga	X	--	--	X	--	--	--	--	--	--	--	--
Phocides pigmalion	X	X	X	X	X	X	X	X	X	X	X	X
Polygonus leo	X	X	X	X	X	X	X	X	X	X	X	X
Pyrgus oileus	X	X	X	X	X	X	X	X	X	X	X	X
Staphylus hayhurstii	--	--	--	--	X	--	--	X	X	--	X	X
Urbanus dorantes	X	X	X	X	X	X	X	X	X	X	X	X
Urbanus proteus	X	X	X	X	X	X	X	X	X	X	X	X
LIBYTHEIDAE												
Libytheana bachmanii	--	--	--	--	--	--	--	--	--	X	X	--
LYCAENIDAE: EUMAEINAE												
Calycopis cecrops	X	X	X	X	X	X	--	X	X	X	X	X
Chlorostrymon maesites	X	--	X	--	X	X	X	X	X	X	X	X
Chlorostrymon simaethis	X	X	X	--	X	X	X	--	X	--	X	X
Electrostrymon angelia	X	X	--	X	X	X	X	X	X	X	X	X
Electrostrymon endymion	--	X	--	--	--	--	--	--	--	--	--	--
Eumaeus atala	--	--	X	--	--	X	--	--	--	--	--	--
Strymon acis	X	--	X	X	X	X	X	X	X	X	X	X
Strymon columella	X	X	X	X	X	X	X	X	X	X	X	X
Strymon limenia	--	--	--	X	X	--	--	--	--	--	--	X
Strymon martialis	X	X	X	X	X	X	--	X	X	X	X	X
Strymon melinus	X	X	X	X	X	X	X	X	X	X	X	X
Tmolus azia	X	--	X	--	X	--	X	X	X	X	X	X
LYCAENIDAE: POLYOMMATINAE												
Brephidium isophthalma	X	X	X	X	X	X	X	X	X	X	X	X
Hemiargus ammon	--	--	--	--	--	--	--	--	--	--	--	--
Hemiargus ceraunus	X	X	X	X	X	X	X	X	X	X	X	X
Hemiargus thomasi	X	X	X	X	X	X	X	X	X	X	X	X
Leptotes cassius	X	X	X	X	X	X	X	X	X	X	X	X
NYMPHALIDAE: CHARAXINAE												
Anaea troglodyta	X	X	X	X	X	X	X	X	X	X	X	X
NYMPHALIDAE: DANAINAE												
Danaus eresimus	--	--	--	--	X	X	--	--	--	--	X	--
Danaus gilippus	X	X	X	X	X	X	X	X	X	X	X	X
Danaus plexippus	X	--	X	--	--	--	--	--	X	X	X	X

SPECIES	J	F	M	A	M	J	J	A	S	O	N	D
NYMPHALIDAE: HELICONIINAE												
Agraulis vanillae	X	X	X	X	X	X	X	X	X	X	X	X
Dryadula phaetusa	--	X	--	--	--	--	--	--	--	--	--	--
Dryas iulia	X	X	X	X	X	X	X	X	X	X	X	X
Heliconius charitonius	X	X	X	X	X	X	X	X	X	X	X	X
NYMPHALIDAE: NYMPHALINAE												
Anartia chrysopelea	--	X	--	X	--	--	--	--	--	--	--	--
Anartia jatrophae	X	X	X	X	X	X	X	X	X	X	X	X
Diaethria clymena	--	--	--	--	--	--	X	--	--	--	--	--
Eresia frisia	X	--	X	X	X	X	X	X	X	X	X	X
Eunica monima	--	--	X	--	X	--	X	X	--	X	X	X
Eunica tatila	X	X	X	X	X	X	X	X	X	X	X	X
Euptoieta claudia	--	--	X	--	X	--	--	X	--	X	--	--
Hamadryas amphichloe	--	--	--	--	--	--	X	--	--	--	--	--
Junonia coenia	X	X	X	X	X	X	X	X	X	X	--	X
Junonia evarete	X	X	X	X	X	X	X	X	X	X	X	X
Junonia genoveva	X	X	--	--	--	--	--	--	X	X	X	X
Limenitis archippus	--	--	--	--	X	--	--	X	--	--	--	--
Marpesia chiron	--	--	--	--	--	--	--	--	--	X	--	--
Marpesia eleuchea	--	--	--	--	--	--	--	--	--	X	--	--
Marpesia petreus	X	X	--	--	X	X	X	X	X	X	X	--
Phyciodes phaon	X	X	X	X	X	X	X	X	X	X	X	X
Phyciodes tharos	X	X	X	X	X	X	X	X	X	X	X	X
Siproeta stelenes	X	X	X	X	X	X	--	--	X	X	X	X
Vanessa atalanta	X	X	X	--	X	--	--	--	--	X	--	--
Vanessa cardui	--	--	--	X	--	--	--	--	X	X	X	X
Vanessa virginiensis	--	--	--	--	X	X	--	--	--	X	--	--
NYMPHALIDAE: SATYRINAE												
Hermeuptychia sosybius	--	--	--	--	--	--	--	--	--	X	--	--
Neonympha areolata	--	--	--	--	--	--	--	--	--	X	--	--
PAPILIONIDAE: PAPILIONINAE												
Battus polydamas	--	--	--	X	X	X	--	--	--	--	--	--
Eurytides celadon	--	--	--	--	--	--	--	--	--	--	--	--
Eurytides marcellus	--	--	--	--	--	--	--	--	--	--	--	--
Papilio andraemon	--	--	--	--	X	X	X	X	X	X	X	--
Papilio aristodemus	--	--	X	X	X	X	X	X	--	--	--	--
Papilio cresphontes	X	X	X	X	X	X	X	X	X	X	X	X
Papilio palamedes	--	--	X	X	--	--	--	--	--	--	--	--
Papilio polyxenes	--	X	--	--	--	--	--	--	--	--	--	--
PIERIDAE: COLIADINAE												
Anteos maerula	--	--	--	X	--	--	X	X	X	--	--	--
Aphrissa orbis	--	--	--	X	--	--	--	--	--	--	--	--
Aphrissa statira	--	--	--	--	--	--	--	--	--	--	--	--
Colias eurytheme	--	--	--	--	--	--	X	--	--	X	--	--
Eurema boisduvaliana	--	--	--	--	--	--	--	--	X	--	--	--
Eurema daira	X	X	X	X	X	X	X	X	X	X	X	X
Eurema dina	--	--	--	--	--	--	--	--	--	--	--	--
Eurema lisa	X	X	X	X	X	X	X	--	X	X	X	X
Eurema nicippe	--	--	--	--	X	--	X	X	X	X	X	--
Eurema nise	--	--	--	X	--	X	X	--	X	--	--	--
Kricogonia lyside	--	--	--	--	--	--	X	X	X	X	--	--
Nathalis iole	X	--	X	X	X	X	X	X	X	X	X	X
Phoebis agarithe	X	X	X	X	X	X	X	X	X	X	X	X
Phoebis philea	X	X	--	X	X	X	X	--	X	X	X	X
Phoebis sennae	X	X	X	X	X	X	X	X	X	X	X	X
PIERIDAE: PIERINAE												
Appias drusilla	X	X	X	X	X	X	X	X	X	X	X	X
Ascia monuste	X	X	X	X	X	X	X	X	X	X	X	X
Pieris rapae	X	--	--	--	--	--	--	--	--	--	--	--
Pontia protodice	--	--	X	--	X	--	--	--	--	--	--	--
RIODINIDAE: RIODININAE												
Calephelis virginiensis	--	--	--	--	--	--	--	X	--	--	--	--

Table 4. The distribution of butterflies in the Florida Keys. (An "X" indicates that an individual species has been recorded from an island; dashes represent absence or lack of data.)

Columns are grouped as **UPPER KEYS** (Sands Key, Elliott Key, Adams Key, Totten Key, Old Rhodes Key, Key Largo, Plantation Key, Windley Key, Upper Matecumbe Key, Lignumvitae Key), **MIDDLE KEYS** (Lower Matecumbe Key, Craig Key, Long Key, Grassy Key, Fat Deer Key, Key Vaca Key, Bahia Honda Key), and **LOWER KEYS** (No Name Key, Big Pine Key, Big Torch Key, Ramrod Key, Summerland Key, Cudjoe Key, Sugarloaf Key, Geiger Key, Boca Chica Key, Stock Island, Key West, Fleming Island, Ballast Key).

Species	Sands	Elliott	Adams	Totten	Old Rhodes	Key Largo	Plantation	Windley	Upper Matecumbe	Lignumvitae	Lower Matecumbe	Craig	Long	Grassy	Fat Deer	Key Vaca	Bahia Honda	No Name	Big Pine	Big Torch	Ramrod	Summerland	Cudjoe	Sugarloaf	Geiger	Boca Chica	Stock Island	Key West	Fleming	Ballast
HESPERIIDAE: HESPERIINAE																														
Asbolis capucinus	-	X	X	-	-	X	X	-	X	X	X	-	-	-	-	X	-	X	X	-	-	X	X	X	-	X	X	X	-	-
Atalopedes campestris	-	X	-	-	-	X	X	-	X	-	-	-	-	-	-	X	-	X	X	-	X	X	X	X	X	X	X	X	-	-
Calpodes ethlius	-	X	-	-	-	X	-	-	-	-	-	-	-	-	-	-	-	-	X	-	-	-	-	-	-	-	X	X	-	-
Copaeodes minima	-	X	-	-	-	X	-	-	-	-	-	-	-	-	-	-	-	-	-	-	-	-	-	-	-	-	-	-	-	-
Cymaenes tripunctus	-	X	-	-	-	X	X	-	X	-	-	-	X	-	-	X	-	X	X	-	-	X	-	X	-	-	X	X	-	-
Euphyes arpa	-	-	-	-	-	-	-	-	-	-	-	-	-	-	-	-	-	-	X	-	-	-	-	X	-	-	-	-	-	-
Euphyes pilatka	-	-	-	-	-	X	-	-	-	-	-	-	-	-	-	-	-	X	X	X	-	-	X	X	-	-	X	-	-	-
Hesperia meskei	-	-	-	-	-	-	-	-	-	-	-	-	-	-	-	-	-	-	X	-	-	-	-	X	-	-	-	-	-	-
Hylephila phyleus	-	X	-	-	-	X	X	-	X	-	-	-	-	-	-	-	-	-	X	-	-	X	X	-	X	-	X	X	-	-
Lerema accius	-	X	-	-	-	X	X	-	X	-	-	-	-	-	-	X	-	-	X	-	-	-	-	X	-	-	X	-	-	-
Lerodea eufala	-	-	-	-	-	X	X	X	X	-	-	-	-	-	-	-	-	-	X	-	X	X	X	X	-	-	X	-	-	-
Nastra neamathla	-	X	-	-	-	X	-	-	-	-	-	-	-	-	-	-	-	-	-	-	-	-	-	-	-	-	-	-	-	-
Nyctelius nyctelius	-	-	-	-	-	-	-	-	-	-	-	-	-	-	-	-	-	-	X	-	-	-	-	-	-	-	-	-	-	-
Oligoria maculata	-	-	-	-	-	-	-	-	-	-	-	-	-	-	-	-	-	X	X	-	-	X	X	X	-	-	-	-	-	-
Panoquina ocola	-	X	-	-	-	X	X	-	-	-	-	-	-	-	-	-	-	-	X	-	-	-	-	-	-	-	-	-	-	-
Panoquina panoquin	-	-	-	-	-	-	-	-	-	-	-	-	-	-	-	-	-	-	X	X	-	-	-	-	-	-	-	-	-	-
Panoquina panoquinoides	-	X	-	-	-	X	X	-	-	X	-	-	-	-	-	X	-	X	X	X	-	X	-	X	X	-	X	X	-	-
Polites vibex	-	-	-	-	-	X	-	-	-	-	-	-	-	-	-	-	-	-	-	-	-	-	-	-	-	-	-	X	-	-
Wallengrenia otho	-	X	-	-	-	X	X	X	X	-	X	-	X	-	-	X	-	X	X	-	X	X	X	X	X	-	X	X	-	-
HESPERIIDAE: PYRGINAE																														
Epargyreus zestos	-	X	-	-	-	X	X	-	X	X	-	-	X	-	-	X	-	-	X	-	-	-	-	X	X	-	X	X	-	-
Ephyriades brunnea	-	-	-	-	-	X	-	-	-	-	X	-	-	-	-	-	-	X	X	-	X	X	X	-	X	-	X	-	-	-
Erynnis zarucco	-	-	-	-	-	-	-	-	-	X	-	-	-	-	-	-	-	-	X	-	-	X	-	X	X	-	X	X	X	-
Gorgythion begga	-	-	-	-	-	X	-	-	-	-	-	-	-	-	-	-	-	-	-	-	-	-	-	-	-	-	-	-	-	-
Phocides pigmalion	-	X	X	X	X	X	X	-	X	X	-	-	-	-	-	X	X	X	X	-	-	X	X	X	-	X	X	X	-	-
Polygonus leo	-	X	-	-	-	X	X	X	X	-	-	-	-	-	-	X	X	X	X	-	-	-	-	X	X	-	X	X	-	-
Pyrgus oileus	-	X	-	-	-	X	X	-	X	X	X	-	-	-	-	-	-	-	X	-	-	-	-	-	-	-	X	X	-	-
Staphylus hayhurstii	-	-	-	-	-	X	-	-	-	-	-	-	-	-	-	-	-	-	-	-	-	-	-	-	-	-	-	-	-	-
Urbanus dorantes	-	X	-	-	-	X	X	X	-	X	-	-	-	-	-	X	-	X	X	-	-	X	X	X	-	-	X	X	-	-
Urbanus proteus	-	X	X	-	-	X	X	X	X	X	-	-	-	-	-	X	-	X	X	-	-	-	-	X	X	-	X	X	-	-
LIBYTHEIDAE																														
Libytheana bachmanii	-	X	-	-	-	X	-	-	-	-	-	-	-	-	-	-	-	-	-	-	-	-	-	-	-	-	-	-	-	-
LYCAENIDAE: EUMAEINAE																														
Calycopis cecrops	-	X	-	-	-	X	X	-	-	-	-	-	-	-	-	-	-	X	X	-	-	X	X	X	-	-	X	-	-	-
Chlorostrymon maesites	-	-	-	-	-	X	X	-	-	-	-	-	-	-	-	-	-	-	-	-	-	-	-	-	-	-	X	X	-	-
Chlorostrymon simaethis	-	X	-	-	-	X	X	-	-	-	-	-	-	-	-	-	-	-	-	-	-	-	-	-	-	-	X	X	-	-
Electrostrymon angelia	-	-	-	-	-	-	-	-	-	-	-	-	-	-	-	-	-	-	X	-	-	-	-	-	-	-	X	X	-	-
Electrostrymon endymion	-	-	-	-	-	-	-	-	-	-	-	-	-	-	X	-	-	-	-	-	-	-	-	-	-	-	-	-	-	-
Eumaeus atala	-	X	-	-	-	X	-	-	-	-	-	-	-	-	-	-	-	-	-	-	-	-	-	-	-	-	-	-	-	-
Strymon acis	-	-	-	-	-	X	-	-	-	-	-	-	-	-	-	-	-	-	X	-	-	-	-	-	-	-	-	-	-	-
Strymon columella	-	X	-	-	-	X	X	-	-	X	X	-	-	-	-	X	-	-	X	-	-	X	X	X	X	X	X	X	X	X
Strymon limenia	-	-	-	-	-	-	-	-	-	-	-	X	-	-	-	-	-	-	X	-	-	-	-	-	-	-	X	X	-	-
Strymon martialis	-	X	-	-	-	X	-	-	-	X	-	-	-	-	-	X	-	-	X	-	-	X	X	X	-	-	X	X	-	X
Strymon melinus	-	X	-	-	-	X	X	X	X	X	X	-	-	-	-	X	-	-	X	-	-	X	X	X	-	-	X	X	-	-
Tmolus azia	-	-	-	-	-	X	X	-	-	-	-	-	-	-	-	-	-	-	-	-	-	-	-	-	-	-	-	X	-	-
LYCAENIDAE: POLYOMMATINAE																														
Brephidium isophthalma	-	X	-	-	-	X	X	-	X	X	-	-	-	-	-	-	-	-	X	-	-	-	-	X	X	-	X	X	-	-
Hemiargus ammon	-	-	-	-	-	-	-	-	-	-	-	-	-	-	-	-	-	-	X	-	-	-	-	-	-	-	-	-	-	-
Hemiargus ceraunus	-	X	-	-	-	X	X	-	-	X	-	-	-	-	-	X	-	-	X	-	-	-	-	X	-	-	X	X	-	-
Hemiargus thomasi	-	X	X	-	X	X	X	-	-	X	-	-	-	-	-	-	-	-	X	-	-	-	-	X	X	-	X	-	-	-
Leptotes cassius	-	X	-	-	-	X	X	X	X	X	X	-	X	-	-	X	X	X	X	-	-	X	X	X	X	X	X	X	-	-
NYMPHALIDAE: CHARAXINAE																														
Anaea troglodyta	-	-	-	-	-	-	-	-	-	-	-	-	-	-	-	-	-	-	X	-	-	-	-	-	-	-	-	-	-	-

	Sands Key	Elliott Key	Adams Key	Totten Key	Old Rhodes Key	Key Largo	Plantation Key	Windley Key	Upper Matecumbe Key	Lignumvitae Key	Lower Matecumbe Key	Craig Key	Long Key	Grassy Key	Fat Deer Key	Key Vaca Key	Bahia Honda Key	No Name Key	Big Pine Key	Big Torch Key	Ramrod Key	Summerland Key	Cudjoe Key	Sugarloaf Key	Geiger Key	Boca Chica Key	Stock Island	Key West	Fleming Island	Ballast Key
NYMPHALIDAE: DANAINAE																														
Danaus eresimus	--	X	--	--	--	X	--	--	X	--	X	--	--	--	--	--	--	--	--	--	--	--	--	--	--	--	--	--	--	--
Danaus gilippus	--	X	--	--	X	X	X	--	X	X	--	--	--	--	--	X	--	--	X	--	--	--	X	--	U	--	--	X	X	--
Danaus plexippus	--	X	X	--	--	X	--	--	--	X	--	X	--	--	--	X	--	X	X	--	--	--	X	--	--	--	--	X	X	--
NYMPHALIDAE: HELICONIINAE																														
Agraulis vanillae	--	X	--	--	X	X	X	X	X	X	X	--	--	--	--	X	X	--	X	--	--	--	X	--	--	--	--	X	X	--
Dryadula phaetusa	--	--	--	--	U	--	--	--	--	--	--	--	--	--	--	--	--	--	--	--	--	--	--	--	--	--	--	--	--	--
Dryas iulia	--	X	X	X	--	X	--	--	--	X	--	--	--	--	--	X	--	X	X	--	--	--	X	--	--	--	--	X	--	--
Heliconius charitonius	--	X	X	X	X	X	X	X	X	X	--	--	X	--	--	X	X	X	X	--	--	--	X	X	--	--	--	X	--	--
NYMPHALIDAE: NYMPHALINAE																														
Anartia chrysopelea	--	--	--	--	--	--	--	--	--	--	--	--	--	--	--	--	--	--	X	--	--	--	--	--	--	--	--	X	--	--
Anartia jatrophae	--	X	--	--	--	X	X	--	--	X	--	--	--	--	--	X	--	--	X	--	--	--	--	--	--	--	--	X	--	--
Diaethria clymena	--	--	--	--	--	--	--	--	--	--	--	--	--	--	--	--	--	--	--	--	--	--	--	--	--	--	--	--	X	--
Eresia frisia	X	X	X	--	X	X	X	--	X	X	X	--	--	--	--	X	--	--	X	--	--	--	--	--	--	--	--	X	X	--
Eunica monima	--	--	--	--	--	X	--	--	X	--	--	--	--	--	--	--	--	--	X	--	--	--	--	--	--	--	--	X	X	--
Eunica tatila	--	X	X	X	X	X	X	--	X	X	X	--	X	--	--	--	--	--	X	--	--	--	--	--	--	--	--	X	--	--
Euptoieta claudia	--	--	--	--	--	X	--	--	--	--	--	--	--	--	--	--	--	--	X	--	--	--	--	--	--	--	--	X	--	--
Hamadryas amphichloe	--	--	--	--	--	X	X	--	--	--	--	--	--	--	--	--	--	--	X	--	--	--	--	--	--	--	--	--	--	--
Junonia coenia	--	X	--	--	--	--	--	--	--	--	--	--	--	--	--	--	--	X	X	--	X	X	X	--	X	X	--	X	--	--
Junonia evarete	--	X	X	--	--	X	X	X	--	X	X	--	--	--	--	X	--	X	X	--	X	X	X	X	X	X	X	X	--	--
Junonia genovea	--	--	--	--	--	X	X	--	--	--	--	--	--	--	--	--	--	--	U	--	--	--	--	--	--	--	--	--	--	--
Limenitis archippus	--	X	--	--	--	X	--	--	--	--	--	--	--	--	--	--	--	--	X	--	--	--	--	--	--	--	--	--	--	--
Marpesia chiron	--	--	--	--	--	--	--	--	--	--	--	--	--	--	--	--	--	--	X	--	--	--	--	--	--	--	--	--	--	--
Marpesia eleuchea	--	--	--	--	--	--	--	--	--	--	--	--	--	--	--	--	--	--	--	--	--	--	--	X	--	--	--	--	--	--
Marpesia petreus	--	X	--	--	X	X	X	--	X	X	--	--	--	--	--	--	--	--	--	--	--	--	U	X	--	--	--	X	--	--
Phyciodes phaon	--	X	--	--	X	X	X	--	X	X	--	--	--	--	--	--	--	--	X	--	--	--	--	--	--	--	--	X	X	--
Phyciodes tharos	--	X	--	--	X	X	--	--	--	--	X	--	--	--	--	X	--	--	X	--	--	--	--	--	--	--	--	X	--	--
Siproeta stelenes	--	X	X	--	--	X	X	--	--	X	--	--	--	--	--	--	--	--	X	--	--	--	X	--	--	--	--	X	--	--
Vanessa atalanta	--	X	--	--	X	X	--	--	--	--	--	--	--	--	--	X	--	--	X	--	--	--	--	--	--	--	--	X	X	--
Vanessa cardui	--	--	--	--	--	--	--	--	--	X	--	--	--	--	--	--	--	--	X	--	--	--	--	--	--	--	--	X	X	--
Vanessa virginiensis	--	X	--	--	--	X	--	--	--	--	--	--	--	--	--	--	--	--	X	--	--	--	--	--	--	--	--	X	--	--
NYMPHALIDAE: SATYRINAE																														
Hermeuptychia sosybius	--	--	--	--	--	X	--	--	--	--	--	--	--	--	--	--	--	--	X	--	--	--	--	--	--	--	--	--	--	--
Neonympha areolata	--	--	--	--	--	X	--	--	--	X	--	--	--	--	--	--	--	--	X	--	--	--	--	--	--	--	--	--	--	--
PAPILIONIDAE: PAPILIONINAE																														
Battus polydamas	--	X	--	--	--	X	--	--	--	--	--	--	--	--	--	--	--	--	--	--	--	--	--	--	--	--	--	--	--	--
Eurytides celadon	--	U	--	--	--	--	--	--	--	--	--	--	--	--	--	--	--	--	--	--	--	--	--	--	--	--	--	X	--	--
Eurytides marcellus	--	--	--	--	--	X	--	--	--	--	--	--	--	--	--	--	--	--	--	--	--	--	--	--	--	--	--	--	--	--
Papilio andraemon	X	X	X	--	X	X	--	--	--	--	--	--	X	--	--	--	--	--	--	--	--	--	--	--	--	--	--	X	--	--
Papilio aristodemus	X	X	X	X	X	X	--	--	X	--	X	--	--	--	--	--	--	--	--	--	--	--	--	--	--	--	--	X	--	--
Papilio cresphontes	--	X	--	X	X	X	X	--	X	X	--	--	--	--	X	X	X	X	X	--	--	--	--	--	--	X	--	X	--	--
Papilio palamedes	--	--	--	--	--	X	--	--	--	--	--	--	--	--	--	--	--	--	--	--	--	--	--	--	--	--	--	X	--	--
Papilio polyxenes	--	--	--	--	--	--	--	--	--	X	--	--	--	--	--	--	--	--	--	--	--	--	--	--	--	--	--	--	--	--
PIERIDAE: COLIADINAE																														
Anteos maerula	--	--	--	--	--	X	--	--	--	--	--	--	--	--	--	--	--	--	X	--	--	--	--	--	--	--	--	X	--	--
Aphrissa orbis	--	--	--	--	--	X	--	--	--	--	--	--	--	--	--	--	--	--	X	--	--	--	--	--	--	--	--	--	--	--
Aphrissa statira	--	U	--	--	--	X	--	--	--	X	--	--	--	--	--	--	--	--	X	--	--	--	--	--	--	--	--	--	--	--
Colias eurytheme	--	--	--	--	X	X	--	--	--	--	--	--	--	--	--	--	--	--	--	--	--	--	--	--	--	--	--	--	--	--
Eurema boisduvaliana	--	--	--	--	--	X	--	--	--	--	--	--	--	--	--	--	--	--	--	--	--	--	--	--	--	--	--	X	--	--
Eurema daira	--	X	--	--	--	X	X	X	X	X	X	--	--	--	--	X	--	--	X	--	--	X	X	X	X	X	X	X	X	--
Eurema dina	--	--	--	--	--	X	--	--	--	--	--	--	--	--	--	--	--	--	X	--	--	--	--	--	--	--	--	--	--	--
Eurema lisa	--	X	X	--	--	X	X	--	--	X	--	--	--	--	--	--	--	--	X	--	--	X	X	X	--	--	X	X	--	--
Eurema nicippe	--	X	--	--	--	X	X	--	--	--	--	--	--	--	--	--	--	--	X	--	--	--	X	--	U	--	--	X	--	--
Eurema nise	--	X	--	--	--	X	X	--	--	--	--	--	--	--	--	--	--	--	X	--	--	--	--	--	--	--	--	--	--	--
Kricogonia lyside	--	X	X	--	--	X	X	--	X	--	--	--	--	--	--	--	--	--	X	--	--	--	--	--	--	--	--	--	--	--
Nathalis iole	--	X	X	--	--	X	--	--	--	X	--	--	--	--	--	--	--	--	X	--	--	--	--	--	--	--	X	X	X	--
Phoebis agarithe	X	X	X	--	X	X	X	X	X	X	X	--	X	--	--	X	X	X	X	X	--	X	--	--	--	--	--	X	--	--
Phoebis philea	--	X	--	--	--	X	X	--	--	--	--	--	--	--	--	--	--	X	X	--	--	--	--	--	--	--	--	X	--	--
Phoebis sennae	--	X	X	--	--	X	X	X	X	X	--	--	--	--	--	X	--	X	X	--	--	--	--	--	--	--	--	X	--	--
PIERIDAE: PIERINAE																														
Appias drusilla	--	X	X	X	X	X	X	X	X	X	--	--	--	--	--	--	--	X	X	X	--	X	--	--	--	--	--	X	--	--
Ascia monuste	X	X	--	--	X	X	X	--	X	X	X	--	X	--	--	X	X	X	X	--	--	--	X	--	X	X	--	X	--	--
Pieris rapae	--	--	--	--	--	--	--	--	--	--	--	--	--	--	--	--	--	--	--	--	--	--	--	--	--	--	--	--	X	--
Pontia protodice	--	X	--	--	--	X	--	--	--	X	--	--	--	--	--	--	--	--	--	--	--	--	--	--	--	--	--	--	--	--
RIODINIDAE: RIODININAE																														
Calephelis virginiensis	--	--	--	--	--	--	--	--	--	--	--	--	--	--	--	--	--	--	X	--	--	--	--	--	--	--	--	--	--	--

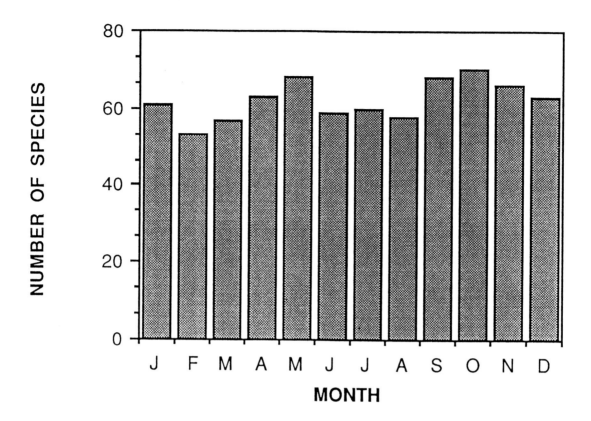

Fig. 49. Graph of the number of butterfly species in the Florida Keys recorded for each month of the year.

of large numbers of insectivorous birds, and high probability of hurricanes. Yet even one of the smallest of Florida's butterflies, *Copaeodes minima*, was able to make its way to Elliott Key, which lies approximately 8 km from the mainland.

PHENOLOGY

Adult butterflies occur all months of the year in the Florida Keys (Figure 49). The number of species recorded for each month varies from a low of 54 in February to a high of 72 in October. Two small peaks of diversity seem evident, corresponding to the monthly distribution of rainfall (Figures 5 and 7). The first peak occurs in April and May at the beginning of the wet season. Some tropical butterflies, such as the univoltine Schaus Swallowtail, are highly synchronized to eclose at this time of year. Multiple-brooded species also become much more abundant after the summer rains begin. The exact timing of this increased butterfly emergence may vary some two or three weeks in any one year, depending upon the mildness of the winter and the amount, frequency, and timing of precipitation.

Another peak of diversity occurs at the end of the wet season, during September and October. This is the time of year when migrant species begin to appear in numbers in south Florida. Many multiple-brooded butterflies also seem to reach their peak abundance in the fall. *Liatris tenuifolia* and other composites bloom in September and October in the tropical pinelands of the Lower Keys and provide a seasonal abundance of nectar. The monthly occurrence of individual species of butterflies in the Florida Keys is listed in Table 3.

DISTRIBUTION

Many butterflies are widely distributed throughout the Florida Keys. Others are limited to the more northern or southern parts of the chain (Table 4). Apparently, elevation and the slight decrease in rainfall from Key Largo to Key West has a large effect upon the distribution and abundance of plants and animals in the Keys. The hammocks of the Upper Keys are taller and have fewer thatch palms (*Thrinax* spp.) than those of the Middle or Lower Keys. Disturbed sites and vacant lots on Key Largo have a variety of herbs and grasses, while those of the Lower Keys are mostly grassy. *Anaea t. floridalis, Strymon acis bartrami, Hesperia meskei, Euphyes arpa, Euphyes pilatka klotsi, Oligoria maculata,* and *Ephyriades brunnea floridansis* are butterflies associated with the tropical pinelands of the Lower Keys. Some other species such as *Electrostrymon angelia* and *Erynnis zarucco* are more often found in disturbed sites, but mostly in the Lower Keys.

White's (1970) distinction between the higher Upper Keys and the lower Middle Keys at the Upper Matecumbe/Lower Matecumbe line seems to have some biological relevance. Butterflies such as *Staphylus hayhurstii, Battus polydamas, Papilio aristodemus ponceanus, Papilio andraemon bonhotei, Eurema nise, Kricogonia lyside, Chlorostrymon simaethis, Tmolus azia, Dryas iulia, Eunica tatila,* and *Junonia genoveva* either drop out completely or become much reduced in abundance below White's Line.

Although some butterflies, such as the pineland species mentioned above, may be limited by the abundance and distribution of their larval host plants, this is not the case for all species of restricted distribution in the Keys. For example, the host plant of the Zestos Skipper, *Galactia striata,* is widespread and abundant throughout the islands, but this butterfly occurs mostly in the Lower Keys. Similarly, the host plant of the Schaus and Bahama Swallowtails, torchwood, commonly grows in hammocks at least to Big Pine Key, yet these butterflies are primarily limited to the islands north of Key Largo.

RECENT CHANGES

The butterfly fauna of the Florida Keys has changed in recent times. Some native species such as *Hesperia meskei, Euphyes arpa, Staphylus hayhurstii, Epargyreus zestos,* and *Papilio aristodemus ponceanus* have declined in abundance. The first three skippers have not been seen in a number of years and may no longer occur in the Keys. The Zestos Skipper seems to have mostly disappeared from the mainland and Upper Keys. The Schaus Swallowtail was listed by the U. S. Fish and Wildlife Service as Endangered in 1984 based on declining population levels and rapidly disappearing habitat.

On the other hand, at least 10 species of butterflies are thought to have become established in Florida during this century. This list includes *Asbolis capucinus, Chlorostrymon simaethis, Danaus eresimus, Electrostrymon angelia, Eunica monima, Junonia genoveva, Phoebis philea, Siproeta stelenes, Tmolus azia,* and *Urbanus dorantes.* Another 15 tropical species have been recorded from the Keys, but failed to become established (Table 5). It is interesting to note that most of these strays seem to have come from Cuba, not the Bahamas.

Table 5. Exotic tropical butterflies that have been recorded from the Florida Keys.

SPECIES	ESTABLISHED	MOST PROBABLE AREA OF ORIGIN
HESPERIIDAE		
Asbolis capucinus	YES	Cuba
Gorgythion begga	NO	Mexico or Central America
Nyctelius nyctelius	NO	Cuba
Urbanus dorantes	YES	Mexico or Central America
PAPILIONIIDAE		
Eurytides celadon	NO	Cuba
PIERIDAE		
Anteos maerula	NO	Cuba
Aphrissa orbis	NO	Cuba
Eurema boisduvaliana	NO	Cuba
Phoebis philea	YES	Central or South America
LYCAENIDAE		
Chlorostrymon simaethis	YES	Cuba
Electrostrymon angelia	YES	Cuba
Electrostrymon endymion	NO	Mexico or Central America
Strymon limenia	NO	Cuba
Hemiargus ammon	NO	Cuba
Tmolus azia	YES	Central or South America
NYMPHALIDAE		
Anartia chrysopelea	NO	Cuba
Danaus eresimus	YES	Cuba
Diaethria clymena	NO	South America
Dryadula phaetusa	NO	Mexico or Central America
Eunica monima	YES	Cuba
Hamadryas amphichloe	NO	Cuba
Junonia genoveva	YES	Cuba
Marpesia chiron	NO	Cuba
Marpesia eleuchea	NO	Cuba
Siproeta stelenes	YES	Cuba

CONSERVATION

The Florida Keys are rapidly changing. As urban areas expand, natural areas are increasingly destroyed, fragmented, or degraded. Many animals in the Keys such as the American Crocodile (*Crocodylus acutus*), Key Largo Woodrat (*Neotoma floridana smalli*), Key Largo Cotton Mouse (*Peromyscus gossypinus allapaticola*), Key Deer (*Odocoileus virginianus clavium*, Fig. 37), and the Schaus Swallowtail are endangered to a point dangerously near extinction and have been placed on the State and Federal lists of threatened and endangered wildlife (Wood, 1990) to help insure their protection.

Conservation groups such as the Nature Conservancy and National and Florida Audubon Societies, together with State and Federal agencies (Florida Department of Natural Resources, Florida Department of Environmental Regulation, Florida Game and Fresh Water Fish Commission, U. S. Fish and Wildlife Service, and National Park Service) are working toward saving critical habitats in the Keys, in part by acquiring natural areas. Many tracts once open to exploration and collecting (such as on northern Key Largo) are now restricted. We strongly suggest that the naturalist contact the Florida Department of Natural Resources (address: State of Florida, Department of Natural Resources, 3900 Commonwealth Boulevard, Tallahassee, Florida 32399) or specific parks of interest before attempting field work in the Keys. One or more permits are usually required in order to collect butterflies and other organisms on State or Federal land. Collecting of endangered wildlife is prohibited under Federal and State Law.

PRECAUTIONS

Life for the early settlers of the Keys must have been miserable much of the year due to the great abundance of mosquitos (Culicidae), sand flies (Ceratopogonidae), and deer flies (Tabanidae). Without proper protective clothing, and strong repellent, our past two decades of work in Biscayne National Park and other natural areas of the Keys would not have been possible because of these noxious biting insects. Urban areas of the Keys are heavily sprayed with insecticides during the breeding season in order to reduce adult mosquito populations. To the chagrin of many environmentalists, the adulticides used may be affecting other organisms, such as the endangered Schaus Swallowtail (Emmel and Minno, 1988) and other butterflies as well as the general insect community diversity (Emmel, Ponce, Minno, and Eliazar, unpublished).

Two plants to avoid contact with in the Keys are poisonwood (*Metopium toxiferum*, Fig. 26) in the family Anacardiaceae and manchineel *(Hippomane mancinella*, Fig. 30) in the Euphorbiaceae. Poisonwood is a very common tree in tropical hardwood hammocks and tropical pinelands. The sap of this plant causes severe skin irritation. Manchineel is a rare tree that grows on shell mounds and coastal uplands in the Keys. Manchineel is similar in appearance to the common wild figs in the genus *Ficus* that also grow in upland areas. The sap of manchineel is known to cause extremely severe allergic reactions that may require hospitalization in some cases.

In spite of Charlotte Niedhauk's (1969) comments to the contrary, eastern diamondback rattlesnakes are present on the Keys in Biscayne National Park, Key Largo, Big Pine Key, and perhaps other areas. Not all of the snakes will sound a warning if approached. Luckily, rattlesnakes are not very abundant in the Keys. Coral snakes are also present on the islands, but are rarely seen. In contrast, scorpions of several different species are plentiful, especially under the drifts of debris along beaches and in trash piles. None of the scorpions from the Keys is especially venomous, but the stings do hurt! Ticks are uncommon in the Upper Keys, but are more frequent in the pinelands of the Lower Keys where the Endangered Key Deer live. Lyme Disease, carried by certain ticks, has not yet been reported from the Keys (Butler and Denmark, 1990), but may become established in the future. Chigger mites are also abundant in pinelands and grassy areas throughout the Keys.

NOTE ON SPECIES ACCOUNTS

In the section following the color plates we discuss all 106 butterflies reported from the Florida Keys. Each entry presents characteristics useful in identification, species range, habitat preferences, host plants, immature stages, adult flight period, flowers visited, and abundance. Much of these data are from our own field research conducted in the Keys from 1982 until present. A number of lepidopterists (cited in the acknowledgements) also contributed a great deal of previously unpublished information. Works consulted for species distributions include Brown and Heineman (1972), Howe (1975), Kimball (1965), Klots (1951), Opler and Krizek (1984), Riley (1975), and Scott (1970, 1986a,b). Schwartz (1987) also provided recent data on distribution, abundance, and flowers visited. The nomenclature adopted in this book generally follows that of Hodges *et al.* (1983) for butterflies and Wunderlin (1982) for plants. Long and Lakela (1971) and Correll and Correll (1982) are additional, useful plant references.

Abbreviations used in the text and plates are AM (Allyn Museum of Entomology, Sarasota), FSCA (Florida State Collection of Arthropods, Gainesville), HDB (H. D. Baggett collection, Palatka), TCE (T. C. Emmel collection, Gainesville), MCM (M. C. Minno collection, Gainesville), FW (forewing).

Butterflies of the Florida Keys

PLATE 1. HESPERIIDAE

1a. *Epargyreus zestos zestos* (Geyer)
      Dorsal male, FW = 24 mm, Florida: Monroe Co., Stock Island (MCM).
1b. *Epargyreus zestos zestos* (Geyer)
      Ventral female, FW = 25 mm, Florida: Monroe Co., Stock Island (MCM).
5a. *Phocides pigmalion okeechobee* (Worthington)
      Dorsal male, FW = 28 mm, Florida: Monroe Co., Key Largo (MCM).
5b. *Phocides pigmalion okeechobee* (Worthington)
      Ventral female, FW = 33 mm, Florida: Monroe Co., Key Largo (MCM).
6a. *Polygonus leo savigny* (Latreille)
      Dorsal female, FW = 25 mm, Florida: Monroe Co., Upper Matecumbe Key (MCM).
6b. *Polygonus leo savigny* (Latreille)
      Ventral male, FW = 24 mm, Florida: Dade Co., (MCM).
9a. *Urbanus dorantes dorantes* (Stoll)
      Dorsal female, FW = 22 mm, Florida: Alachua Co., (MCM).
9b. *Urbanus dorantes dorantes* (Stoll)
      Ventral male, FW = 22 mm, Florida: Monroe Co., Key Largo (MCM).
10a. *Urbanus proteus proteus* (Linnaeus)
      Dorsal female, FW = 21 mm, Florida: Monroe Co., Stock Island (MCM).
10b. *Urbanus proteus proteus* (Linnaeus)
      Ventral female, FW = 24.5 mm, Florida: Broward Co., (MCM).
11a. *Asbolis capucinus* (Lucas)
      Dorsal male, FW = 21 mm, Florida: Broward Co., (MCM).
11b. *Asbolis capucinus* (Lucas)
      Ventral female, FW = 24 mm, Florida: Broward Co., (MCM).
13a. *Calpodes ethlius* (Stoll)
      Dorsal male, FW = 25.5 mm, Florida: Indian River Co., (MCM).
13b. *Calpodes ethlius* (Stoll)
      Ventral male, FW = 26.5 mm, Florida: Indian River Co., (MCM).

PLATE 2. HESPERIIDAE

2a. *Ephyriades brunnea floridensis* Bell and Comstock
   Dorsal male, FW = 18 mm, Florida: Monroe Co., Big Pine Key (MCM).
2b. *Ephyriades brunnea floridensis* Bell and Comstock
   Dorsal female, FW = 18.5 mm, Florida: Monroe Co., Big Pine Key (MCM).
2c. *Ephyriades brunnea floridensis* Bell and Comstock
   Ventral female, FW = 17 mm, Florida: Monroe Co., Big Pine Key (MCM).
3a. *Erynnis zarucco* (Lucas)
   Dorsal male, FW = 18 mm, Florida: Monroe Co., Key West (MCM).
3b. *Erynnis zarucco* (Lucas)
   Dorsal female, FW = 19 mm, Florida: Monroe Co., Key West (MCM).
3c. *Erynnis zarucco* (Lucas)
   Ventral female, FW = 20 mm, Florida: Monroe Co., Key West (MCM).
4a. *Gorgythion begga pyralinus* (Möschler)
   Dorsal female, FW = 13.5 mm, El Salvador: La Perla (AM).
4b. *Gorgythion begga pyralinus* (Möschler)
   Ventral male, FW = 13.5 mm, Mexico: Nayarit (AM).
7a. *Pyrgus oileus oileus* (Linnaeus)
   Dorsal male, FW = 13.5 mm, Florida: Broward Co. (MCM).
7b. *Pyrgus oileus oileus* (Linnaeus)
   Dorsal female, FW = 14 mm, Florida: Broward Co. (MCM).
7c. *Pyrgus oileus oileus* (Linnaeus)
   Ventral male, FW = 14 mm, Florida: Broward Co. (MCM).
8a. *Staphylus hayhurstii* (W. H. Edwards)
   Dorsal female, FW = 12 mm, Florida: Alachua Co. (MCM).
8b. *Staphylus hayhurstii* (W. H. Edwards)
   Ventral female, FW = 11 mm, Florida: Monroe Co., Key Largo (FSCA).
15a. *Cymaenes tripunctus tripunctus* (Herrich-Schäffer)
   Dorsal male, FW = 13 mm, Florida: Broward Co. (MCM).
15b. *Cymaenes tripunctus tripunctus* (Herrich-Schäffer) Ventral female, FW = 14 mm, Florida: Broward Co.
   (MCM).
21a. *Lerodea eufala* (W. H. Edwards)
   Dorsal male, FW = 12 mm, Florida: Monroe Co., Key Largo (MCM).
21b. *Lerodea eufala* (W. H. Edwards)
   Ventral male, FW = 12 mm, Florida: Monroe Co., Key Largo (MCM).
22a. *Nastra neamathla* (Skinner and Williams)
   Dorsal male, FW = 13 mm, Florida: Broward Co. (MCM).
22b. *Nastra neamathla* (Skinner and Williams)
   Ventral female, FW = 12 mm, Florida: Broward Co. (MCM).
27a. *Panoquina panoquinoides panoquinoides* (Skinner)
   Dorsal male, FW = 13.5 mm, Florida: Dade Co., Elliott Key
   (MCM).
27b. *Panoquina panoquinoides panoquinoides* (Skinner)
   Ventral female, FW = 13.5 mm, Florida: Lee Co. (MCM).

3a

7a

8a

2a

3b

7b

8b

2b

3c

7c

4a

2c

4b

15a

22a

21a

27a

15b

22b

21b

27b

PLATE 3. HESPERIIDAE

12a. *Atalopedes campestris huron* (W. H. Edwards)
Dorsal male, FW = 17.5 mm, Florida: Monroe Co., Key Largo (MCM).
12b. *Atalopedes campestris huron* (W. H. Edwards)
Dorsal female, FW = 16.5 mm, Florida: Putman Co. (MCM).
12c. *Atalopedes campestris huron* (W. H. Edwards)
Ventral male, FW = 15.5 mm, Florida: Monroe Co., Big Pine Key (MCM).
16a. *Euphyes arpa* (Boisduval and Leconte)
Dorsal male, FW = 19 mm, Florida: Monroe Co., Big Pine Key (HDB).
16b. *Euphyes arpa* (Boisduval and Leconte)
Dorsal female, FW = 19 mm, Florida: Monroe Co., Big Pine Key (HDB).
16c. *Euphyes arpa* (Boisduval and Leconte)
Ventral male, FW = 17 mm, Florida: Highlands Co. (MCM).
17a. *Euphyes pilatka klotsi* Miller, Harvey, and Miller
Dorsal male, FW = 18 mm, Florida: Monroe Co., Big Pine
Key (MCM).
17b. *Euphyes pilatka klotsi* Miller, Harvey, and Miller
Dorsal female, FW = 20 mm, Florida: Monroe Co., Big Pine Key (MCM).
17c. *Euphyes pilatka klotsi* Miller, Harvey, and Miller
Ventral male, FW = 19 mm, Florida: Monroe Co., Big Pine Key (MCM).
17d. *Euphyes pilatka pilatka* (W. H. Edwards)
Dorsal male, FW = 18.5 mm, Florida: Dade Co. (MCM).
17e. *Euphyes pilatka pilatka* (W. H. Edwards)
Dorsal female, FW = 21.5 mm, Florida: Monroe Co., Key Largo (TCE).
17f. *Euphyes pilatka pilatka* (W. H. Edwards)
Ventral male, FW = 20.5 mm, Florida: Dade Co. (MCM).
18a. *Hesperia meskei* (W. H. Edwards)
Dorsal male, FW = 14.5 mm, Florida: Monroe Co., Big Pine Key (HDB).
18b. *Hesperia meskei* (W. H. Edwards)
Dorsal female, FW = 16 mm, Florida: Monroe Co., Big Pine Key (MCM).
18c. *Hesperia meskei* (W. H. Edwards)
Ventral male, FW = 14 mm, Florida: Monroe Co., Big Pine Key (HDB).
19a. *Hylephila phyleus phyleus* (Drury)
Dorsal male, FW = 14 mm, Florida: Monroe Co., Key Largo (MCM).
19b. *Hylephila phyleus phyleus* (Drury)
Dorsal female, FW = 15 mm, Florida: Alachua Co. (MCM).
19c. *Hylephila phyleus phyleus* (Drury)
Ventral male, FW = 13.5 mm, Florida: Alachua Co. (MCM).

17a

17d

16a

17b

17e

16b

17c

17f

16c

12a

18a

19a

12b

18b

19b

12c

18c

19c

PLATE 4. HESPERIIDAE

14a. *Copaeodes minima* (W. H. Edwards)
Dorsal male, FW = 8 mm, Florida: Putnam Co. (MCM).

14b. *Copaeodes minima* (W. H. Edwards)
Dorsal female, FW = 9.5 mm, Florida: Dade Co., Elliott Key (MCM).

14c. *Copaeodes minima* (W. H. Edwards)
Ventral male, FW = 9.5 mm, Florida: Alachua Co. (MCM).

20a. *Lerema accius accius* (J. E. Smith)
Dorsal male, FW = 16 mm, Florida: Broward Co. (MCM).

20b. *Lerema accius accius* (J. E. Smith)
Dorsal female, FW = 18 mm, Florida: Broward Co. (MCM).

20c. *Lerema accius accius* (J. E. Smith)
Ventral female, FW = 17 mm, Florida: Alachua Co. (MCM).

23a. *Nyctelius nyctelius nyctelius* (Latreille)
Dorsal male, FW = 18 mm, Dominican Republic: Puerto Plata Province (MCM).

23b. *Nyctelius nyctelius nyctelius* (Latreille)
Ventral female, FW = 18 mm, Florida: Monroe Co., Key Largo (FSCA).

24a. *Oligoria maculata* (W. H. Edwards)
Dorsal female, FW = 16.5 mm, Florida: Monroe Co., Big Pine Key (MCM).

24b. *Oligoria maculata* (W. H. Edwards)
Ventral female, FW = 16 mm, Florida: Monroe Co., Big Pine Key (MCM).

25a. *Panoquina ocola ocola* (W. H. Edwards)
Dorsal male, FW = 17 mm, Florida: Dade Co., Elliott Key (MCM).

25b. *Panoquina ocola ocola* (W. H. Edwards)
Ventral male, FW = 16 mm, Florida: Broward Co. (MCM).

26a. *Panoquina panoquin* (Scudder)
Dorsal male, FW = 14 mm, Florida: Levy Co., Yankeetown (MCM).

26b. *Panoquina panoquin* (Scudder)
Dorsal female, FW = 14 mm, Florida: Levy Co., Yankeetown (MCM).

26c. *Panoquina panoquin* (Scudder
Ventral male, FW = 14 mm, Florida: Levy Co., Yankeetown (MCM).

28a. *Polites vibex vibex* (Geyer)
Dorsal male, FW = 13 mm, Florida: Levy Co. (MCM).

28b. *Polites vibex vibex* (Geyer)
Dorsal female, FW = 14 mm, Florida: Alachua Co. (MCM).

28c. *Polites vibex vibex* (Geyer)
Ventral male, FW = 13.5 mm, Florida: Levy Co. (MCM).

29a. *Wallengrenia otho* (J. E. Smith)
Dorsal male, FW = 14 mm, Florida: Dade Co., Elliott Key (MCM).

29b. *Wallengrenia otho* (J. E. Smith)
Dorsal female, FW = 15 mm, Florida: Dade Co., Elliott Key (MCM).

29c. *Wallengrenia otho* (J. E. Smith)
Ventral female, FW = 14 mm, Florida: Dade Co. (MCM).

29a

14a

28a

20a

29b

14b

28b

20b

29c

14c

28c

20c

25a

23a

24a

25b

23b

24b

26a

26b

26c

PLATE 5. PAPILIONIDAE

30. *Battus polydamas lucayus* Rothschild and Jordan
        Dorsal female, FW = 45 mm, Florida: Dade Co. (MCM).
31. *Eurytides celadon* Lucas
        Dorsal male, FW = 33 mm, Cuba (AM).
32. *Eurytides marcellus floridensis* (Holland)
        Dorsal female, FW = 33 mm, Florida: Lake Co. (MCM).
33. *Papilio andraemon bonhotei* Sharpe
        Dorsal male, FW = 41.5 mm, Florida: Monroe Co., Key Largo (FSCA).
37a. *Papilio polyxenes asterius* Stoll
        Dorsal male, FW = 46 mm, Florida: Broward Co. (MCM).
37b. *Papilio polyxenes asterius* Stoll
        Dorsal female, FW = 49 mm, Florida: Broward Co. (MCM).

PLATE 6. PAPILIONIDAE

30. *Battus polydamas lucayus* Rothschild and Jordan
        Ventral female, FW = 45 mm, Florida: Dade Co. (MCM).
31. *Eurytides celadon* Lucas
        Ventral male, FW = 33 mm, Cuba (AM).
32. *Eurytides marcellus floridensis* (Holland)
        Ventral female, FW = 33 mm, Florida: Lake Co. (MCM).
33. *Papilio andraemon bonhotei* Sharpe
        Ventral male, FW = 41.5 mm, Florida: Monroe Co., Key Largo (FSCA).
37a. *Papilio polyxenes asterius* Stoll
        Ventral male, FW = 46 mm, Florida: Broward Co. (MCM).
37b. *Papilio polyxenes asterius* Stoll
        Ventral female, FW = 49 mm, Florida: Broward Co. (MCM).

37a

31

33

37b

32

30

37a

31

33

37b

32

30

PLATE 7. PAPILIONIDAE

34a. *Papilio aristodemus ponceanus* Schaus
        Dorsal female, FW = 50 mm, Florida: Monroe Co., Key Largo (FSCA).
34b. *Papilio aristodemus ponceanus* Schaus
        Ventral female, FW = 50 mm, Florida: Monroe Co., Key Largo (FSCA).
35a. *Papilio cresphontes* Cramer
        Dorsal male, FW = 56 mm, Florida: Monroe Co., Plantation Key (MCM).
35b. *Papilio cresphontes* Cramer
        Ventral female, FW = 61.5 mm, Texas: Bexar Co. (MCM).
36a. *Papilio palamedes* Drury
        Dorsal male, FW = 54.5 mm, Florida: Broward Co. (MCM).
36b. *Papilio palamedes* Drury
        Ventral male, FW = 48 mm, Florida: Broward Co. (MCM).

36a

36b

35a

35b

34a

34b

PLATE 8. PIERIDAE

38a. *Appias drusilla neumoegenii* (Skinner)
  Dorsal male, FW = 34.5 mm, Florida: Monroe Co., Key Largo (MCM).
38b. *Appias drusilla neumoegenii* (Skinner)
  Dorsal female, FW = 33 mm, Florida: Monroe Co., Key Largo (MCM).
38c. *Appias drusilla neumoegenii* (Skinner)
  Ventral male, FW = 34 mm, Florida: Monroe Co., Key Largo (MCM).
39a. *Ascia monuste phileta* (Fabricius)
  Dorsal male, FW = 31.5 mm, Florida: Indian River Co. (MCM).
39b. *Ascia monuste phileta* (Fabricius)
  Ventral male, FW = 30 mm, Florida: Monroe Co., Upper Matecumbe Key (MCM).
39c. *Ascia monuste evonima* (Boisduval)
  Ventral male, FW = 31 mm, Florida: Dade Co., Elliott Key (MCM).
39d. *Ascia monuste phileta* (Fabricius)
  Dorsal female, FW = 28 mm, Florida: Dade Co., Elliott Key (MCM).
39e. *Ascia monuste phileta* (Fabricius)
  Dorsal female (dark form), FW = 28 mm, Florida: Dade Co., Elliott Key (MCM).
39f. *Ascia monuste phileta* (Fabricius)
  Ventral female, FW = 30 mm, Florida: Broward Co. (MCM).

39a

38a

39d

39b

38b

39e

39c

38c

39f

PLATE 9. PIERIDAE

40a. *Pieris rapae* (Linnaeus)
      Dorsal male, FW = 26 mm, Florida: Alachua Co. (MCM).

40b. *Pieris rapae* (Linnaeus)
      Dorsal female, FW = 23.5 mm, Florida: Alachua Co. (MCM).

40c. *Pieris rapae* (Linnaeus)
      Ventral male, FW = 26 mm, Florida: Alachua Co. (MCM).

41a. *Pontia protodice* (Boisduval and Leconte)
      Dorsal male, FW = 22 mm, Florida: Monroe Co., Key Largo (HDB).

41b. *Pontia protodice* (Boisduval and Leconte)
      Dorsal female, FW = 24 mm, Florida: Dade Co., Elliott Key (MCM).

41c. *Pontia protodice* (Boisduval and Leconte)
      Ventral female, FW = 23.5 mm, Florida: Monroe Co., Key Largo (HDB).

45a. *Colias eurytheme* Boisduval
      Dorsal male, FW = 24 mm, Florida: Broward Co. (MCM).

45b. *Colias eurytheme* Boisduval
      Dorsal female (white form), FW = 28 mm, Florida: Broward Co. (MCM).

45c. *Colias eurytheme* Boisduval
      Ventral female, FW = 25 mm, Florida: Broward Co. (MCM).

50a. *Eurema nicippe* (Cramer)
      Dorsal male, FW = 26 mm, Florida: Broward Co. (MCM).

50b. *Eurema nicippe* (Cramer)
      Dorsal female, FW = 24 mm, Florida: Broward Co. (MCM).

50c. *Eurema nicippe* (Cramer)
      Ventral male, FW = 22 mm, Florida: Broward Co. (MCM).

52a. *Kricogonia lyside* (Godart)
      Dorsal male, FW = 23 mm, Florida: Monroe Co., Key Largo (MCM).

52b. *Kricogonia lyside* (Godart)
      Dorsal female, FW = 24 mm, Florida: Dade Co., Elliott Key (MCM).

52c. *Kricogonia lyside* (Godart)
      Ventral male, FW = 23 mm, Florida: Dade Co., Elliott Key (MCM).

40a

40b

40c

41a

41b

41c

52a

52b

52c

45a

45b

45c

50a

50b

50c

PLATE 10. PIERIDAE

43. *Aphrissa orbis orbis* (Poey)
        Dorsal male, FW = 30.5 mm, Florida: Monroe Co., Big Pine Key (FSCA).
44a. *Aphrissa statira floridensis* (Neumoegen)
        Dorsal male, FW = 32 mm, Florida: Broward Co. (MCM).
44b. *Aphrissa statira floridensis* (Neumoegen)
        Dorsal female, FW = 34.5 mm, Florida: Broward Co. (MCM).
44c. *Aphrissa statira floridensis* (Neumoegen)
        Ventral male, FW = 34 mm, Florida: Broward Co. (MCM).
54a. *Phoebis agarithe maxima* (Neumoegen)
        Dorsal male, FW = 36 mm, Florida: Monroe Co., Key Largo (MCM).
54b. *Phoebis agarithe maxima* (Neumoegen)
        Dorsal female (white form), FW = 35 mm, Florida: Broward Co. (MCM).
54c. *Phoebis agarithe maxima* (Neumoegen)
        Dorsal female, FW = 29 mm, Florida: Monroe Co., Big Pine Key (MCM).
54d. *Phoebis agarithe maxima* (Neumoegen)
        Ventral male, FW = 34.5 mm, Florida: Dade Co., Elliott Key (MCM).
56a. *Phoebis sennae eubule* (Linnaeus)
        Dorsal male, FW = 34 mm, Florida: Broward Co. (MCM).
56b. *Phoebis sennae eubule* (Linnaeus)
        Dorsal female, FW = 34 mm, Florida: Levy Co. (MCM).
56c. *Phoebis sennae sennae* (Linnaeus)
        Dorsal female, FW = 31 mm, Florida: Monroe Co., Stock Island (HDB).
56d. *Phoebis sennae eubule* (Linnaeus)
        Ventral male, FW = 33 mm, Florida: Broward Co. (MCM).

44a

54a

56a

44b

54b

56b

44c

54c

56c

43

54d

56d

PLATE 11. PIERIDAE

42a. *Anteos maerula* (Fabricius)
> Dorsal male, FW = 38 mm, Jamaica: St. Thomas Parrish (TCE).

42b. *Anteos maerula* (Fabricius)
> Ventral male, FW = 42 mm, Florida: Monroe Co., Key Largo (FSCA).

55a. *Phoebis philea philea* (Johansson)
> Dorsal male, FW = 41 mm, Florida: Broward Co. (MCM).

55b. *Phoebis philea philea* (Johansson)
> Ventral male, FW = 38 mm, Florida: Broward Co. (MCM).

55c. *Phoebis philea philea* (Johansson)
> Dorsal female (white form), FW = 37.5 mm, Florida: Monroe Co., Stock Island (MCM).

55d. *Phoebis philea philea* (Johansson)
> Dorsal female, FW = 39 mm, Florida: Broward Co. (MCM).

55a

55b

55c

55d

42a

42b

PLATE 12. PIERIDAE

46a. *Eurema boisduvaliana* (Felder and Felder)
      Dorsal male, FW = 20 mm, Mexico: San Luis Potosi (TCE).
46b. *Eurema boisduvaliana* (Felder and Felder)
      Ventral male, FW = 22 mm, Mexico: San Luis Potosi (TCE).
47a. *Eurema daira daira* (Godart)
      Dorsal male (wet season form), FW = 14 mm, Florida: Dade Co., Elliott Key (MCM).
47b. *Eurema daira daira* (Godart)
      Dorsal female (wet season form), FW = 17 mm, Florida: Broward Co. (MCM).
47c. *Eurema daira daira* (Godart)
      Ventral male (wet season form), FW = 17 mm, Florida: Monroe Co., Key Largo (MCM).
47d. *Eurema daira palmira* (Poey)
      Dorsal male (wet season form), FW = 16.5 mm, Florida: Monroe Co., Key Largo (MCM).
47e. *Eurema daira palmira* (Poey)
      Dorsal female (wet season form), FW = 16 mm, Florida: Monroe Co., Big Pine Key (MCM).
47f. *Eurema daira palmira* (Poey)
      Ventral male (wet season form), FW = 15 mm, Florida: Broward Co. (MCM).
47g. *Eurema daira daira* (Godart)
      Dorsal male (dry season form), FW = 16.5 mm, Florida: Marion Co. (MCM).
47h. *Eurema daira daira* (Godart)
      Dorsal female (dry season form), FW = 18 mm, Florida: Monroe Co., Key Largo (MCM).
47i. *Eurema daira daira* (Godart)
      Ventral male (dry season form), FW = 17 mm, Florida: Broward Co. (MCM).
48a. *Eurema dina helios* M. Bates
      Dorsal male, FW = 19.5 mm, Florida: Dade Co. (MCM).
48b. *Eurema dina helios* M. Bates
      Dorsal female, FW = 19 mm, Florida: Dade Co. (MCM).
48c. *Eurema dina helios* M. Bates
      Ventral male, FW = 20 mm, Florida: Dade Co. (MCM).
49a. *Eurema lisa lisa* Boisduval and Leconte
      Dorsal male, FW = 17 mm, Florida: Levy Co. (MCM).
49b. *Eurema lisa lisa* Boisduval and Leconte
      Dorsal female, FW = 19 mm, Florida: Alachua Co. (MCM).
49c. *Eurema lisa lisa* Boisduval and Leconte
      Ventral male, FW = 15 mm, Florida: Dade Co., Elliott Key (MCM).
51a. *Eurema nise nise* (Cramer)
      Dorsal male, FW = 16 mm, Florida: Dade Co., Elliott Key (MCM).
51b. *Eurema nise nise* (Cramer)
      Dorsal female, FW = 15.5 mm, Florida: Dade Co., Elliott Key (MCM).
51c. *Eurema nise nise* (Cramer)
      Ventral male, FW = 14 mm, Florida: Dade Co., Elliott Key (MCM).
53a. *Nathalis iole* Boisduval
      Dorsal male, FW = 13 mm, Florida: Monroe Co., Key Largo (MCM).
53b. *Nathalis iole* Boisduval
      Dorsal female, FW = 13 mm, Florida: Monroe Co., Key Largo (MCM).
53c. *Nathalis iole* Boisduval
      Ventral male, FW = 13 mm, Florida: Dade Co., Elliott Key (MCM).

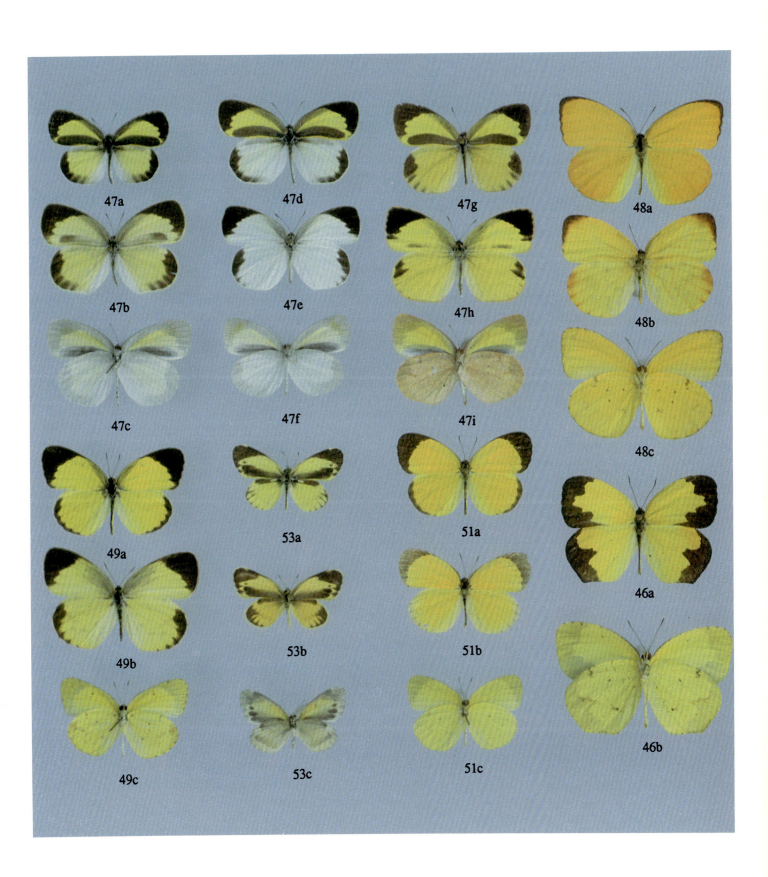

47a

47d

47g

48a

47b

47e

47h

48b

47c

47f

47i

48c

49a

53a

51a

49b

53b

51b

46a

49c

53c

51c

46b

PLATE 13. LYCAENIDAE

58a. *Chlorostrymon maesites* (Herrich-Schäffer)
        Dorsal male, FW = 10 mm, Florida: Dade Co. (FSCA).
58b. *Chlorostrymon maesites* (Herrich-Schäffer)
        Dorsal female, FW = 9.5 mm, Florida: Monroe Co., Key Largo (HDB).
58c. *Chlorostrymon maesites* (Herrich-Schäffer)
        Ventral male, FW = 10 mm, Florida: Dade Co. (FSCA).
59a. *Chlorostrymon simaethis simaethis* (Drury)
        Dorsal male, FW = 11 mm, Florida: Monroe Co., Key Largo (MCM).
59b. *Chlorostrymon simaethis simaethis* (Drury)
        Dorsal female, FW = 10 mm, Florida: Monroe Co., Key Largo (MCM).
59c. *Chlorostrymon simaethis simaethis* (Drury)
        Ventral female, FW = 11 mm, Florida: Monroe Co., Key Largo (MCM).
62a. *Eumaeus atala florida* Röber
        Dorsal male, FW = 21 mm, Florida: Dade Co. (MCM).
62b. *Eumaeus atala florida* Röber
        Dorsal female, FW = 23 mm, Florida: Dade Co. (MCM).
62c. *Eumaeus atala florida* Röber
        Ventral male, FW = 22 mm, Florida: Dade Co. (MCM).
64. *Strymon columella modestus* (Maynard)
        Ventral male, FW = 11.5 mm, Florida: Broward Co. (MCM).
65. *Strymon limenia* (Hewitson)
        Ventral male, FW = 12 mm, Cuba: Oriente Province (AM).
68a. *Tmolus azia* (Hewitson)
        Dorsal male, FW = 8 mm, Florida: Monroe Co., Key Largo (MCM).
68b. *Tmolus azia* (Hewitson)
        Dorsal female, FW = 9 mm, Florida: Monroe Co., Key Largo (MCM).
68c. *Tmolus azia* (Hewitson)
        Ventral male, FW = 8 mm, Florida: Monroe Co., Key Largo (MCM).
69a. *Brephidium isophthalma pseudofea* (Morrison)
        Dorsal male, FW = 6 mm, Florida: Monroe Co., Big Pine Key (MCM).
69b. *Brephidium isophthalma pseudofea* (Morrison)
        Dorsal female, FW = 9 mm, Florida: Broward Co. (MCM).
69c. *Brephidium isophthalma pseudofea* (Morrison)
        Ventral female, FW = 8 mm, Florida: Monroe Co., Big Pine Key (MCM).
71a. *Hemiargus ceraunus antibubastus* Hübner
        Dorsal male, FW = 9.5 mm, Florida: Monroe Co., Key Largo (MCM).
71b. *Hemiargus ceraunus antibubastus* Hübner
        Dorsal female, FW = 11 mm, Florida: Monroe Co., Key West (MCM).
71c. *Hemiargus ceraunus antibubastus* Hübner
        Ventral male, FW = 10 mm, Florida: Monroe Co., Key Largo (MCM).
72a. *Hemiargus thomasi bethunebakeri* Comstock and Huntington
        Dorsal male, FW = 11 mm, Florida: Monroe Co., Key Largo (MCM).
72b. *Hemiargus thomasi bethunebakeri* Comstock and Huntington
        Dorsal female, FW = 12 mm, Florida: Monroe Co., Key Largo (MCM).
72c. *Hemiargus thomasi bethunebakeri* Comstock and Huntington
        Ventral male, FW = 11 mm, Florida: Monroe Co., Big Pine Key (MCM).
73a. *Leptotes cassius theonus* (Lucas)
        Dorsal male, FW = 11.5 mm, Florida: Broward Co. (MCM).
73b. *Leptotes cassius theonus* (Lucas)
        Dorsal female, FW = 12 mm, Florida: Highlands Co. (MCM).
73c. *Leptotes cassius theonus* (Lucas)
        Ventral female, FW = 12 mm, Florida: Broward Co. (MCM).

73a

71a

72a

65

73b

71b

72b

64

73c

71c

72c

58a

68a

69a

59a

58b

68b

69b

59b

58c

68c

69c

59c

62a

62b

62c

PLATE 14. LYCAENIDAE

57a. *Calycopis cecrops* (Fabricius)
   Dorsal male, FW = 13 mm, Florida: Monroe Co., No Name Key (MCM).
57b. *Calycopis cecrops* (Fabricius)
   Dorsal female, FW = 13 mm, Florida: Monroe Co., No Name Key (MCM).
57c. *Calycopis cecrops* (Fabricius)
   Ventral male, FW = 12 mm, Florida: Marion Co. (MCM).
60a. *Electrostrymon angelia angelia* (Hewitson)
   Dorsal male, FW = 13 mm, Florida: Monroe Co., Stock Island (MCM).
60b. *Electrostrymon angelia angelia* (Hewitson)
   Dorsal female, FW = 11 mm, Florida: Broward Co. (MCM).
60c. *Electrostrymon angelia angelia* (Hewitson)
   Ventral male, FW = 11 mm, Florida: Broward Co. (MCM).
61a. *Electrostrymon endymion* (Fabricius)
   Dorsal male, FW = 10.5 mm, Mexico: San Luis Potosi (AM).
61b. *Electrostrymon endymion* (Fabricius)
   Ventral male, FW = 10 mm, Florida: Monroe Co., vicinity of Crawl Key (FSCA).
63a. *Strymon acis bartrami* (Comstock and Huntington)
   Dorsal male, FW = 11 mm, Florida: Monroe Co., Big Pine Key (MCM).
63b. *Strymon acis bartrami* (Comstock and Huntington)
   Dorsal female, FW = 12 mm, Florida: Monroe Co., Big Pine Key (MCM).
63c. *Strymon acis bartrami* (Comstock and Huntington)
   Ventral male, FW = 12 mm, Florida: Monroe Co. Big Pine Key (MCM).
64a. *Strymon columella modestus* (Maynard)
   Dorsal male, FW = 11.5 mm, Florida: Broward Co. (MCM).
64b. *Strymon columella modestus* (Maynard)
   Dorsal female, FW = 12.5 mm, Florida: Broward Co. (MCM).
64c. *Strymon columella modestus* (Maynard)
   Ventral female, FW = 10.5 mm, Florida: Monroe Co., Key Largo (MCM).
65. *Strymon limenia* (Hewitson)
   Dorsal male, FW = 12 mm, Cuba: Oriente Province (AM).
66a. *Strymon martialis* (Herrich-Schäffer)
   Dorsal male, FW = 13 mm, Florida: Monroe Co., Key Largo (FSCA).
66b. *Strymon martialis* (Herrich-Schäffer)
   Dorsal female, FW = 13 mm, Florida: Monroe Co., Big Pine Key (MCM).
66c. *Strymon martialis* (Herrich-Schäffer)
   Ventral male, FW = 12.5 mm, Florida: Monroe Co., Key Largo (FSCA).
67a. *Strymon melinus melinus* Hübner
   Dorsal male, FW = 13.5 mm, Florida: Monroe Co., Key Largo (MCM).
67b. *Strymon melinus melinus* Hübner
   Dorsal female, FW = 13.5 mm, Florida: Monroe Co., Key Largo (MCM).
67c. *Strymon melinus melinus* Hübner
   Ventral female (variant with pale eyespot), FW = 12 mm, Florida: Monroe Co., Key Largo (MCM).
74a. *Calephelis virginiensis* (Guérin-Ménéville)
   Dorsal male, FW = 10 mm, Florida: Alachua Co. (MCM).
74b. *Calephelis virginiensis* (Guérin-Ménéville)
   Dorsal female, FW = 10.5 mm, Florida: Broward Co. (MCM).
74c. *Calephelis virginiensis* (Guérin-Ménéville)
   Ventral male, FW = 10 mm, Florida: Broward Co. (MCM).

59

PLATE 15. NYMPHALIDAE: HELICONIINAE

76a. *Agraulis vanillae nigrior* Michener
        Dorsal male, FW = 37 mm, Florida: Broward Co. (MCM).
76b. *Agraulis vanillae nigrior* Michener
        Ventral male, FW = 36 mm, Florida: Putnam Co. (MCM).
77a. *Dryadula phaetusa* (Linnaeus)
        Dorsal male, FW = 40.5 mm, Mexico (TCE).
77b. *Dryadula phaetusa* (Linnaeus)
        Ventral female, FW = 43 mm, Mexico (TCE).
78a. *Dryas iulia largo* Clench
        Dorsal male, FW = 42.5 mm, Florida: Broward Co. (MCM).
78b. *Dryas iulia largo* Clench
        Ventral female, FW = 42 mm, Florida: Dade Co., Elliott Key (MCM).
79a. *Heliconius charitonius tuckeri* Comstock and Brown
        Dorsal male, FW = 44 mm, Florida: Alachua Co. (MCM).
79b. *Heliconius charitonius tuckeri* Comstock and Brown
        Ventral female, FW = 43.5 mm, Florida: Broward Co. (MCM).

76a

76b

79a

79b

78a

78b

77a

77b

PLATE 16. NYMPHALIDAE: NYMPHALINAE

80a. *Anartia chrysopelea* Hübner
Dorsal male, FW = 18.5 mm, Florida: Monroe Co., Big Pine Key (FSCA).
80b. *Anartia chrysopelea* Hübner
Ventral male, FW = 21 mm, Florida: Monroe Co., Stock Island (AM).
81a. *Anartia jatrophae guantanamo* Munroe
Dorsal male, FW = 28 mm, Florida: Dade Co., Elliott Key (MCM).
81b. *Anartia jatrophae guantanamo* Munroe
Ventral male, FW = 28 mm, Florida: Dade Co., Elliott Key (MCM).
86a. *Euptoieta claudia* (Cramer)
Dorsal male, FW = 27 mm, Bahamas: Great Abaco (MCM).
86b. *Euptoieta claudia* (Cramer)
Ventral male, FW = 28 mm, Florida: Broward Co. (MCM).
98a. *Vanessa atalanta rubria* (Fruhstorfer)
Dorsal male, FW = 23 mm, Florida: Alachua Co.(MCM).
98b. *Vanessa atalanta rubria* (Fruhstorfer)
Ventral female, FW = 28 mm, Florida: Broward Co. (MCM).
99a. *Vanessa cardui* (Linnaeus)
Dorsal female, FW = 31 mm, Florida: Collier Co. (MCM).
99b. *Vanessa cardui* (Linnaeus)
Ventral male, FW = 31 mm, New Mexico: Santa Fe Co. (MCM).
100a. *Vanessa virginiensis* (Drury)
Dorsal male, FW = 27 mm, Florida: Alachua Co. (MCM).
100b. *Vanessa virginiensis* (Drury)
Ventral female, FW = 29 mm, Florida: Dade Co., Elliott Key (MCM).

PLATE 17. NYMPHALIDAE: NYMPHALINAE

83a. *Eresia frisia frisia* (Poey)
> Dorsal male, FW = 14.5 mm, Florida: Monroe Co., Upper Matecumbe Key (MCM).

83b. *Eresia frisia frisia* (Poey)
> Dorsal female, FW = 17.5 mm, Florida: Dade Co., Elliott Key (MCM).

83c. *Eresia frisia frisia* (Poey)
> Ventral male, FW = 15 mm, Florida: Monroe Co., Upper Matecumbe Key (MCM).

95a. *Phyciodes phaon* (W. H. Edwards)
> Dorsal male, FW = 14 mm, Florida: Monroe Co., Key Largo (MCM).

95b. *Phyciodes phaon* (W. H. Edwards)
> Dorsal female, FW = 15 mm, Florida: Monroe Co., Key Largo (MCM).

95c. *Phyciodes phaon* (W. H. Edwards)
> Ventral male, FW = 15 mm, Florida: Dade Co., Elliott Key (MCM).

96a. *Phyciodes tharos tharos* (Drury)
> Dorsal male, FW = 15.5 mm, Florida: Monroe Co., Elliott Key (MCM).

96b. *Phyciodes tharos tharos* (Drury)
> Dorsal female, FW = 16.5 mm, Florida: Lake Co. (MCM).

96c. *Phyciodes tharos tharos* (Drury)
> Ventral male, FW = 14 mm, Florida: Monroe Co., Elliott Key (MCM).

96a

95a

83a

96b

95b

83b

96c

95c

83c

PLATE 18. NYMPHALIDAE: NYMPHALINAE

88a. *Junonia coenia coenia* (Hübner)
    Dorsal male, FW = 24 mm, Florida: Dade Co., Elliott Key (MCM).
88b. *Junonia coenia coenia* (Hübner)
    Dorsal female, FW = 24 mm, Florida: Broward Co., (MCM).
88c. *Junonia coenia coenia* (Hübner)
    Ventral male, FW = 26 mm, Florida: Leon Co. (MCM).
88d. *Junonia coenia coenia* (Hübner)
    Ventral female (dry season form), FW = 27.5 mm, Florida: Alachua Co. (MCM).
89a. *Junonia evarete* (Cramer)
    Dorsal male, FW = 27 mm, Florida: Broward Co. (MCM).
89b. *Junonia evarete* (Cramer)
    Dorsal female, FW = 28 mm, Florida: Dade Co., Elliott Key (MCM).
89c. *Junonia evarete* (Cramer)
    Ventral male, FW = 27 mm, Florida: Dade Co., Elliott Key (MCM).
89d. *Junonia evarete* (Cramer)
    Ventral male (dry season form), FW = 26 mm, Florida: Dade Co., Elliott Key (MCM).
90a. *Junonia genoveva* (Stoll)
    Dorsal male, FW = 24 mm, Florida: Monroe Co., Key Largo (MCM).
90b. *Junonia genoveva* (Stoll)
    Dorsal female, FW = 26 mm, Florida: Monroe Co., Key Largo (MCM).
90c. *Junonia genoveva* (Stoll)
    Ventral male, FW = 26 mm, Dominican Republic: La Vega Province (MCM).
90d. *Junonia genoveva* (Stoll)
    Ventral male, FW = 24 mm, Florida: Monroe Co., Key Largo (MCM).

90a

89a

88a

90b

89b

88b

90c

89c

88c

90d

89d

88d

PLATE 19. NYMPHALIDAE: NYMPHALINAE

87a. *Hamadryas amphichloe diasia* (Fruhstorfer)
        Dorsal female, FW = 35 mm, Dominican Republic: La Vega Province (MCM).
87b. *Hamadryas amphichloe diasia* (Fruhstorfer)
        Ventral male, FW = 35.5 mm, Dominican Republic: Puerto Plata Province (MCM).
91a. *Limenitis archippus floridensis* (Strecker)
        Dorsal male, FW = 38 mm, Florida: Alachua Co. (MCM).
91b. *Limenitis archippus floridensis* (Strecker)
        Ventral male, FW = 34 mm, Florida: Broward Co. (MCM).
92a. *Marpesia chiron* (Fabricius)
        Dorsal male, FW = 29 mm, Costa Rica: Meredia Province (TCE).
92b. *Marpesia chiron* (Fabricius)
        Ventral female, FW = 29 mm, Mexico: San Luis Potosi (TCE).
93a. *Marpesia eleuchea eleuchea* Hübner
        Dorsal male, FW = 31 mm, Florida: Monroe Co., Sugarloaf Key (AM).
93b. *Marpesia eleuchea eleuchea* Hübner
        Ventral female, FW = 27 mm, Bahamas: North Andros Island (AM).
94a. *Marpesia petreus petreus* (Cramer)
        Dorsal male, FW = 40 mm, Florida: Broward Co. (MCM).
94b. *Marpesia petreus petreus* (Cramer)
        Ventral male, FW = 36 mm, Florida: Dade Co., Elliott Key (MCM).
97a. *Siproeta stelenes biplagiata* (Fruhstorfer)
        Dorsal male, FW = 41.5 mm, Florida: Dade Co. (MCM).
97b. *Siproeta stelenes biplagiata* (Fruhstorfer)
        Ventral male, FW = 40 mm, Florida: Broward Co. (MCM).

PLATE 20. LIBYTHEIDAE, NYMPHALIDAE: NYMPHALINAE AND SATYRINAE

75a. *Libytheana bachmanii* (Kirtland)
      Dorsal male, FW = 22 mm, Florida: Alachua Co. (MCM).
75b. *Libytheana bachmanii* (Kirtland)
      Ventral female, FW = 22 mm, Florida: Dade Co., Elliott Key (MCM).
82a. *Diaethria clymena* (Cramer)
      Dorsal male, FW = 22 mm, Peru: Huanuco Province (TCE).
82b. *Diaethria clymena* (Cramer)
      Ventral male, FW = 21 mm, Peru: Huanuco Province (TCE).
84a. *Eunica monima* (Stoll)
      Dorsal male, FW = 21 mm, Florida: Dade Co. (HDB).
84b. *Eunica monima* (Stoll)
      Ventral male, FW = 20 mm, Florida: Dade Co. (MCM).
85a. *Eunica tatila tatilista* Kaye
      Dorsal female, FW = 29 mm, Florida: Monroe Co., Key Largo (MCM).
85b. *Eunica tatila tatilista* Kaye
      Ventral male, FW = 28 mm, Florida: Monroe Co., Key Largo (MCM).
101a. *Anaea troglodyta floridalis* Johnson and W. P. Comstock
      Dorsal male, FW = 34 mm, Florida: Monroe Co., Big Pine Key (MCM).
101b. *Anaea troglodyta floridalis* Johnson and W. P. Comstock
      Dorsal female, FW = 38 mm, Florida: Monroe Co., Big Pine Key (MCM).
101c. *Anaea troglodyta floridalis* Johnson and W. P. Comstock
      Ventral male, FW = 34 mm, Florida: Monroe Co., Big Pine Key (MCM).
102. *Hermeuptychia sosybius* (Fabricius)
      Ventral female, FW = 17.5 mm, Florida: Monroe Co., Key Largo (HDB).
103. *Neonympha areolata areolata* (J. E. Smith)
      Ventral female, FW = 18 mm, Florida: Dade Co. (MCM).

84a

84b

103

85a

85b

101a

101b

101c

75a

75b

102

82a

82b

PLATE 21. NYMPHALIDAE: DANAINAE

104a. *Danaus eresimus tethys* Forbes
                Dorsal male, FW = 41 mm, Florida: Dade Co., Elliott Key (MCM).
104b. *Danaus eresimus tethys* Forbes
                Ventral female, FW = 37.5 mm, Florida: Highlands Co. (MCM).
105a. *Danaus gilippus berenice* (Godart)
                Dorsal male, FW = 40.5 mm, Florida: Monroe Co., Big Pine Key (MCM).
105b. *Danaus gilippus berenice* (Godart)
                Ventral female, FW = 40 mm, Florida: Dade Co., Elliott Key (MCM).
106a. *Danaus plexippus plexippus* (Linnaeus)
                Dorsal male, FW = 53 mm, Florida: Marion Co. (MCM).
106b. *Danaus plexippus plexippus* (Linnaeus)
                Ventral female, FW = 48 mm, Florida: Dade Co., Elliott Key (MCM).

105a

104a

105b

104b

106a

106b

PLATE 22. HESPERIIDAE IMMATURES AND BIOLOGY

1. Mature larva of *Epargyreus zestos zestos*, on Stock Island, Monroe Co., Florida.

2. Mature larva of *Ephyriades brunnea floridensis*, on Stock Island, Monroe Co., Florida.

3. Mature larva of *Erynnis zarucco*, on Stock Island, Monroe Co., Florida.

5. Adult *Phocides pigmalion okeechobee*, in Cactus Hammock at Big Pine Key, Monroe Co., Florida.

5b. Third instar larva of *Phocides pigmalion okeechobee*, in leaf nest on red mangrove at Big Pine Key, Monroe Co., Florida.

6. Mature larva of *Polygonus leo savigny*, on Big Pine Key, Monroe Co., Florida.

PLATE 23. HESPERIIDAE IMMATURES AND BIOLOGY

11a. Mature larva of *Asbolis capucinus*, on Key West, Monroe Co., Florida.

11b. Pupa of *Asbolis capucinus*, on Key West, Monroe Co., Florida.

15a. Mature larva of *Cymaenes tripunctus tripunctus* from La Vega Province, Dominican Republic.

15b. Pupa of *Cymaenes tripunctus tripunctus* on Stock Island, Monroe Co., Florida.

27. Mature larva of *Panoquina panoquinoides panoquinoides*, on Elliott Key, Dade Co., Florida.

PLATE 24. LARVAE AND PUPAE OF PAPILIONIDAE

33a. Mature larva (lateral view) of *Papilio andraemon bonhotei* on Elliott Key, Dade Co., Florida.

33b. Mature larva (dorsal view) of *Papilio andraemon bonhotei* on Elliott Key, Dade Co., Florida.

33c. Green and brown phases of the pupae (lateral views) of *Papilio andraemon bonhotei* on Elliott Key, Dade Co., Florida.

34a. Mature larva (dorsal view) of *Papilio aristodemus ponceanus* on Elliott Key, Dade Co., Florida.

34b. Mature larva (lateral view) of *Papilio aristodemus ponceanus* on Elliott Key, Dade Co., Florida.

34c. Pupa (lateral view) of *Papilio aristodemus ponceanus* on Elliott Key, Dade Co., Florida.

33a

33b

33c

34a

34c

34b

PLATE 25. LARVAE AND PUPAE OF PAPILIONIDAE

35a. Mature larva (lateral view) of *Papilio cresphontes* in Gainesville, Alachua Co., Florida.

35b. Pupa (lateral view) of *Papilio cresphontes* in northern Key Largo, Monroe Co., Florida.

35c. Comparison of pupae (lateral views) of *Papilio cresphontes* (left), *P. aristodemus ponceanus* (center), and *P. andraemon bonhotei* (right), all on Elliott Key, Monroe Co., Florida.

35a

35c

35b

PLATE 26. IMMATURES AND ADULTS OF PIERIDAE

38a. Mature larva of *Appias drusilla neumoegenii* on *Capparis flexuosa* in Broward Co., Florida.

38b. Pupa of *Appias drusilla neumoegenii* from a larva found on *Drypetes diversifolia* at the Bartlett Estate, Broward Co., Florida.

39a. Mature larva of *Ascia monuste phileta* on *Lepidium virginicum* (Broward Co., Florida).

39b. The pupa of *Ascia monuste phileta* (Broward Co., Florida) resembles a bird dropping.

54a. Mature larva of *Phoebis agarithe* on *Pithecellobium keyense* (Key Largo, Monroe Co., Florida).

54b. Pupa (lateral view) of *Phoebis agarithe* from eggs collected on *Lysiloma latisiliquum* at Arch Creek, Dade Co., Florida.

54c. *Phoebis agarithe* males drinking at moist pavement on northern Key Largo, Monroe Co., Florida.

38a

38b

39a

39b

54a

54b

54c

PLATE 27. LARVAE AND PUPAE OF LYCAENIDAE

59a. Mature larva (dorsal view) of *Chlorostrymon simaethis simaethis* in the fruit of balloon vine, *Cardiospermum halicacabum,* on Plantation Key, Monroe Co., Florida.

59b. Pupa (dorsal view) of *Chlorostrymon simaethis simaethis* reared from a larva on balloon vine, north Key Largo, Monroe Co., Florida.

63. Mature larva of *Strymon acis bartrami* feeding on the leaves of woolly croton on Big Pine Key, Monroe Co., Florida.

64. Mature larva of *Strymon columella modestus* on Key Largo, Monroe Co., Florida.

66. Mature larva (dorsal view) of *Strymon martialis* found on the flowers of bay cedar, *Suriana maritima*, on Elliott Key, Dade Co., Florida.

68. Mature larva of *Tmolus azia* on the flower buds of *Leucaena leucocephala* on Key Largo, Monroe Co., Florida.

85

59a

59b

63

64

66

68

PLATE 28.   LARVAE AND PUPAE OF LYCAENIDAE

68. Pupae of *Tmolus azia* reared from larvae found on the flowers of lead plant (*Leucaena leucocephala*) on Key Largo, Monroe Co., Florida.

72a. Two pods of balloon vine (*Cardiospermum halicacabum*) on north Key Largo, showing frass accumulation from the larvae of *Hemiargus thomasi bethunebakeri* in the pod on the left and an exit hole at the base of the pod on the right.

72b. Mature larva (dorsal view) of *Hemiargus thomasi bethunebakeri* in a balloon vine pod on north Key Largo, Monroe Co., Florida.

72c. Two pupae (dorsolateral and dorsal views) of *Hemiargus thomasi bethunebakeri* on north Key Largo, Monroe Co., Florida.

73a. Mature larva (green and red phase) of *Leptotes cassius theonus* on the flowers of *Lysiloma latisiliquum* (Fabaceae) on Elliott Key, Dade Co., Florida.

73b. Mature larva (red and gray phase) of *Leptotes cassius theonus*, found feeding on *Lysiloma* flowers on Elliott Key, Dade Co., Florida.

68

72a

2b

72c

73a

73b

PLATE 29. LARVAE AND PUPAE OF NYMPHALIDAE

78. Mature larva of *Dryas iulia largo* feeding on passion vine in Broward Co., Florida.

79. Mature larvae of *Heliconius charitonius tuckeri* on *Passiflora suberosa* vine in Broward Co., Florida.

81. The White Peacock, *Anartia jatrophae guatanamo*, is commonly encountered across south Florida and the Keys throughout the year.

83. Mature larva of *Eresia frisia frisia* feeding on the *Dicliptera assurgens* host plant, Elliott Key, Dade Co., Florida.

94. Pupa of *Marpesia petreus petreus* in Broward Co., Florida.

97. Pupa of *Siproeta steneles biplagiata* reared from eggs found on *Blechum brownei* (Acanthaceae) in Broward Co., Florida. Note the elongate silk pad from which the pupa is hanging.

101. Mature larva of *Anaea troglodyta floridalis* on woolly croton on Big Pine Key, Monroe Co., Florida.

78

79

81

83

94

97

101

CLASSIFICATION OF THE BUTTERFLIES

PAPILIONOIDEA

HESPERIIDAE
    *Megathyminae
    *Coeliadinae
    *Pyrrhopyginae
    Pyrginae
    *Trapezitinae
    *Heteropterinae
    Hesperiinae

PAPILIONIDAE
    *Baroniinae
    *Parnassiinae
    Papilioninae

PIERIDAE
    *Pseudopontiinae
    *Dismorphiinae
    Pierinae
    Coliadinae

LYCAENIDAE
    *Lipteninae
    *Poritiinae
    *Liphyrinae
    *Miletinae
    *Curetinae
    *Lycaeninae
    Eumaeinae
    Polyommatinae

RIODINIDAE
    *Euselasiinae
    Riodininae

LIBYTHEIDAE

NYMPHALIDAE
    *Ithomiinae
    *Acraeinae
    Heliconiinae
    Nymphalinae
    *Calinaginae
    *Apaturinae
    Charaxinae
    *Amathusiinae
    *Morphinae
    *Brassolinae
    Satyrinae
    Danainae

1. Classification modified from Heppner (1992).
* Exotic, not in south Florida.

FAMILY HESPERIIDAE
(Skipper Butterflies)

Nearly one-third of the butterflies found in the Florida Keys are skippers. Skipper butterflies (Hesperiidae) may be recognized by the antennae, which are usually hooked or bent at the tip. Whereas the last segments of the antenna (the apiculus) of most skippers taper to a point, other butterfly groups have a rounded club. The robust body, broad head, and dark, opaque eyes are additional distinguishing characteristics. The forewings often have white, yellowish, or translucent spots. The ground color of the upper surfaces is frequently a uniform dark brown, or in some groups, golden-yellow with dark borders. A few tropical species found in the Keys have iridescent blue markings. All six legs are used for perching. Eggs are dome-shaped or conical, and may be ribbed, sculptured, or smooth. The larvae of most species cut and fold portions of leaves or tie leaves together to form a shelter in which they hide. Skipper caterpillars have large heads, a narrow neck, and often a dark hardened plate on top of the first thoracic segment, the prothoracic shield. The larvae are slow moving and usually do not try to get away if disturbed. Pupation usually takes place in the last larval shelter. The pupa is secured to the shelter by a silk girdle around the middle and the caudal end is attached to a silk pad. Adult males often have pheromone producing and disseminating structures on the wings. Adults range in size from very small to medium-sized butterflies.

SUBFAMILY PYRGINAE (Broad-Winged Skippers)

As their name suggests, broad-winged skippers or pyrgines often have larger wings relative to the other major group of hesperiids in the Keys, the branded skippers. Most pyrgines feed on dicotyledonous plants, especially legumes, in the larval stages. The caterpillars may be brightly marked with red or yellow, and live in rather roomy leaf shelters on the host. The prothoracic shield is large and dark in some genera, and absent in others. Males and females tend to have similar color patterns. However, males of many species may be easily distinguished by the costal fold, a flap covering specialized pheromone-releasing scales (androconia) along the costal margin of the dorsal forewings. Adults of many species freqently land on the undersides of leaves. Ten species of pyrgines have been reported from the Keys. Those most likely to be encountered are the Zestos Skipper, Florida Dusky Wing, Mangrove Skipper, Hammock Skipper, Tropical Checkered Skipper, Dorantes Skipper, and Long-Tailed Skipper.

1. ZESTOS SKIPPER
Epargyreus zestos zestos (Geyer)

Pl. 1, Fig. 1

DESCRIPTION: FW = 24-27.5 mm. The Zestos Skipper is readily distinguished from other butterflies in the Keys by the golden band on the forewings, the short tails, and the simple pattern of light and dark brown bands on the ventral hindwings. The ground color is yellowish-brown, with a faint purplish iridescence on the under surfaces. The sexes are similar, but males have a narrow costal fold.
DISTRIBUTION: Big Pine Key, Elliott Key, Geiger Key, Key Largo, Key Vaca, Key West, Lignumvitae Key, Long Key, Plantation Key, Stock Island, Sugarloaf Key, Upper Matecumbe Key.

Epargyreus zestos zestos is also found in the Bahamas and most of the eastern Antilles, but not on Cuba or Jamaica. Clench and Bjorndal (1980) recently described the populations from Great Inagua, Little Inagua, and Caicos Islands as a separate race.

NATURAL HISTORY: The Zestos Skipper frequents tropical hardwood hammocks. Males perch along trails or hammock edges. Adults sometimes alight on the undersides of leaves. The eggs are laid singly on the leaves of *Galactia striata* (= *Galactia spiciformis*; Wunderlin, 1982), a legume. The larvae partially cut and fold over sections of leaves to build shelters when small, or tie several leaves together in later instars. The caterpillar is green with a rounded, black head marked with two yellow eye patches (Plate 22). The prothoracic shield is black. Pupae are brown. Adults have been reported for every month except January in the Keys.

FLOWERS VISITED: *Bidens alba, Lantana involucrata, Morinda royoc, Senecio mexicana.*

STATUS: Although locally abundant in the Lower Keys, the Zestos Skipper occurs sporadically in the Upper Keys and has largely disappeared from the mainland (Lenczewski, 1980). The host plant is quite common on Elliott Key and Key Largo, but this butterfly has not been seen in the northernmost Keys since the 1970's, in spite of intensive field observation.

2. FLORIDA DUSKY WING   Pl. 2, Fig. 2
Ephyriades brunnea floridensis Bell and Comstock

DESCRIPTION: FW = 15-19 mm. Adults of the Florida Dusky Wing are black with whitish spots on the forewings. Females tend to have larger spots than males and are patterned with pale bands having a purplish iridescence. Males are very darkly-colored and have conspicuous costal folds on the forewings. The outer margin of the hindwing is rounder than in *Erynnis zarucco*.

DISTRIBUTION: Big Pine Key, Cudjoe Key, Key Largo, Lower Matecumbe Key, No Name Key, Stock Island, Sugarloaf Key, Summerland Key.

The type specimens of *E. brunnea floridensis* are from Key Largo (Miller & Brown, 1981), and this race is endemic to Florida. *Ephyriades brunnea brunnea* Herrich-Schäffer is found in Cuba and the Bahamas. Other races of *E. brunnea* occur on Jamaica and the Leeward Islands.

NATURAL HISTORY: Adults have a swift flight, low to the ground. The eggs are laid on locust berry, *Byrsonima lucida* (Malpighiaceae), a common shrub in tropical pinelands. An exotic shrub in the same family grown for its tart, edible fruit, Barbados cherry (*Malpighia glabra*), may also be used in urban areas of the Keys. The larvae feed on leaves and construct shelters by folding over sections of leaves or tying several leaves together. The caterpillar is light green with a few narrow yellow lines running down the body (Plate 22). The head is dark brown or black with patches of orange. The pupa is green. Adults occur all months of the year and readily visit flowers for nectar. One individual was found being eaten by an unidentified crab spider (Thomisidae) on the flowers of *Croton linearis* on Big Pine Key (19 Feb. 1990).

FLOWERS VISITED: *Bidens alba, Bumelia salicifolia, Byrsonima lucida, Coccoloba uvifera, Croton linearis, Flaveria linearis, Lantana involucrata, Morinda royoc, Pithecellobium keyense, Pluchea odorata, Senecio mexicana.*

STATUS: The Florida Dusky Wing is abundant in the pineland areas of the Lower Keys. It is also found in low numbers on North Key Largo in the area that was once pine forest, but is now tropical hardwood hammock. Locust berry is present at this site. This skipper is also abundant in the pinelands of Everglades National Park and other areas of southern Dade County.

3. ZARUCCO DUSKY WING
Erynnnis zarucco (Lucas)

Pl. 2, Fig. 3

DESCRIPTION: FW = 15-20 mm. The Zarucco Dusky Wing is a medium-sized, darkly-colored skipper with small white spots on the forewings. Females have a distinctive pale patch between the white spots on the uppersides of the forewings. Males have conspicuous costal folds. The hindwings are relatively broad. There is considerable variation in the coloration of the hindwing fringes. Most specimens have a mixture of brown and white scales, although some may be nearly pure white, especially females. Another skipper found in the Keys, the Florida Dusky Wing, is similar in appearance, but that species has a noticeably rounder outer margin of the hindwing.

DISTRIBUTION: Big Pine Key, Fleming Island, Geiger Key, Key West, Lignumvitae Key, Stock Island, Sugarloaf Key, Summerland Key.

Erynnis zarucco also occurs in Cuba, Hispaniola, Puerto Rico, and as other races, on the mainland and in North, Central, and South America.

NATURAL HISTORY: The Zarucco Dusky Wing is found in open, weedy fields and along roadsides. The flight pattern is swift and low to the ground. The orange eggs are laid on the new growth of *Sesbania macrocarpa* (Fabaceae). Immatures may at times be very abundant on isolated plants of the host and are easily reared. The larvae tie leaflets together to form shelters. The caterpillar is green with a dark and pale yellow lateral line (Plate 22). The head is light brown with orange patches and a dark "W" on the front. Pupae are green. Adults can be found during all months of the year on the Lower Keys.

FLOWERS VISITED: *Bidens alba.*

STATUS: Adults of *E. zarucco* occur in low to medium abundance in the Lower Keys. The Zarucco Dusky Wing has not been reported from the northernmost Keys, and the brown-fringed mainland race is rare on the southern tip of Florida. Although both Riley (1975) and Schwartz (1987) state that Caribbean populations of *E. zarucco* are brown-fringed, specimens that we have examined from Hispaniola and Cuba are like the Keys population in having brown and white fringes. According to Miller and Miller (1989), the current distribution of *E. zarucco* in the Caribbean is best explained by a disperalist model. However, a vicariance model could also easily apply, in which populations of *Erynnis zarucco* in the Antilles were originally derived from white-fringed *Erynnis zarucco funeralis* of southwestern North America. We believe that the Keys population today is most closely related to Cuban, not mainland, stock, and the partially white fringes are the result of genes from distant *E. zarucco funeralis* kinship. If this is indeed true, then the situation becomes taxomonically complex, because the types of *E. zarucco* are from Cuba. If three races are to be recognized, then *E. zarucco funeralis* is the white-fringed taxon of western North America, Central America, and South America, *E. zarucco zarucco* is the Caribbean race, and the eastern North American population is undescribed!

4. VARIEGATED SKIPPER
Gorgythion begga pyralinus (Möschler)

Pl. 2, Fig. 4

DESCRIPTION: FW = 13.5 mm. As its common name implies, the Variegated Skipper is complexly patterned with light and dark brown on the upper wings. A short row of small white spots occurs near the apex of the forewing. The upper wings have a purplish luster. The hindwings are mostly dark brown below. The sexes are similar in appearance.

STATUS: A few specimens of this smallish skipper, apparently accidental imports from Mexico or Central America, were taken on 28 April 1968 and 3 January 1970 on Key Largo (H. D. Baggett, pers. comm.). These are the only reports of *G. begga pyralinus* from Florida, and the Variegated Skipper does not occur elsewhere in the Caribbean. Although several specimens were collected on each occasion, this species has failed to become permanently established.

5. MANGROVE SKIPPER   Pl. 1, Fig. 5
Phocides pigmalion okeechobee (Worthington)

DESCRIPTION: FW = 24.5-33 mm. This is the largest skipper in Florida and cannot be mistaken for any other species. The wings are black with iridescent blue markings (Plate 22). The sexes are similar in appearance, but males have narrow costal folds.

DISTRIBUTION: Adams Key, Bahia Honda Key, Big Pine Key, Boca Chica Key, Cudjoe Key, Elliott Key, Key Largo, Key Vaca, Key West, Lignumvitae Key, No Name Key, Old Rhodes Key, Plantation Key, Stock Island, Sugarloaf Key, Summerland Key, Totten Key, Upper Matecumbe Key.

The Florida population is distinct from *Phocides pigmalion batabano* Lucas of Cuba, Cayman Islands, and Bahamas. Other races, which are very differently colored from Florida specimens, occur in Hispaniola, Puerto Rico, and in Mexico, Central America, and South America.

NATURAL HISTORY: Adults of this robust skipper are powerful flyers. Males can often be seen patrolling over the tops of mangroves. Females are more often found along the edges of mangrove forests. Both sexes visit flowers readily and are rather docile and easily-collected while feeding. Adults often perch on the undersides of leaves. The eggs are laid singly on the leaves of red mangrove (*Rhizophora mangle*, Rhizophoraceae). Larvae cut and fold over sections of leaves. Young larvae are brilliantly colored, being red with transverse yellow stripes (Plate 22), but they change to white in the last instar. The brown head capsule bears two yellow eye patches. The pupa is greenish white. The Mangrove Skipper flies all year in the Keys.

FLOWERS VISITED: *Bauhinia variegata, Bidens alba, Bourreria ovata, Bougainvillea glabra, Casasia clusiifolia, Eupatorium odoratum, Ipomoea indica, Lantana camara, Lysiloma latisiliquum, Metopium toxiferum, Morinda royoc, Pithecellobium keyense, Pluchea odorata, Senecio mexicana, Solanum blodgettii.*

STATUS: The Mangrove Skipper is abundant throughout the Florida Keys and in coastal areas of the southern mainland.

6. HAMMOCK SKIPPER   Pl. 1, Fig. 6
Polygonus leo savigny (Latreille)

DESCRIPTION: FW = 22-25 mm. The Hammock Skipper is a relatively large species with large white spots on the forewings. The ground color of the uppersides is blackish with a steely luster. The undersides of the hindwings are paler with two dark bands and a purplish sheen. The hindwings have two very short tails.

DISTRIBUTION: Bahia Honda Key, Big Pine Key, Cudjoe Key, Elliott Key, Key Largo, Key Vaca, Key West, Lignumvitae Key, No Name Key, Old Rhodes Key, Plantation Key, Stock Island, Sugarloaf Key, Summerland Key, Windley Key.

Polygonus leo savigny is found in southern Florida, Cuba, the Bahamas, Virgin Islands, and Leeward Islands. Other subspecies of *Polygonus leo* occur in Hispaniola, Jamaica, Mexico,

Central America, and South America.

NATURAL HISTORY: Adults of the Hammock Skipper frequent wooded areas. Males perch along trails and hammock edges. Like many other tropical pyrgines, this species often alights on the undersides of leaves. Eggs are laid singly on the new growth of Jamaica dogwood (*Piscidia piscipula*, Fabaceae). An exotic ornamental tree in the same family, *Pongamia pinnata*, is probably also used as a host in urban areas. The caterpillar is light green with a pale yellow lateral line on each side (Plate 22). The head is whitish with two black spots on the upper front and a black line along the side. The larvae are frequently parasitized by a small black braconid wasp (*Apanteles* species?). Dozens of these wasps may emerge from each parasitized caterpillar. Dyar (1897) described the egg and larval stages in greater detail. The pupa is green with a short horn on the head. Adults occur all months of the year in the Keys.

FLOWERS VISITED: *Bidens alba, Galactia striata, Lantana camara, Lantana involucrata, Morinda royoc, Pithecellobium keyense, Pluchea odorata, Senecio mexicana.*

STATUS: The Hammock Skipper is abundant in tropical hammocks throughout the Keys and in coastal areas of the southern mainland. A similar species, *Polygonus manueli*, has been reported from Florida (Kimball, 1965) but does not currently occur in the state and probably never did. We have examined the dos Passos specimens listed in Kimball and they are all *P. leo*. Older valid specimens of *P. manueli*, including a paratype from Royal Palm Hammock on the mainland (Bell and Comstock, 1948), are probably mislabelled. The known distribution of *P. manueli* is confined to Mexico, Central America, and South America.

7. TROPICAL CHECKERED SKIPPER
Pl. 2, Fig. 7

Pyrgus oileus oileus (Linnaeus)

DESCRIPTION: FW = 13-15 mm. The Tropical Checkered Skipper has a distinctive color pattern of black banding on a white ground. Males have numerous long bluish-white hairs on the uppersides of the wings and costal folds. Females are darker above than males. A similar species found in northern Florida, *Pyrgus communis* (Grote), has been reported from Key West (Kimball, 1965), but the record is probably based on a misidentified female *P. oileus* or a mislabelled specimen.

DISTRIBUTION: Big Pine Key, Elliott Key, Key Largo, Key West, Lignumvitae Key, Lower Matecumbe Key, Plantation Key, Stock Island, Upper Matecumbe Key.

The Tropical Checkered Skipper is found throughout mainland Florida, the Keys, and the Greater Antilles, but is absent from most of the Bahamas. Another subspecies is found in the Lesser Antilles and South America.

NATURAL HISTORY: Males of the Tropical Checkered Skipper patrol for females, flying low to the ground in weedy disturbed sites. Both sexes often feed at flowers. The pale greenish eggs are laid singly on the young leaves of malvaceous plants. *Sida acuta, Sida rhombifolia*, and *Malvastrum corchorifolium* are probably the main hosts in the Keys. Larvae are green with faint whitish striations. The head is black and hairy. Behind the head is a light brown prothoracic shield. The caterpillars fold and tie leaves to form shelters in which they hide. Pupae are greenish with a sparse covering of relatively long hairs. Tropical Checkered Skipper adults have been reported for every month in the Keys.

FLOWERS VISITED: *Bidens alba, Lippia nodiflora, Melanthera aspera, Morinda royoc, Sida acuta.*

STATUS: *Pyrgus oileus* is variable in abundance and distribution in the Keys, but seems to be consistently present in weedlots and along roadsides on Key Largo.

8. SOUTHERN SOOTY WING   Pl. 2, Fig. 8
Staphylus hayhurstii (W. H. Edwards)

DESCRIPTION: FW = 10.5-13.5 mm. The Southern Sooty Wing is a small dark skipper that has some white spots near the apex and usually also a spot near the middle of the forewing. The outer margin of the hindwing is scalloped. The sexes are similar, but males have costal folds. *Gorgythion begga* is somewhat similar in appearance, but a careful comparison of the color figures will show the differences in pattern.

DISTRIBUTION: *Staphylus hayhurstii* occurs throughout Florida and much of the eastern and midwestern United States. The only records in the Keys are from Key Largo. This species does not occur elsewhere in the Caribbean.

NATURAL HISTORY: The adults occur in wooded areas near the host plant. The wings are held out to the sides rather than over the back at rest. The Southern Sooty Wing often perches on the undersides of leaves. Eggs are laid singly on the host. We suspect that *Iresine canescens* (Amaranthaceae) is the food plant in the Keys. Like other pyrgines, the larvae construct shelters from and feed on the leaves of the host. The larva has a black head covered with numerous hairs and a very narrow neck. The prothoracic shield is light brown. The body is light green with numerous small whitish spots. Pupae are brown with a thick covering of white wax. Adults have been found in May, August, September, November, and December on Key Largo.

STATUS: This drab little butterfly was locally distributed on Key Largo, but there have been no records of it from the Keys in recent years, and it may no longer be present.

9. DORANTES SKIPPER   Pl. 1, Fig. 9
Urbanus dorantes dorantes (Stoll)

DESCRIPTION: FW = 19.5-22.5 mm. The Dorantes Skipper is one of two long-tailed skipper butterflies found in Florida, but it may easily be distinguished from *Urbanus proteus* by the plain brown dorsal surfaces. The forewings bear large spots, and a pattern of dark brown bands on a lighter ground mark the undersides of the hindwings. The sexes are similar, but males have costal folds.

DISTRIBUTION: Big Pine Key, Cudjoe Key, Elliott Key, Key Largo, Key Vaca, Key West, Lignumvitae Key, No Name Key, Plantation Key, Stock Island, Sugarloaf Key, Summerland Key, Windley Key.

The Dorantes Skipper is found throughout Florida, Mexico, and Central and South America. Other races occur on Cuba and on Hispaniola, Puerto Rico, and the Virgin Islands.

NATURAL HISTORY: Adults occur both in open areas and forests. Males frequently perch along trails and hammock edges or patrol weedy areas for females. The flight is erratic and low to the ground. Both sexes visit flowers freely. At rest, the wings are held closed over the back, and adults sometimes perch on the undersides of leaves. The greenish eggs are laid singly on the young leaves and pedicels of beggar ticks, *Desmodium incanum* and *Desmodium tortuosum* (Fabaceae). Larvae feed on leaves and make leaf shelters in which to hide. The caterpillar is brown with a black head and prothoracic shield (Heppner, 1975). The brown-colored pupa is thinly covered by a white wax. Adults occur all months of the year in the Keys.

FLOWERS VISITED: *Bidens alba, Flaveria linearis, Lantana involucrata, Melanthera aspera, Senecio mexicana, Stachytarpheta jamaicensis.* One adult was seen feeding on a bird dropping, 23 July 1987, on Elliott Key.

STATUS: The Dorantes Skipper is sporadic in distribution and abundance in the Keys, but may be numerous on occasion. This species only recently has become established in Florida (Clench, 1970), but is now quite widespread and abundant, especially in south Florida.

10. LONG-TAILED SKIPPER
Urbanus proteus proteus (Linnaeus)

Pl. 1, Fig. 10

DESCRIPTION: FW = 20-24.5 mm. *Urbanus proteus* is readily distinguished by the long tails on the hindwings, and the iridescent blue flush on the upper surfaces of the wings (Plate 33). Males are very similar to females but have small costal folds on the forewings.

DISTRIBUTION: Adams Key, Big Pine Key, Elliott Key, Geiger Key, Key Largo, Key Vaca, Key West, Lignumvitae Key, No Name Key, Plantation Key, Stock Island, Sugarloaf Key, Upper Matecumbe Key, Windley Key.

Urbanus proteus proteus occurs throughout Florida and the southern United States, Mexico, Central America, and South America. A different race, *Urbanus proteus domingo* (Scudder), is found in the West Indies.

NATURAL HISTORY: This butterfly is similar to the Dorantes Skipper in behavior and ecology. Adults sometimes perch on the undersides of leaves and often visit flowers. Unlike the Dorantes Skipper, the Long-Tailed Skipper tends to perch with the wings partly open. The yellowish eggs are laid singly or one on top of the other in short strings. The larvae eat the leaves of *Desmodium incanum, Desmodium tortuosum,* and *Galactia striata* (Fabaceae). The caterpillar is brightly colored, being yellowish green with black striations (see color plate 47 in Pyle, 1981). The supraspiracular line is light yellow most of the length of the body, but changes to orange on the last two segments. Each proleg is marked with an orange spot. The prothorax is red ventrally and bears a black dorsal shield. The head is mostly light brown with a black front and reddish eye patches (Heppner, 1975). The pupa is brown with a coating of white wax. Adults occur all months of the year in the Keys.

FLOWERS VISITED: *Alternanthera ramosissima, Bidens alba, Bougainvillea glabra, Eupatorium odoratum, Lantana camara, Lantana involucrata, Melanthera aspera, Pluchea odorata, Senecio mexicana, Schinus terebinthifolius, Stachytarpheta jamaicensis.*

STATUS: The Long-Tailed Skipper is widespread and abundant on the mainland (especially during the fall), but is sporadic in distribution and abundance in the Keys.

SUBFAMILY HESPERIINAE
(Branded Skippers)

Branded skippers may have either relatively short stubby wings or somewhat longer and narrower wings, depending on the group. The males of many species have dark patches or lines of androconial scales (stigmas or sex-brands) on the dorsal side of the forewings. Ground colors may be dark brown or golden-yellow with dark borders. The darker species frequently have spots on the forewings. Hesperiines are also known as grass skippers, because the larvae feed on monocots, especially grasses. The caterpillars of most species construct shelters by tying the edges of leaves together. Some species do not make shelters. Larval color depends in part upon the habitat preference. Those that live near the ground or at the base of the host plant are usually brown with dark heads. Species that live up on the leaves of host are more often green with light-colored heads that may be patterned with disruptive stripes, lines, and spots. The prothoracic shield is usually much narrower than that of pyrgines. In some genera, the pupa has a sharp point on the head. At least 19 species of hesperiines have been found in the Florida Keys. The branded skippers most likely to be encountered are the Monk Skipper, Field Skipper, Three Spot Skipper, Klots' Sawgrass Skipper, Fiery Skipper, Twin Spot Skipper, Obscure Skipper, and the Broken Dash.

11. MONK SKIPPER
Asbolis capucinus (Lucas)

Pl. 1, Fig. 11

DESCRIPTION: FW = 21-24 mm. The Monk Skipper is a robust species with plain brown wings. Males have a long narrow stigma running across the middle of each forewing and are smaller than females.

DISTRIBUTION: Adams Key, Big Pine Key, Boca Chica Key, Cudjoe Key, Elliott Key, Key Biscayne, Key Largo, Key Vaca, Key West, Lignumvitae Key, Lower Matecumbe Key, No Name Key, Plantation Key, Stock Island, Sugarloaf Key, Summerland Key, Upper Matecumbe Key.

Asbolis capucinus is abundant in southern Florida and in the Keys. This species is native to Cuba.

NATURAL HISTORY: The Monk Skipper is a powerful flyer, but often visits flowers. This butterfly is most abundant in urban areas near palms. Males perch on vegetation and fly out to investigate passing butterflies. The eggs are laid singly on the leaves of palms (Arecaceae). Coconut palm (*Cocos nucifera*) seems to be the preferred host, but silver palm (*Coccothrinax argentata*, Fig. 38), thatch palm (*Thrinax radiata*, Fig. 45), saw palmetto (*Serenoa repens*), areca palm (*Chrysalidocarpus lutescens*), and Christmas palm (*Veitchia merrillii*) are also used. The larvae feed on the mature leaves and construct shelters by tying the edges of an individual leaflet together. Feeding takes place toward the tip of the leaflet, but the midrib is usually left intact. The caterpillar is light bluish-green with a yellowish flush and black spiracles (Plate 23). The head is pale orange-brown. On the prothorax, the dorsal shield is a narrow black line. The anal plate is broad, rounded, and outlined in black. Pupae are olive green and black. Adults occur all months of the year in the Keys.

FLOWERS VISITED: *Allamanda cathartica, Bidens alba, Catheranthus roseus, Flaveria linearis, Ipomoea indica, Pluchea odorata, Senecio mexicana.*

STATUS: The monk skipper became established in Florida in the 1940's (Klots, 1951), and is now abundant as far north as Tampa. Its dispersal has undoubtedly been facilitated by the widespread planting of introduced palms in urban landscaping.

12. FIELD SKIPPER
Atalopedes campestris huron (W. H. Edwards)

Pl. 3, Fig. 12

DESCRIPTION: FW = 13.5-18 mm. Males of the Field Skipper are readily identified by the large oval stigma on each forewing. The uppersides are mostly golden-yellow with dark brown borders. Females are much darker above, but are easily distinguished from other species by the squarish translucent spot near the middle of the forewing.

DISTRIBUTION: Big Pine Key, Boca Chica Key, Cudjoe Key, Elliott Key, Geiger Key, Key Largo, Key Vaca, Key West, No Name Key, Plantation Key, Ramrod Key, Stock Island, Sugarloaf Key, Summerland Key, Upper Matecumbe Key.

The Field Skipper is a common species in the warmer parts of North, Central, and South America. Despite being such a widely distributed butterfly, *A. campestris* does not occur in the West Indies. Several other endemic species in the same genus occur in the Greater Antilles and a few of the Bahama Islands.

NATURAL HISTORY: The Field Skipper frequents weedy disturbed sites, salt marshes, and grassy tropical pinelands. Males perch on the ground or low vegetation and fly out to investigate passing insects. Females fly near the ground in grassy areas. The whitish eggs are laid singly on low grasses (Poaceae). Larvae are a drab olive color with black heads and prothoracic shields. Silken tubes mixed with detritus are constructed by the larvae along the ground, at the bases of grass stalks. The caterpillars live in these tubes, but come out to feed on the leaves of the host. Pupae are brown with sparse hairs. Adults have been recorded every month except July in the Keys.

FLOWERS VISITED: *Bidens alba, Flaveria linearis, Lantana camara, Lantana ovatifolia, Lippia nodiflora, Melanthera aspera, Sida hederacea, Senecio mexicana.*

STATUS: The Field Skipper is sporadic in distribution and abundance in the Keys, but seems to be most numerous in the pinelands of the Lower Keys.

13. CANNA SKIPPER   Pl. 1, Fig. 13
Calpodes ethlius (Stoll)

DESCRIPTION: FW = 23-26.5 mm. *Calpodes ethlius* is a large brownish skipper with translucent spots on the wings. Diagnostic features include the rather narrow pointy forewings, the spot in the forewing cell, and the short row of small translucent spots on the hindwings.

DISTRIBUTION: Big Pine Key, Elliott Key, Key Largo, Key West, Stock Island.

The Canna Skipper is found throughout Florida, much of the West Indies, and in the more tropical parts of Mexico, Central America, and South America.

NATURAL HISTORY: The adults are active at dawn and dusk, but also fly at other times of the day. Richard Anderson (pers. comm.) collected one at a light in Key West. They are good dispersers, and isolated hosts will frequently have numerous immatures. The small grayish eggs are laid singly on the leaves of *Canna* species and related plants. There are no natural food plants in the Keys, but ornamental *Canna* species and hybrids are sometimes used in landscaping. Immatures may be abundant on cannas in urban areas. Larvae have light brown heads with a black spot on the front. The prothoracic shield is a narrow black line, and the body cuticle is transparent. Pupae are light green and have an exceeding long tongue case, extending beyond the body, and a sharp point on the head. Adults have been taken in January, September, October, November, and December in the Keys, a pattern exhibited by many migratory butterflies.

FLOWERS VISITED: *Ipomoea indica, Senecio mexicana.*

STATUS: Adults of *Calpodes ethlius* are usually uncommon in the Keys, but have been seen in good numbers on occasion.

14. SOUTHERN SKIPPERLING

Pl. 4, Fig. 14

Copaeodes minima (W. H. Edwards)

DESCRIPTION: FW = 8-10 mm. The Southern Skipperling is one of the smallest butterflies in Florida. Adults are mostly golden-yellow in color. The underside of the hindwing is yellow with a narrow whitish streak from the base to the outer margin. Females tend to be slightly larger and darker than males.

DISTRIBUTION: Elliott Key, Key Largo.

Copaeodes minima is found in the southeastern United States, Mexico, and Central America. Other species in the same genus occur in the Greater Antilles.

NATURAL HISTORY: The Southern Skipperling is found in disturbed grassy areas. Adults have a rapid darting flight close to the ground and may be easily overlooked due to their small size. Eggs are laid singly on weedy grasses (Poaceae) such as Bermuda grass (*Cynodon dactylon*), but host plants in the Keys have not been determined. Caterpillars and pupae are mostly green in color. The pupa has a sharp point on the head. The few adults reported from the Keys were found in May and November.

STATUS: There was only one record of *C. minima* from the Keys (a single female that we found on Elliott Key) before 1989, but Richard Boscoe (pers. comm.) saw many on Key Largo during November of that year. This abundance must have been the result of migration or temporary colonization, however, as no additional records have turned up. The Southern Skipperling is locally abundant on the mainland.

15. THREE SPOT SKIPPER

Pl. 2, Fig. 15

Cymaenes tripunctus tripunctus (Herrich-Schäffer)

DESCRIPTION: FW = 12-15 mm. The Three Spot Skipper is a small drab butterfly that may be easily confused with other similar skippers. The main distinguishing features are the long antennae, the small white spots (usually more than three) near the apex and the middle of the forewings (but not in the cell), and the faint row of spots on the undersides of the hindwings.

DISTRIBUTION: Big Pine Key, Elliott Key, Key Largo, Key Vaca, Key West, Long Key, No Name Key, Plantation Key, Stock Island, Sugarloaf Key, Summerland Key, Upper Matecumbe Key.

The Three Spot Skipper is found in southern Florida, the Greater Antilles, and the Virgin Islands. Another subspecies of *C. tripunctus* is widely distributed in Mexico, Central America, and South America.

NATURAL HISTORY: *Cymaenes tripunctus* is usually found in or near wooded, disturbed sites. Adults perch on low vegetation and visit flowers. Eggs are laid singly on grasses (Poaceae) such as Guineagrass (*Panicum maximum*) and *Digitaria sanguinalis*. Larvae live in shelters formed by tying the edges of an individual leaf together. The caterpillar is light green with faint white lines and striations on the body (Plate 23). The head is whitish with dark brown edges and stripes. The pupa is green with a sharp point on the head. Adults occur all months of the year in the Keys.

FLOWERS VISITED: *Bidens alba, Cirsium horridulum, Eupatorium coelestinum, Flaveria linearis, Pithecellobium keyense.*

STATUS: The Three Spot Skipper is locally abundant in the Keys, especially in weedy urban areas.

16. PALMETTO SKIPPER
Euphyes arpa (Boisduval and Leconte)

DESCRIPTION: FW = 16.5-20 mm. Males of the Palmetto Skipper are golden-yellow above, with dark brown borders and a dark stigma across the middle of each forewing. Females are mostly dark brown, with some golden spots on the forewings. Both sexes are golden-yellow below.

DISTRIBUTION: Big Pine Key, Sugarloaf Key.

   The Palmetto Skipper occurs mostly in peninsular Florida.

NATURAL HISTORY: Open tropical pineland is the usual habitat of the Palmetto Skipper in the Keys. Adults are often found at flowers. Eggs are laid on the leaves of palmettos (Arecaceae), especially saw palmetto (*Serenoa repens*). The color of the eggs is light green with a red swirl about the middle. The larva folds and ties segments of a mature leaf together to form a shelter. The caterpillar is green with a small white and black prothoracic shield. The head is whitish with light brown stripes and bears a black spot on the upper front. A plug of white wax is used to block the entrance of the shelter before pupation. Adults have been found in January, March, April, May, October, and December in the Keys.

FLOWERS VISITED: *Cirsium horridulum*.

STATUS: The Palmetto Skipper was fairly abundant in the tropical pinelands of the Lower Keys in the 1970's (R. Anderson and H. D. Baggett, pers. comm.), but it seems to have recently disappeared and may no longer occur in the Keys. We have not seen it on Big Pine Key in spite of many surveys conducted since 1982 in pineland habitats with saw palmetto. Neither did Schwartz (1987) find any specimens.

17. SAWGRASS SKIPPER
Euphyes pilatka (W. H. Edwards)

DESCRIPTION: FW = 17.5-22 mm. Males of the Sawgrass Skipper are golden-yellow, with dark brown borders and a short black stigma in the middle of each forewing. Two different races of the Sawgrass Skipper occur in the Keys. The endemic Lower Keys population (*Euphyes pilatka klotsi* Miller, Harvey and Miller, 1985) is darker than the mainland race. Females are especially dark above and resemble females of the Palmetto Skipper. Unlike this species, however, the ventral hindwings of both sexes of *E. pilatka* are brownish.

DISTRIBUTION: *Euphyes pilatka pilatka*: Key Largo. *Euphyes pilatka klotsi*: Big Pine Key, Big Torch Key, Cudjoe Key, No Name Key, Stock Island, Sugarloaf Key.

   The Sawgrass Skipper occurs throughout most of Florida, and north along the coastal plain to Virginia.

NATURAL HISTORY: Males perch near clumps of the host plant and fly out to investigate passing insects. Both sexes often come to flowers for nectar. The light green eggs are laid singly on the leaves of sawgrass *Cladium jamaicense* (Cyperaceae), a large sedge armed with small sharp teeth along the margins of the leaves. Eggs develop a red swirl about the middle after they are laid. Larvae tie the edges of leaves together (especially those near the central growing point) to form shelters in which they hide. The caterpillar is similar to that of the Palmetto Skipper, but has three black lines separated by white on the head. Before pupation, the entrance to the shelter is plugged with particles of wax. Tachinid flies frequently parasitize the immature stages of Klots' Sawgrass Skipper on Big Pine Key. Adults of Klots' Sawgrass

Skipper have been taken in December, January, February, March, April, May, September, and October.

FLOWERS VISITED: *Bidens alba, Cirsium horridulum, Croton linearis, Flaveria linearis, Pithecellobium keyense, Senecio mexicana.*

STATUS: Klots' Sawgrass Skipper is usually uncommon in the tropical pinelands of the Lower Keys, but immatures are often relatively easy to find. Individuals of the mainland race occasionally turn up on northern Key Largo, but do not seem to breed there although sawgrass is present.

18. ROCKLAND GRASS SKIPPER   Pl. 3, Fig. 18
Hesperia meskei (W. H. Edwards)

DESCRIPTION: FW = 13-16.5 mm. Adults of *Hesperia meskei* are golden-yellow and dark brown on the upper surfaces. Males have a dark stigma in the middle of the forewings. The undersides are greenish-yellow with a row of yellow spots.

DISTRIBUTION: Big Pine Key, Sugarloaf Key.

The Keys population of *Hesperia meskei* seems to represent an unnamed subspecies. This species occurs locally from southern Florida northward into North Carolina. Another population is found in the southern Great Plains.

NATURAL HISTORY: Adults of the Rockland Grass Skipper perch on low vegetation and occasionally visit flowers. H. D. Baggett has observed oviposition on the grass, *Aristida purpurascens* (McGuire, 1982), but the life history is unknown. Adults have been taken in every month except February, July, and August.

FLOWERS VISITED: *Bidens alba.*

STATUS: As with *E. arpa*, the Rockland Grass Skipper was abundant in grassy tropical pinelands on some of the Lower Keys in the 1970's, but it seems to have disappeared in recent times. No specimens have been reported from the Keys since 1985.

19. FIERY SKIPPER   Pl. 3, Fig. 19
Hylephila phyleus phyleus (Drury)

DESCRIPTION: FW = 12-17.5 mm. The Fiery Skipper gets its name from the bright golden-yellow color of the males. Females, however, are mostly dark brown with golden-yellow spots above. Diagnostic features include the very short antennae, and the pattern of small dark spots on the undersides of the hindwings (Fig. 41).

DISTRIBUTION: Big Pine Key, Cudjoe Key, Elliott Key, Geiger Key, Key Largo, Key West, Plantation Key, Stock Island, Summerland Key, Upper Matecumbe Key.

Hylephila phyleus is very widely distributed in the warmer areas of North, Central, and South America. This butterfly also occurs throughout the West Indies.

NATURAL HISTORY: Adults perch on low vegetation in weedy disturbed sites and visit flowers freely. The white eggs are laid singly on grasses (Poaceae) such as Bermuda grass, *Cynodon dactylon*, but the hosts used in the Keys are not known. The larvae are brown with black heads and prothoracic shields. They live in silken tubes near the base of the plants. Pupae are cream-colored with dark brown markings on the dorsum. Adults fly every month of the year in the Keys.

FLOWERS VISITED: *Bidens alba, Flaveria linearis, Lantana ovatifolia, Lippia nodiflora,*

Melanthera aspera, Pithecellobium keyense, Sida acuta, Sida hederacea, Stachytarpheta jamaicensis.

STATUS: The Fiery Skipper is variable in abundance in the Keys, but may be numerous on occasion.

20. CLOUDED SKIPPER   Pl. 4, Fig. 20
Lerema accius accius (J. E. Smith)

DESCRIPTION: FW = 13-18 mm. *Lerema accius* is a medium-sized blackish skipper. Males usually have some small white spots and a black stigma on the forewings. Females are larger than males and have larger white spots on the forewings. The undersides of the hindwings of both sexes are obscurely patterned, with a dark band toward the middle and blue-gray shading along the outer margin.

DISTRIBUTION: Big Pine Key, Elliott Key, Key Largo, Key Vaca, Plantation Key, Stock Island, Summerland Key, Upper Matecumbe Key.

   The Clouded Skipper is found throughout Florida, the southeastern United States, Mexico, and Central America, but does not occur in the West Indies.

NATURAL HISTORY: Adults are found in wooded disturbed sites with weedy grasses (Poaceae) such as *Panicum maximum*. We found one adult in a spider web around the ruins of an abandoned house on Plantation Key. The eggs are laid singly on grasses including *Setaria macrosperma* and probably *P. maximum*. The caterpillars live in shelters on the leaves of the host. The head is whitish with black stripes on the front and a black line around the margin. The body is light green with faint white stripes and striations. The pupa is green with a sharp point on the head. Adults have been reported for every month but May, June, and December in the Keys.

FLOWERS VISITED: *Bidens alba.*

STATUS: Although abundant on the mainland, the Clouded Skipper is usually uncommon in the Keys. The species seems to be most numerous in weedy urban areas.

21. EUFALA SKIPPER   Pl. 2, Fig. 21
Lerodea eufala (W. H. Edwards)

DESCRIPTION: FW = 11.5-14 mm. *Lerodea eufala* is another obscurely marked butterfly that is easily confused with other skippers. Both sexes are grayish-brown with white spots on the forewings. Often there are one or two characteristic white spots in the forewing cell.

DISTRIBUTION: Big Pine Key, Cudjoe Key, Key Largo, Key Vaca, Key West, Plantation Key, Ramrod Key, Stock Island, Sugarloaf Key, Summerland Key, Upper Matecumbe Key, Windley Key.

   The Eufala Skipper is found throughout Florida and the warmer parts of North, Central, and South America. It also occurs in the Greater Antilles.

NATURAL HISTORY: The Eufala Skipper frequents open weedy areas. Adults fly low to the ground and visit flowers occasionally. The eggs are laid singly on grasses (Poaceae), but the host plants used in the Keys are not known. The caterpillars are green with brown heads. The pupa is green with a sharp point on the head. The Eufala Skipper has been reported for every month except May and June in the Keys.

FLOWERS VISITED: *Bidens alba, Flaveria linearis.*

STATUS: The Eufala Skipper is usually uncommon in the Keys, but occurs in vacant lots in the City of Key Largo with regularity.

22. NEAMATHLA SKIPPER   Pl. 2, Fig. 22
Nastra neamathla (Skinner and Williams)

DESCRIPTION: FW = 11-13 mm. The Neamathla Skipper is a small dark brown butterfly. The wings are nearly unmarked, except for some small faint spots on the forewings.
DISTRIBUTION: Elliott Key, Key Largo.
   This species is found in Florida, Mexico, and Central America.
NATURAL HISTORY: Adults fly low to the ground in grassy areas such as along roadsides and in vacant lots. The host plants used in the Keys are unknown, but grasses (Poaceae) in the genus *Andropogon* are fed upon elsewhere in Florida. The larvae are green, with reddish-brown stripes on the head. Pupae are also green and have a sharp point on the head. Adults have been reported from September and October in the Keys.
STATUS: The Neamathla Skipper seems to occur as stray specimens in the Keys, and is local on the southern mainland.

23. NYCTELIUS SKIPPER   Pl. 4, Fig. 23
Nyctelius nyctelius nyctelius (Latreille)

DESCRIPTION: FW = 17-18 mm. *Nyctelius nyctelius* is a robust, dark brown skipper with transluscent spots on the forewings, including two in the cell. The ventral hindwing has two dark bands and a purplish luster.
DISTRIBUTION: Key Largo.
   The Nyctelius Skipper is found in Mexico, Central America, South America, and throughout the West Indies.
STATUS: This skipper occurs in grassy disturbed areas. The only specimen known from Florida was taken by Abner Towers, 10 May 1974, on northern Key Largo (FSCA).

24. TWIN SPOT SKIPPER   Pl. 4, Fig. 24
Oligoria maculata (W. H.Edwards)

DESCRIPTION: FW = 15-19 mm. The Twin Spot Skipper is named for the two characteristic white spots that lie adjacent to one another on the ventral hindwing. The size of these white spots is quite variable. Some specimens are nearly unmarked, while others are similar to the mainland population. The Clouded Skipper is similar in appearance, but does not have the hindwing spots of *O. maculata*.
DISTRIBUTION: Big Pine Key, Cudjoe Key, No Name Key, Sugarloaf Key, Summerland Key.
   Oligoria maculata is a common species in Florida and is found in other parts of the southeastern United States from Texas to New Jersey.
NATURAL HISTORY: This dark skipper occurs in the tropical pinelands of the Lower Keys. Adults often visit flowers. The larvae are grass-feeders, but the exact host plant is not known. The brownish eggs are laid singly in the lab. Larvae are pinkish-green with brown heads and black prothoracic shields. Pupae are cream-colored. Adults have been reported for every month but August in the Keys.

FLOWERS VISITED: *Bidens alba, Cirsium horridulum, Flaveria linearis, Pithecellobium keyense, Senecio mexicana.*
STATUS: The Twin Spot Skipper is usually uncommon in the Lower Keys, but may be numerous on occasion.

25. OCOLA SKIPPER
Panoquina ocola ocola (W. H. Edwards)

Pl. 4, Fig. 25

DESCRIPTION: FW = 13.5-18 mm. This brownish skipper has a few spots on the forewing and a faint row of small spots on the underside of the hindwing. Unlike some other related species, the Ocola Skipper rarely has a spot in the forewing cell. Some individuals have a purplish sheen to the ventral hindwing.
DISTRIBUTION: Big Pine Key, Elliott Key, Key Largo, Plantation Key.
   Panoquina ocola ocola occurs in the warmer parts of North, Central, and South America. It is absent from the Bahamas, but is found in the Greater Antilles. A recently described race, *Panoquina ocola distipuncta* Johnson and Matusik, occurs in one range of mountains in southern Hispaniola.
NATURAL HISTORY: The Ocola Skipper frequents many habitats, including roadsides, vacant lots, marshes, old fields, and open woods. Adults avidly visit flowers for nectar. The eggs are laid singly on aquatic and semiaquatic grasses (Poaceae). Larvae and pupae are green. The pupa has a sharp point on the head. Adults have been reported in the Keys from June, September, October, and December.
STATUS: This butterfly is widespread and abundant on the southern mainland during the fall, but is less common to rare at other times. The Ocola Skipper is strangely uncommon in the Keys, even during the fall. The only specimen we have seen was a male taken 24 October 1987 on Elliott Key. This individual (illustrated on Plate 4, Fig. 25a) is larger than normal and has a small hyaline spot in the forewing cell. Although tentatively identified as *Panoquina hecebolus* (Scudder) (Southern Lepidopterist's News 9(2):11; 10(1):9), S. R. Steinhauser examined the genitalia and determined it to be *P. ocola*. There are no authentic records of either *P. hecebolus* or *Panoquina sylvicola* (Herrich-Schäffer) from Florida. We have examined the specimen listed by Kimball (1965) from Key Largo (July 19, 1939, Beamer) and it is *P. panoquinoides*, not *P. sylvicola*.

26. SALT MARSH SKIPPER
Panoquina panoquin (Scudder)

Pl. 4, Fig. 26

DESCRIPTION: FW = 12-14.5 mm. The Salt Marsh Skipper is easily identified by the pale veins and white streak on the underside of the hindwings. The forewings have the usual whitish spots, including a conspicuous one in the cell. The ground color of the upper wings is yellowish-brown.
DISTRIBUTION: Big Pine Key, Big Torch Key, Sugarloaf Key.
   Panoquina panoquin is also occasionally taken along Card Sound Road on the extreme southern mainland, near northern Key Largo. This butterfly is found in coastal areas of Florida north to New Jersey and west to Texas.
NATURAL HISTORY: *Panoquina panoquin* lives exclusively in salt marshes and adjacent areas. Adults visit roadside flowers readily. The flight is erratic and low to the ground.

Although this is an abundant species along the Atlantic coast, little is known of the immature stages. The few specimens that have been reported from the Keys were taken in October and December.

STATUS: Although locally abundant in salt marshes on the mainland, especially in northern and central Florida, this skipper is rare in the Keys. A few specimens (apparently strays) have been taken in the Lower Keys.

27. OBSCURE SKIPPER
Panoquina panoquinoides panoquinoides (Skinner)

Pl. 2, Fig. 27

DESCRIPTION: FW = 12-14 mm. The Obscure Skipper is yellowish-brown with white spots on the forewings and ventral hindwings. Often, however, the ventral spots are greatly reduced in size or are absent. Males tend to have smaller spots on the forewings than females. There is a characteristic yellowish dash on the underside of the forewings near the inner margin. This species is similar to *Nastra neamathla* in coloration.

DISTRIBUTION: Big Pine Key, Big Torch Key, Elliott Key, Geiger Key, Key Largo, Key Vaca, Key West, Lignumvitae Key, No Name Key, Plantation Key, Stock Island, Sugarloaf Key, Summerland Key.

The type specimens of *P. panoquinoides* are from Key West (Miller and Brown, 1981). This butterfly is widely distributed in coastal areas of southern Florida, Louisiana, Texas, Mexico, Central America, northern South America, the Bahamas, and Greater Antilles. A different subspecies occurs in the Lesser Antilles.

NATURAL HISTORY: The Obscure Skipper flies near the ground in salt marshes. Males perch on low vegetation or bare patches of soil and fly out to investigate other butterflies. The eggs are laid singly on grasses (Poaceae) such as *Distichlis spicata* and *Sporobolus virginicus* (Fig. 9). Larvae and pupae are green (Plate 23). There is a sharp point on the head of the pupa. Adults have been reported for every month but August in the Keys.

FLOWERS VISITED: *Eupatorium coelestinum, Flaveria linearis, Tournefortia volubilis.*

STATUS: *Panoquina panoquinoides* is often abundant in salt marshes and along shorelines throughout the Keys.

28. WHIRLABOUT
Polites vibex vibex (Geyer)

Pl. 4, Fig. 28

DESCRIPTION: FW = 12-14 mm. Males of *Polites vibex* are mostly golden-yellow, with dark borders and a stigma near the center of the forewing. Females are mostly blackish, with yellow spots on the forewing. The ventral hindwing has a characteristic pattern of dark spots.

DISTRIBUTION: Key Largo, Key West.

Polites vibex vibex occurs throughout Florida and the southeastern United States. Other subspecies are found in Mexico, Central America, and South America.

NATURAL HISTORY: Vacant lots, roadsides, and similar open disturbed sites are the preferred habitat of the Whirlabout. Males perch on low vegetation and fly out to investigate passing butterflies. Both sexes visit flowers for nectar readily. The eggs are laid singly on weedy grasses or nearby plants. The larva is green with a black head and prothoracic shield. The pupa is also light green. The few specimens from the Keys were taken in June.

STATUS: Although the Whirlabout is one of the most abundant and widespread butterflies on the mainland, there are only a few records (apparently strays) from the Keys.

29. BROKEN DASH   Pl. 4, Fig. 29
Wallengrenia otho (J. E. Smith)

DESCRIPTION: FW = 12-15 mm. The Broken Dash is named for the male's stigma, which, unlike other skippers in the Keys, consists of two discontinuous patches. The male is mostly dark brown, with some yellowish spots and an orange flush along the costal margin on the upperside of the forewings. Females are similar, but lack the dark stigma and the orange flush. The ventral hindwing is reddish, with a central band of faint yellowish spots.

DISTRIBUTION: Big Pine Key, Cudjoe Key, Elliott Key, Geiger Key, Key Largo, Key Vaca, Key West, Long Key, Lower Matecumbe Key, No Name Key, Plantation Key, Ramrod Key, Stock Island, Sugarloaf Key, Summerland Key, Upper Matecumbe Key, Windley Key.

The Broken Dash occurs in the southeastern United States.

NATURAL HISTORY: Grassy trails, disturbed sites, and tropical pinelands are the favorite haunts of the Broken Dash in the Keys. Males usually perch on low vegetation, while females fly near the ground in grassy areas. This species readily comes to flowers. The eggs are laid singly on grasses such as *Paspalum caespitosum*. The larva is brown with a yellowish lateral stripe on the thorax. The head and prothoracic shield are black. The shelter is a case made of grass leaves that the larva attaches to the host with silk and carries to new locations as needed. Adults occur all months of the year in the Keys.

FLOWERS VISITED: *Bidens alba, Borrichia frutescens, Bourreria ovata, Coreopsis leavenworthi, Eupatorium coelestinum, Flaveria linearis, Jacquemontia* sp., *Lantana ovatifolia, Metopium toxiferum, Morinda royoc, Pithecellobium keyense, Schinus terebinthefolius, Senecio mexicana.*

STATUS: The Broken Dash is usually abundant in the tropical pinelands of the Lower Keys. It is less common and more localized in the Middle and Upper Keys.

FAMILY PAPILIONIDAE
(Swallowtails)

Swallowtails are among the largest butterflies found in the Florida Keys. All of our species, except the Polydamas Swallowtail, have distinctive tails on the hindwings. The eyes are large and opaque. All six legs are functional for perching. The flight is usually strong and high, making them difficult to catch. Adults often visit flowers, but feed quickly and usually continue to flutter the wings as they sip nectar. Many swallowtails are attracted to bright red or yellow flowers. Swallowtail eggs are relatively large, round, and smooth. The caterpillars feed on aromatic plants, especially in the Rutaceae, and bear a concealed defensive gland behind the head, the osmeterium. Normally the osmeterium is not visible, but if the larva is provoked, the gland is inflated and the forked, foul-smelling structure is presented to the attacker. Larvae are thickest at the thorax and taper gradually to the caudal end. Young larvae of *Papilio* species are brown and white, and resemble bird or lizard droppings. Pupae are attached to the substrate by a silk girdle about the middle and caudal hooks entangled in a silk pad. Although eight swallowtails have been reported from the Keys, the Giant Swallowtail is the only common species. More detailed accounts of North American species can be found in Emmel and Heppner (1992).

30. POLYDAMAS SWALLOWTAIL   Pl. 5-6, Figs. 30
Battus polydamas lucayus Rothschild and Jordan

DESCRIPTION: FW = 39-48 mm. This handsome butterfly is black with a band of greenish-yellow spots along the outer margin of wings above. Red spots adorn the underside of the body and the outer margin of the hindwings. This is the only swallowtail in the Keys that lacks tails.

DISTRIBUTION: Elliott Key, Key Largo.

Battus polydamas lucayus is found in southern Florida and the Bahamas. At least twelve additional subspecies occur in other parts of the West Indies, and the mainland race is widely distributed in Mexico, Central America, and South America.

NATURAL HISTORY: The Polydamas Swallowtail may be locally common near patches of the larval host plants, *Aristolochia* species (Aristolochiaceae) in southern Florida. The native host in the Keys is probably *Aristolochia pentrandra*. Other exotic species of pipevines, such as *Aristolochia gigantea* and *Aristolochia littoralis*, are sometimes planted as ornamentals in urban areas of south Florida and are used by this butterfly. The yellowish-brown eggs are laid in small groups on the young leaves. The larvae are gregarious when young, but become more solitary in the later instars. The caterpillar is dark brown with several rows of orange, fleshy tubercles. The osmeterium is yellow. The pupa is light brown, with some orange markings on the dorsum. Adults have been found in April, May, and June in the Keys.

STATUS: The Polydamas Swallowtail is local in occurrence and variable in abundance in the Keys. It is sometimes abundant near sandy beaches on the ocean side of Elliott Key, but we have not found it elsewhere in the Keys.

31. CUBAN KITE SWALLOWTAIL
Eurytides celadon Lucas

Pl. 5-6, Figs. 31

DESCRIPTION: FW = 33 mm. The Cuban Kite Swallowtail has a pattern of black stripes on a white ground. The second band from the base of the forewing consists of a single black stripe. The tails are long and narrow. The Zebra Swallowtail is similar, but the banding pattern is much different.
DISTRIBUTION: Kimball (1965) listed a questionable record of *E. celadon* from Key West. More recently (May 16, 1978), Charles V. Covell, Jr. (pers. comm.) saw but could not catch a possible Cuban Kite Swallowtail flying along the oceanside shore of Elliott Key. This butterfly is endemic to Cuba.
STATUS: The Cuban Kite Swallowtail apparently strays to Florida on occasion.

32. ZEBRA SWALLOWAIL
Eurytides marcellus floridensis (Holland)

Pl. 5-6, Figs. 32

DESCRIPTION: FW = 33-47 mm. Like the preceding species, the Zebra Swallowtail is white with black stripes, but the second band from the base of the forewing consists of two stripes that coalesce toward the inner margin. There is also a conspicuous red anal spot on the upperside of the hindwing, and a red line through the middle of the hindwing below.
DISTRIBUTION: Kimball (1965) listed a record of the Zebra Swallowtail from Key Largo.

This butterfly is local in scrub habitats on the Atlantic coastal ridge in south Florida, but is abundant and widespread in more northern parts of the state. Similar species in the genus *Eurytides* are endemic to Cuba, Jamaica, and Hispaniola.
STATUS: Individuals of *Eurytides marcellus* may occasionally stray to the Upper Keys from the Florida mainland. The larval host plant, pawpaw (*Asimina* spp., Annonaceae), does not occur in the Keys.

33. BAHAMA SWALLOWTAIL
Papilio andraemon bonhotei Sharpe

Pl. 5-6, Fig. 33

DESCRIPTION: FW = 39-50 mm. The Bahama Swallowtail is black with a yellow band on the upperside of the wings (Fig. 24). There is also a characteristic yellow bar across the forewing cell, and yellow marginal spots on the hindwing. On the underside of the hindwing, there is a squarish rusty patch. The tail is relatively long and has a yellow spot in the middle of the expanded tip. The sexes are similar in color pattern, but males have black and yellow antennal clubs while females have solid black antennal clubs.
DISTRIBUTION: Adams Key, Elliott Key, Key Largo, Key West, Long Key, Old Rhodes Key, Sands Key.

Papilio andraemon bonhotei occurs in the Upper Florida Keys and the Bahamas. Other subspecies are found in Cuba and the Cayman Islands. The typical race from Cuba has been accidentally introduced into Jamaica.
NATURAL HISTORY: The Bahama Swallowtail is found locally in tropical hardwood hammocks in the Upper Keys. Males fly along hammock edges and trails. Females search in the hammocks for host plants of the proper growth stage on which to lay eggs. We have found adults being eaten by dragonflies, (*Erythemis vesiculosa*, Libellulidae), twice on Elliott Key. The

pale green eggs are laid singly on the uppersides of the young leaves of torchwood (*Amyris elemifera*, Fig. 29), and occasionally on wild lime (*Zanthoxylum fagara*, Fig. 28), sour orange (*Citrus aurantium*), and key lime (*Citrus aurantifolia*, Fig. 27). All of these plants are in the family Rutaceae. The caterpillar is similar to that of the Giant Swallowtail, brown with whitish patches on the middle and caudal end of the body (Plate 24), but is smaller, and the osmeterium is white. The dorsum of the prothorax is white with two small forward-pointing lobes. The pupa may be brown or green with dark markings (Plates 24, 25), and the upper half of the body is strongly bent away from the substrate. The adults fly from late March until November, but are most abundant in the latter part of the rainy season.

FLOWERS VISITED: *Bourreria ovata, Dalbergia brownei, Heliotropium angiospermum, Lantana involucrata, Melanthera aspera, Metopium toxiferum, Morinda royoc, Stachytarpheta jamaicensis.*

STATUS: This species was formerly considered a rare stray from the Bahamas, but L. N. Brown (1973a, b; 1974) discovered large breeding populations in Biscayne National Park. The Florida population was federally listed as Threatened in 1976, but was later taken off the list when a few surveys failed to find any individuals. We have found the Bahama swallowtail to be quite local in distribution. Abundance varies seasonally and from year to year. Its ecological requirements are very similar to those of the Schaus Swallowtail. Although *P. andraemon* is considered to be a pest of citrus in Jamaica (Lawrence, 1972) where it seems to have been recently introduced, and is an urban butterfly in Nassau, the Florida population has not been able to colonize other areas of the Keys or the mainland in spite of abundant citrus hosts. It is our opinion that the Bahama Swallowtail is a butterfly native to the Florida Keys.

34. SCHAUS SWALLOWTAIL   Pl. 7, Fig. 34
Papilio aristodemus ponceanus Schaus

DESCRIPTION: FW = 40-58 mm. The Schaus Swallowtail is dark brown on the upperside, with a marginal row of yellow spots and a yellow band across the middle of the wings. This band is sharply angled across the end of the cell on the forewings. The ventral side of the hindwing has a large reddish-brown patch and a row of diffuse blue spots across the middle of the wing (Fig. 20). The tail is straight-sided and marked with yellow along the outer edge. The sexes are similar, but males have yellow and black at the tip of the antennae. The antennae of females are entirely black.

DISTRIBUTION: Adams Key, Elliott Key, Key Largo, Key West, Lower Matecumbe Key, Old Rhodes Key, Sands Key, Swan Key, Totten Key, Upper Matecumbe Key.

   Papilio aristodemus ponceanus is found only in the Florida Keys. Other subspecies occur in the Bahamas and the Greater Antilles.

NATURAL HISTORY: The Schaus Swallowtail is found in the tropical hardwood hammocks of the Upper Keys. Males patrol hammock edges and trails. Females usually fly within the hammock, searching for host plants. Both sexes occasionally visit flowers. The greenish eggs are laid on the uppersides of the young leaves of torchwood (*Amyris elemifera*, Rutaceae) and occasionally wild lime (*Zanthoxylum fagara*). Key Lime (*Citrus aurantifolia*) is probably also used. The mature larva is brown with white patches on the caudal end, along the sides, and on the dorsum of the prothorax (Plate 24). There are also several rows of blue spots on the body. The osmeterium is white. The stout pupa is brown and erect rather than bent at the middle (Plates 24, 25). Adults emerge at the beginning of the wet season and are usually univoltine, but a second brood has been reported occasionally (Brown, 1976). The recorded flight period is from the end of March through September; however, the normal single adult brood occurs from late April to mid June.

FLOWERS VISITED: *Alternanthera ramosissima, Borrichia arborescens, Canella winterana, Capraria biflora, Coccoloba diversifolia, Coccoloba uvifera, Cordia sebestena, Dalbergia brownei, Heliotropium angiospermum, Lantana involucrata, Melanthera aspera, Morinda royoc, Psidium guajava, Psychotria nervosa, Randia aculeata, Stachytarpheta jamaicensis.*

STATUS: The range of the Schaus Swallowtail has declined since this butterfly was first described in 1911 from specimens taken in hammocks south of the city of Miami. Other than the types, the last specimens from mainland Florida were taken in 1924. The Schaus Swallowtail was abundant on Upper Matecumbe Key through the 1940's, but none has been found there for many years. The population on Key Largo was doing well in the early 1970's, but declined shortly thereafter, prompting the U. S. Fish and Wildlife Service to list the Schaus Swallowtail as a Threatened species in April of 1976. The status was changed to Endangered in 1984. This butterfly is still rare, but is breeding in the hammocks of northern Key Largo. Populations in Biscayne National Park seem to be doing well, but vary in size from year to year. The small populations currently existing on northern Key Largo may actually be reestablished almost annually by founder individuals flying south from the keys within the Park, inasmuch as county mosquito control spraying is still impacting the Key Largo sites. Collecting of the Schaus Swallowtail is prohibited under State and Federal law.

35. GIANT SWALLOWTAIL
Papilio cresphontes Cramer

Pl. 7, Fig. 35

DESCRIPTION: FW = 51-63 mm. The Giant Swallowtail is one of the largest butterflies in Florida. The dorsal side of the wings is dark brown with yellow spots. The undersides are yellowish with a band of blue spots across the middle of the hindwing and a small rusty patch near the end of the cell. The spatulate tail has a yellow spot in the center of the tip.

DISTRIBUTION: Big Pine Key, Elliott Key, Fat Deer Key, Grassy Key, Key Largo, Key Vaca, Lignumvitae Key, No Name Key, Old Rhodes Key, Plantation Key, Stock Island, Sugarloaf Key, Totten Key, Upper Matecumbe Key.

The Giant Swallowtail is widely distributed in eastern North America, Mexico, Central America, and northern South America. It also occurs in Cuba.

NATURAL HISTORY: The Giant Swallowtail is found in tropical hardwood hammocks and urban areas of the Keys. Adults are strong fliers, and often visit flowers for nectar. The yellowish-brown eggs are laid on the new growth of wild lime (*Zanthoxylum fagara*), citrus, and occasionally torchwood (*Amyris elemifera*). The caterpillar is brown with whitish patches on the caudal end, about the middle, and on the sides of the thorax (Plate 25). The osmeterium is bright red. Pupae are brown and the upper half is only moderately bent away from the substrate (Plate 25). Adults have been recorded every month of the year in the Keys.

FLOWERS VISITED: *Bougainvillea glabra, Bourreria ovata, Carica papaya, Eupatorium odoratum, Lantana involucrata, Metopium toxiferum, Morinda royoc, Pithecellobium keyense, Schinus terebinthefolius, Senecio mexicana.* One was observed on Elliott Key with the undersides of the wings caked with orange pollen, perhaps from *Delonix regia*.

STATUS: The Giant Swallowtail is a common butterfly throughout the Keys. It is the only one of the three rutaceous-feeders in the Keys to occur in urban areas.

36. PALAMEDES SWALLOWTAIL
Papilio palamedes Drury

Pl. 7, Fig. 36

DESCRIPTION: FW = 48-63 mm. The Palmedes Swallowtail is a large dark butterfly with bands of yellow spots on the wings. The underside of the hindwing has bands of orange and blue spots. The tails are straight-sided and may have a yellow line down the center.
DISTRIBUTION: Key Largo, Key West.

Papilio palamedes is found throughout Florida, northward along the coast to Virginia and westward into northern Mexico.
STATUS: Although abundant on the southern mainland, the Palamedes Swallowtail is found in the Keys as rare strays. The larval host plants, bays (*Persea borbonia*, Lauraceae, and *Magnolia virginiana*, Magnoliaceae), do not occur in the Keys (Little, 1978).

37. EASTERN BLACK SWALLOWTAIL
Papilio polyxenes asterius Stoll

Pl. 5-6, Figs. 37

DESCRIPTION: FW = 46-49 mm. Males of the Eastern Black Swallowtail are black with bands of yellow spots on the wings. The hindwings have blue spots above and below. The inner band of yellow spots is much reduced in the female, and the blue spots on the upperside of the hindwing are more pronounced.
DISTRIBUTION: Lignumvitae Key.

The typical race of *Papilio polyxenes* is found in Cuba. *Papilio polyxenes asterius* occurs through much of the United States and southern Canada, primarily east of the Rocky Mountains into northern Mexico but also in the Southwestern U.S. Other subspecies occur in Mexico, Central America, and South America.
STATUS: The Eastern Black Swallowtail is locally abundant on the southern mainland, but is rare in the Keys, apparently due to the lack of larval host plants (Apiaceae). Jeanne Parks took one on Lignumvitae Key on February 24, 1981.

FAMILY PIERIDAE
(WHITES and SULPHURS)

Whites and sulphurs are some of the most abundant and frequently-noticed butterflies in the Keys. Pierids make up about 18% of the Keys butterfly species. The larger species are strong fliers and are difficult to catch. Many pierids exhibit migratory tendencies. Adults have six legs that are used for perching, transparent eyes, and mostly white or yellow wings. The slender eggs are usually white or yellow with ribs. The caterpillars are often green with white, yellow, or reddish lateral lines, and feed on dicotyledonous plants, especially legumes (Fabaceae) and crucifers (Brassicaceae). The pupa is attached to the substrate by hooks entangled in a silk pad at the caudal end, and a silk girdle around the middle. There is a sharp point on the head of the pupa in many genera.

SUBFAMILY PIERINAE
(Whites)

This subfamily of the Pieridae consists of species that are mostly white in color. Larvae of our species may be green or striped with gray and yellow. Pupae tend to be angular, with a ridge on the top of the thorax and thorn-like points on the edges of the wing cases. Of the four species of whites in the Keys, the Florida White and Great Southern White are the most common.

38. FLORIDA WHITE   Pl. 8, Fig. 38
Appias drusilla neumoegenii (Skinner)

DESCRIPTION: FW = 25-34.5 mm. Males of the Florida White are nearly pure white in color but have some dark scaling along the costa of the forewing. Females have black at the tip of the forewing, on the outer margin, and along the costa above. Dry season females have less black, especially along the outer margin of the forewing, than those that developed during the wet season. The dorsal hindwings are yellowish in females. Both sexes have a pearly luster at the base of the forewing on the upperside.
DISTRIBUTION: Adams Key, Big Pine Key, Big Torch Key, Elliott Key, Key Largo, Lignumvitae Key, No Name Key, Old Rhodes Key, Plantation Key, Stock Island, Summerland Key, Totten Key, Upper Matecumbe Key, Windley Key.
Appias drusilla neumoegenii, the Florida population, differs little from *Appias drusilla poeyi* Butler which is found in the Bahamas, Cuba, and the Cayman Islands (Bates, 1934). Other endemic races also occur on Jamaica, Hispaniola, Dominica, and Grenada. The typical race (which has a wide black border along the outer margin of the hindwing in the wet season female) occurs in Texas, Mexico, Central America, and South America.
NATURAL HISTORY: Tropical hardwood hammocks are the home of the Florida White. Males have a fast erratic flight and frequent the upper portion of the canopy. Females flutter more slowly within the hammock looking for host plants. We have found adults trapped in the webs of the golden silk spider (*Nephila clavipes*) on two occasions. The eggs are laid singly on

the new growth of limber caper (*Capparis flexuosa,* Capparaceae) and milkbark (*Drypetes diversifolia,* Euphorbiaceae). Larvae are bluish-green, covered with small yellow tubercles, and have a pair of short tails on the caudal end (Plate 26). The pupa is green with a long curved horn on the head, a ridge on the dorsum of the thorax, and points on the edges of the wing cases. Chermock and Chermock (1947) described the immature stages in greater detail. Adults occur all months of the year in the Keys.

FLOWERS VISITED: *Bidens alba, Eupatorium odoratum, Flaveria linearis, Heliotropium angiospermum, Lantana involucrata, Melanthera aspera, Metopium toxiferum, Morinda royoc, Pithecellobium keyense.*

STATUS: The Florida White is widely distributed in the Keys and coastal areas of the southern mainland. This butterfly undergoes great changes in abundance and may be quite common some years and relatively rare at other times.

39. GREAT SOUTHERN WHITE
Ascia monuste phileta (Fabricius)

Pl. 8, Fig. 39

DESCRIPTION: FW = 24-31.5 mm. Males of *A. monuste phileta* are white with a broken black border along the outer margin and the apex of the forewing. The underside of the hindwing is cream-colored with faint markings. Females have more extensive black borders and a dark spot in the forewing cell. The ground color of females varies from white to dark gray. *Ascia monuste evonima* (Boisduval) is similar, but tends to have bolder dark markings.

DISTRIBUTION: Bahia Honda Key, Big Pine Key, Elliott Key, Geiger Key, Key Biscayne, Key Largo, Key Vaca, Key West, Lignumvitae Key, Long Key, Lower Matecumbe Key, No Name Key, Old Rhodes Key, Plantation Key, Sands Key, Stock Island, Sugarloaf Key, Summerland Key, Upper Matecumbe Key.

Ascia monuste phileta is the Florida race. The typical subspecies occurs in Texas, Mexico, Central America, and South America. *Ascia monuste evonima* is found in the Bahamas and Greater Antilles. We have one specimen of *A. m. evonima* from Elliott Key (Plate 8, Fig. 39c).

NATURAL HISTORY: The Great Southern White is usually found in salt marshes and nearby areas. The flight may be rapid or slow, but is usually near the ground. We have seen adults of this butterfly being eaten by dragonflies (*Erythemis vesiculosa,* Libellulidae) on four different occasions and once by a grayish robberfly (Asilidae) on Elliott Key. The yellowish eggs are laid singly or in clusters on the leaves of saltwort (*Batis maritima,* Bataceae), and occasionally pepper-grass (*Lepidium virginicum,* Brassicaceae) and limber caper (*Capparis flexuosa,* Capparaceae). Larvae are yellow with gray stripes and small black tubercles (Plate 26). The black and white pupa mimics a bird dropping. Adults fly all year in the Keys.

FLOWERS VISITED: *Alternanthera ramosissima, Avicennia germinans, Bidens alba, Borrichia arborescens, Borrichia frutescens, Capraria biflora, Flaveria linearis, Heliotropium angiospermum, Heliotropium curassavicum, Lantana involucrata, Lycium carolinianum, Morinda royoc, Pithecellobium keyense, Psychotria nervosa, Stachytarpheta jamaicensis, Suriana maritima, Yucca aloifolia.*

STATUS: The Great Southern White is a common butterfly in southern Florida and the Keys. There are occasional outbreaks of this species in Florida, followed by northward migrations of vast numbers of adults along the coast (Chermock, 1946). Adults were present in outbreak numbers during March 1988 on Elliott Key, but by late May had returned to normal.

40. EUROPEAN CABBAGE BUTTERFLY
Pieris rapae (Linnaeus)

DESCRIPTION: FW = 23-26 mm. This introduced species is white with black wing tips, and has a black spot on the costa of the hindwing. In addition, males have one, and females have two black spots near the middle of the forewing. The underside of the hindwing is pale yellow.
DISTRIBUTION: Key Biscayne, Key West.
   The European Cabbage Butterfly is now widely distributed in temperate North America, but is rare in tropical south Florida.
STATUS: Kimball (1965) included Key West within the range of *P. rapae* in Florida. More recently, Michael Israel (pers. comm.) captured a specimen on Key Biscayne near Miami. This species is not common in southern Florida and is only rarely present in the Keys.

41. CHECKERED WHITE
Pontia protodice (Boisduval and Leconte)

DESCRIPTION: FW = 18-25 mm. *Pontia protodice* is a white butterfly with black markings. There is a large black spot in the forewing cell. The underside of the hindwing is usually faintly patterned with greenish-yellow. Females have more extensive dark markings than males.
DISTRIBUTION: Elliott Key, Key Largo, Lignumvitae Key.
   The Checkered White is found throughout Florida and much of North America from southern Canada to central Mexico. This butterfly also occasionally strays to Cuba.
NATURAL HISTORY: Weedy, disturbed sites are the favorite habitat of the Checkered White in south Florida. Adults fly low to the ground. The yellowish eggs are laid singly on pepper-grass (*Lepidium virginicum*, Brassicaceae). The caterpillars are yellow with gray stripes and small black tubercles. The pupa is grayish with a ridge on the dorsum of the thorax and with points on the edge of the wing case. Adults have been found in the Keys during March and May.
STATUS: Although abundant in the weedy agricultural areas of the southern mainland, the Checkered White only occasionally strays into the Upper Keys.

SUBFAMILY COLIADINAE
(Sulphurs)

   Members of this subfamily are usually orange, yellow, or white. The larvae are usually green. Pupae are laterally flattened and often have a point on the head. Adults of the larger species are fond of red or yellow flowers and males will often chase falling yellow leaves. Of the 17 species of sulphurs that occur in the Keys, the Barred Sulphur, Little Sulphur, Sleepy Orange, Dainty Sulphur, Large Orange Sulphur, Orange-Barred Sulphur, and Cloudless Sulphur are the most common.

42. GIANT BRIMSTONE
Anteos maerula (Fabricius)

DESCRIPTION: FW = 38-42 mm. The Giant Brimstone is lemon-yellow above, with a small black spot at the end of the forewing cell. Females are paler than males. The underside of the wing is greenish-yellow. The shape of the wings is quite different from our other sulphurs. The tip of the forewing is falcate, and the hindwing has a very short tail.

DISTRIBUTION: Big Pine Key, Key Largo, Stock Island.

Anteos maerula is also found in the Greater Antilles, Mexico, Central America, and South America.

FLOWERS VISITED: *Bidens alba.*

STATUS: The Giant Brimstone is a strong flyer that migrates northward from Cuba into Florida on occasion. Bennett and Knudson (1976) took five specimens on Big Pine Key during August of 1973, and Richard Anderson (pers. comm.) found many during September 1973 on Stock Island. This butterfly is also taken on Key Largo with some regularity (H. D. Baggett, pers. comm.; Leroy Koehn, *Southern Lepidopterists' News* 10:35), but is not known to breed in Florida.

43. ORBED SULPHUR
Aphrissa orbis orbis (Poey)

Pl. 10, Fig. 43

DESCRIPTION: FW = 30.5 mm. Orbed sulphur males are white with a patch of orange at the base of each forewing. The outer margin is bordered by a satiny-white strip of androconial scales. The undersides are pale yellow with some reddish markings. Females are quite different in appearance and resemble females of *Phoebis sennae*, but are pale orange.

DISTRIBUTION: Big Pine Key.

Aphrissa orbis orbis is endemic to Cuba. Another subspecies occurs on Hispaniola.

STATUS: Robert Bennett collected the only known specimen from Florida on Big Pine Key, 25 April 1973 (Bennett and Knudson, 1976). This individual is now in the Florida State Collection of Arthropods.

44. FLORIDA STATIRA SULPHUR
Aphrissa statira floridensis (Neumoegen)

Pl. 10, Fig. 44

DESCRIPTION: FW = 30-34.5 mm. Males of the Florida Statira Sulphur are lemon-yellow with a satiny-white or pale yellow border of androconial scales along the outer margin on the uppersides of the wings. Females are white with a black spot at the end of the cell and a narrow outer border on the forewings. The undersides are pale yellow. In flight, the males resemble those of the much more abundant Cloudless Sulphur.

DISTRIBUTION: Elliott Key (?), Key Largo, Lignumvitae Key.

Aphrissa statira floridensis is limited to coastal southern Florida. Other subspecies occur in the West Indies and in Mexico, Central America, and South America.

NATURAL HISTORY: The Florida Statira Sulphur occurs near patches of the host plant, coinvine (*Dalbergia ecastophyllum*, Fabaceae), which grows at the edge of mangroves and salt marshes. The eggs are laid singly on the young leaves. The larva is yellowish-green with a yellow lateral line, and is covered with numerous small black tubercles. The leaf-like pupa is strongly flattened laterally, is colored green with a pale yellow lateral line that resembles the midrib of a young leaf, and has a long point on the head. The flight season is all year on the southern mainland.

STATUS: Although the host plant occurs on Elliott Key and northern Key Largo, the Florida

Statira Sulphur does not breed in the Keys. Only a few stray individuals have been reported from Key Largo and Lignumvitae Key (Kimball, 1965; Leston *et al.*, 1982). We saw, but could not catch, a probable male flying along the coast of Elliott Key on 5 September 1987.

45. ORANGE SULPHUR
Colias eurytheme Boisduval

Pl. 9, Fig. 45

DESCRIPTION: FW = 22-28 mm. This medium-sized butterfly is orange with dark borders above. There is a black spot at the end of the cell on the forewing and a dark orange spot near the middle of the hindwing. The undersides are greenish-yellow with similar markings. Females have light-colored spots in the marginal black border of the forewing and may be either yellowish-orange or white.
DISTRIBUTION: Key Largo, Plantation Key.
   Colias eurytheme is found across North America from southern Canada to southern Mexico.
STATUS: The Orange Sulphur is sporadic in abundance and distribution in southern Florida, but occasionally breeds south to at least Broward County. A few specimens have been taken in the Upper Keys.

46. BOISDUVAL'S SULPHUR
Eurema boisduvaliana (Felder and Felder)

Pl. 12, Fig. 46

DESCRIPTION: FW = 20-22 mm. Boisduval's Sulphur is yellow, with a wide and irregular black border above. There is a pale orange patch near the apex of the hindwing. The undersides are mostly pale yellow. The hindwings are angled rather than rounded.
DISTRIBUTION: Stock Island.
   Eurema boisduvaliana occurs in Central America, Mexico, and occasionally Cuba.
FLOWERS VISITED: *Schinus terebinthefolius*.
STATUS: Richard Anderson took one on Stock Island, 20 September 1973. The paper describing the discovery (Anderson, 1974) lists the locality as Key West, but the actual site was the Stock Island Botanical Garden, which is near Key West (R. A. Anderson, pers. comm.). This is the only record of *E. boisduvaliana* from the Keys.

47. BARRED SULPHUR
Eurema daira (Godart)

Pl. 12, Fig. 47

DESCRIPTION: FW = 12.5-19 mm. Two different forms of the Barred Sulphur, which are usually treated as subspecies, occur in the Keys. In addition, both subspecies exhibit considerable seasonal variation. The wet season form of *Eurema daira daira* is pale yellow with black borders (Figs. 50, 54). The undersides are whitish. Males have a wide black band along the lower edge of the forewing. This band is faintly present in females. The dry season form of *E. daira daira* is dark yellow with the black border of the hindwing reduced to a squarish apical patch. The undersides of the hindwings vary from light brown to dark reddish brown. *Eurema daira palmira* (Poey) is similar, but the upper hindwings are white in males. Females are white with black borders and lack any trace of a bar along the inner margin of the forewing. The dry season form of *E. d. palmira* has reduced black borders on the hindwing above, and brown scaling below. Calhoun and Anderson (1991) discuss further differences between the two subspecies.

Fig. 50. Comparison of Florida and West Indies forms of males and females of *Eurema daira daira* and *E. d. palmira*, and a closely related species, *E. elathea*: all specimens, DORSAL view. Right column, top to bottom: *E. daira daira*, male (14 May) and female (17 July) **summer forms** (from Broward Co.), male (13 Nov.) and female (11 Nov.) **winter forms** (Broward Co.). Middle column: *E. daira palmira*, two females (Big Pine Key, 6 Sept.); *E. daira daira*, bicolored male (City of Key Largo, 25 Oct.), bicolored male (Broward Co., 14 Aug.). Left column: *E. daira palmira*, male (La Vega Prov., Dominican Republic, 24 June) and female (5 mi. N. of Bath, Jamaica, 26 March); *Eurema elathea*, male (Puerto Plata Prov., Domin. Republic, 20 June) and female (same locality and date).
Fig. 51. Ventral view of the specimens in Figure 50.

DISTRIBUTION: *Eurema daira daira*: Big Pine Key, Boca Chica Key, Cudjoe Key, Elliott Key, Key Biscayne, Key Largo, Key Vaca, Key West, Lignumvitae Key, Lower Matecumbe Key, Plantation Key, Stock Island, Sugarloaf Key, Summerland Key, Upper Matecumbe Key, Windley Key. *Eurema daira palmira* (males): Big Pine Key, Geiger Key, Key Largo, Key West, Lower Matecumbe Key, Sugarloaf Key, Toms Harbor. *Eurema daira palmira* (females): Big Pine Key, Key West.

The Barred Sulphur is widely distributed in tropical America. *E. d. daira* is the southeastern United States population. *E. d. palmira* occurs in the Bahamas and Greater Antilles. Other subspecies occur in Mexico, Central America, and South America. *E. daira daira* is the only population in which the upper hindwings are yellow in the males.

NATURAL HISTORY: The Barred Sulphur occurs in open weedy habitats such as vacant lots and along roadsides. The eggs are laid singly on the new growth of pencil flower (*Stylosanthes hamata*, Fabaceae). Larvae are green with a whitish lateral stripe and are covered with short hairs. Pupae are also green with a pale lateral line and dark markings on the wing cases or are rarely black with a pale lateral line. The head has a small point. Adults occur all months of the year in the Keys.

FLOWERS VISITED: *Bidens alba, Lippia nodiflora, Sida acuta.*

STATUS: *Eurema daira daira* is migratory in Florida. During late summer and fall, individuals from the northern part of the state fly southward in large numbers. In the Keys, the Barred Sulphur is variable in distribution and abundance. It occurs sporadically in Biscayne National Park, although host plants and suitable habitat are present. The Barred Sulphur is often abundant on Key Largo, especially during the fall, but is sporadic in the Lower Keys. Smith *et al.* (1982) sampled populations on Key Largo and the southern mainland, and found that about 6% of the males had white hindwings. Since *E. d. palmira* females were not found, this was interpreted to be a balanced polymorphism in the south Florida populations. However, the Florida State Collection of Arthropods does have males and females of *E. d. palmira* from south Florida, including the Keys. In addition, we collected two *E. d. palmira* females on Big Pine Key, 6 September 1987. Richard Anderson has also taken *E. d. palmira* females in the Lower Keys (Calhoun and Anderson, 1991). The situation seems to be one of occasional temporary establishment of *E. d. palmira* from Cuba and introgression of white hindwing alleles into the resident yellow-hindwing *E. d. daira* population.

48. BUSH SULPHUR
Eurema dina helios M. Bates

Pl. 12, Fig. 48

DESCRIPTION: FW = 16.5-20 mm. Males of the Bush Sulphur are light orange or occasionally yellow, with a narrow black border on the forewing. Females are yellow with an orange patch near the apex of the hindwing. The undersides are yellow with faint markings.

DISTRIBUTION: Key Largo.

Eurema dina helios is found in southern Florida and the Bahamas. Other subspecies occur in the Greater Antilles, Mexico, and Central America.

NATURAL HISTORY: Adults fly in tropical hardwood hammocks in close association with the larval host plant, *Alvaradoa amorphoides* (Fabaceae), a tree of very local occurrence in south Florida. The eggs are laid singly on the young growth. Larvae are green with a pale lateral stripe and are covered with short hairs. The pupa is also green with a short point on the head. Adults occur all year on the southern mainland.

STATUS: A few specimens have been taken on Key Largo (H. D. Baggett, pers. comm.). Little's (1978) range map does not show the host plant occurring in the Keys, but he mentions in the text (p. 11) that it has been reported from Key Largo. We have not found either the butterfly or its host in the Keys.

49. LITTLE SULPHUR

Pl. 12, Fig. 49

Eurema lisa lisa Boisduval and Leconte

DESCRIPTION: FW = 13.5-19 mm. Males of the Little Sulphur are bright yellow with black borders. Females may be either pale yellow or whitish with black borders. In both sexes, the forewings have a dusting of dark scaling along the costal margin, and a small black dot near the end of the cell. The ventral hindwing is yellow with faint markings, and bears a large orange spot near the apex. The dry season form tends to have reduced black borders and crisper markings on the undersides. This species resembles the Jamaican Sulphur, but differs in the fine details of the wing pattern and in habitat preference.

DISTRIBUTION: Adams Key, Big Pine Key, Boca Chica Key, Cudjoe Key, Elliott Key, Key Biscayne, Key Largo, Lignumvitae Key, Plantation Key, Stock Island, Sugarloaf Key, Summerland Key.

Eurema lisa lisa is the continental race found in Florida and much of eastern North America, Mexico, Central America, Bermuda, and the northern Bahamas. The closely similar *Eurema lisa euterpe* Ménétriés is widely distributed in the Antilles.

NATURAL HISTORY: The Little Sulphur flies low to the ground in open weedy areas and disturbed sites. It rarely strays into the shade of forests. The yellowish eggs are laid singly on the young growth of partridge pea (*Cassia fasciculata*, Fabaceae) and other similar *Cassia* species, but host plants used in the Keys have not been determined. *Cassia keyense*, a partridge pea endemic to the tropical pinelands of the Lower Keys, most likely is the main host. The caterpillar is green with a narrow pale yellow lateral line, and is covered with short hairs. Pupae are also green with a short horn on the head. Adults have been reported for every month but August in the Keys.

FLOWERS VISITED: *Bidens alba, Stachytarpheta jamaicensis.*

STATUS: The Little Sulphur occurs sporadically in the Upper Keys, apparently due to the temporary influx of migrants, since the host plants do not seem to occur there. The species is often abundant in the Lower Keys, however, where breeding populations seem to be established.

50. SLEEPY ORANGE

Pl. 9, Fig. 50

Eurema nicippe (Cramer)

DESCRIPTION: FW = 17-26 mm. The Sleepy Orange is a bright orange butterfly with relatively wide black borders, especially on the hindwings. Females are paler than males and have reduced black borders on the hindwing. The undersides are yellowish-orange with faint markings and sometimes a reddish flush. The dry season phenotype has smaller black borders in the female, and is reddish on the ventral side of the hindwing.

DISTRIBUTION: Big Pine Key, Elliott Key, Key Largo, Plantation Key, Stock Island, Sugarloaf Key (?), Summerland Key.

Eurema nicippe is found throughout Florida and the southern United States, Mexico, Central America, the Bahamas, and the Greater Antilles.

NATURAL HISTORY: The Sleepy Orange has an erratic flight low to the ground and occurs in open weedy areas. The eggs are laid on the new growth of shrubby species of *Cassia* (Fabaceae). The hosts used in the Keys are not known, but *Cassia chapmanii (= Cassia bahamense*, Fig. 36), which grows in the Lower Keys, may be eaten. The larvae are green with a pale yellow lateral line. The body is covered with short hairs. Pupae vary in color from mostly green with black markings to entirely black. The head has a sharp point. Adults have been found in May, July, August, September, October, and November in the Keys.
STATUS: The Sleepy Orange is sporadic in distribution and abundance in the Keys. When it does occur, it is usually common, suggesting an influx of migrants at such times.

51. JAMAICAN SULPHUR   Pl. 12, Fig. 51
Eurema nise nise (Cramer)

DESCRIPTION: FW = 12-16 mm. The Jamaican Sulphur is closely similar to the Little Sulphur, but lacks the dark scaling along the costal margin of the forewings, and the black dot at the end of the forewing cell above. The black border on the hindwing is usually narrower than in *E. lisa* and sometimes is nearly absent. The ventral hindwings are mostly yellow.
DISTRIBUTION: Elliott Key, Key Largo, Plantation Key.
   Eurema nise nise is found in southern Florida, Cuba, Jamaica, and Hispaniola. Other races are found in Mexico, Central America, and South America.
NATURAL HISTORY: Adults fly along trails and at the margins of hardwood hammocks. If disturbed, they rapidly head for the shade of the forest. John V. Calhoun observed a female ovipositing on *Lysiloma latisiliquum (= Lysiloma bahamense*, Fig. 31) (*News of the Lepidopterists' Society*, 1984:30; 1989) in Dade County. This leguminous tree grows abundantly in the Keys and on the southern mainland. Adults have been found during April, June, July, and September in the Keys.
STATUS: The Jamaican Sulphur is usually uncommon in the hammocks of the Upper Keys and southern mainland. Although the larval host is widely distributed, populations of this butterfly are ephemeral and sporadic (Calhoun, 1989).

52. GUAYACAN SULPHUR   Pl. 9, Fig. 52
Kricogonia lyside (Godart)

DESCRIPTION: FW = 22-24 mm. The Guayacan Sulphur is whitish above, with pale yellow at the tip of the forewing and along the anal margin of the hindwing. The base of the forewing above is bright lemon-yellow. The underside is greenish-yellow, with a lemon yellow flush along the costal margin of the forewing. The sexes are similar. Males from some populations have a black bar near the apex of the hindwing above, but we have not seen this form from Florida.
DISTRIBUTION: Elliott Key, Key Largo, Plantation Key, Upper Matecumbe Key.
   Kricogonia lyside is also found in the Greater Antilles, the Bahamas, Mexico, Central America, and South America.
NATURAL HISTORY: The Guayacan Sulphur frequents the edges of tropical hardwood hammocks. Trees in the family Zygophyllaceae (*Guaiacum* spp.) have been reported to be the host plants (Riley, 1975; Opler and Krizek, 1984). The most likely food plant in the Keys is lignum vitae (*Guaiacum sanctum*). Lignum vitae grows in the hammocks of the Upper Keys, but in the past was commercially exploited for its dense wood and is now rather rare and local.

Spectacular examples can still be seen on Lignumvitae Key. The caterpillar is green with gray or silvery lines and brown markings (Opler and Krizek, 1984). Adults have been reported from July, August, September, and October in the Keys.

STATUS: It is not known if this butterfly is a permanent resident or a frequent temporary colonizer in Florida. Like *Anteos maerula*, the Guayacan Sulphur may be present in low numbers occasionally in the Keys, but usually is rare. This species is migratory in Mexico and southern Texas. If *Kricogonia lyside* is a breeding resident, it is hard to understand why it has not been found on Lignumvitae Key, where the suspected food plant is abundant. Riley (1975) states that it is rare in Cuba, Jamaica, and Puerto Rico, but abundant on Hispaniola. We saw at least eight individuals on Elliott Key on 23 July 1987, but have not encountered it there again. On Key Largo, we have seen single specimens on a few occasions.

53. DAINTY SULPHUR

Nathalis iole Boisduval

Pl. 12, Fig. 53

DESCRIPTION: FW = 13-16 mm. The Dainty Sulphur is the smallest pierid in Florida. The color pattern is similar to that of the Barred Sulphur, being yellow with black borders and a black bar along the inner margin of the forewing. However, the Dainty Sulphur also has a black bar along the costal margin of the hindwing and is greenish-yellow below (Fig. 40). Males have a conspicuous orange spot on the dorsal hindwing near the base of the costa, but this spot quickly fades to yellow in pinned specimens. The ground color of the females is ochre-yellow.

DISTRIBUTION: Adams Key, Big Pine Key, Elliott Key, Fleming Island, Key Largo, Key West, Lignumvitae Key, Plantation Key, Stock Island, Summerland Key.

Nathalis iole occurs in southern Florida, the Bahamas, the Greater Antilles, southern North America, Central America, and northern South America.

NATURAL HISTORY: The Dainty Sulphur flies low to the ground in weedy disturbed sites. The yellowish eggs are laid singly on the young growth of small Spanish needles plants (*Bidens alba,* Asteraceae). The larvae vary in color from green to blue-green, and usually have a purple stripe on the sides and one on the dorsum. The body is covered with short hairs and there is a pair of small forward-pointing tubercles on the dorsum of the prothorax above the head. Pupae are green and lack a point on the head. Adults have been reported from every month except February in the Keys.

FLOWERS VISITED: *Bidens alba, Lippia nodiflora.*

STATUS: The Dainty Sulphur is sporadic in distribution and abundance in the Keys. In Biscayne National Park, *Nathalis iole* is usually absent, but occasionally appears in abundance for short periods of time. The species is common on the southern mainland.

54. LARGE ORANGE SULPHUR

Phoebis agarithe maxima (Neumoegen)

Pl. 10, Fig. 54

DESCRIPTION: FW = 23.5-36 mm. Males of *Phoebis agarithe* are bright yellowish-orange above, with tiny dark spots on the outer margin at the ends of the veins. Females may be either orange or white, and have larger black spots on the outer margin, a spot in the forewing cell, and black at the apex of the forewing. The undersides are yellowish-orange with reddish-brown markings, including a diagonal postmedial line on the forewing. There are two white spots near the end of the cell on the ventral hindwing of females.

DISTRIBUTION: Adams Key, Bahia Honda Key, Big Pine Key, Cudjoe Key, Elliott Key, Key Biscayne, Key Largo, Key Vaca, Lignumvitae Key, Long Key, Lower Matecumbe Key, No Name Key, Old Rhodes Key, Plantation Key, Sands Key, Stock Island, Sugarloaf Key, Summerland Key, Upper Matecumbe Key, Windley Key.

Phoebis agarithe maxima is endemic to southern Florida. It differs subtly from the typical race, which is widely distributed in southern Texas, Mexico, Central America, and South America. The black discal spot on the forewing of female *P. agarithe maxima* is consistently smaller than that of *P. agarithe agarithe*. Two other races occur in the West Indies. *Phoebis agarithe antilla* Brown from the Bahamas, Cuba, Jamaica, Hispaniola, and Puerto Rico is similar to the Florida race, but is more heavily spotted with reddish-brown below. *Phoebis agarithe pupillata* Dillon from the Lesser Antilles is very different from the other populations, and is most likely a separate species.

NATURAL HISTORY: The Large Orange Sulphur occurs in many habitats in the Keys, particularly the edges of tropical hammocks. The flight is swift and high. We have seen individuals flying over the ocean between the islands of Biscayne National Park on several occasions. Males sometimes sip water from damp sand (Plate 26). The eggs are laid singly on the new growth of blackbead (*Pithecellobium keyense*), cat's-claw (*Pithecellobium unguis-cati*), and wild tamarind (*Lysiloma latisiliquum*). All of these trees are in the family Fabaceae. The caterpillar is yellowish-green with a yellow lateral stripe. Some individuals have small blue spots on the body. The pupa is green with a long point on the head (Plate 26). Adults occur every month of the year in the Keys.

FLOWERS VISITED: *Bidens alba, Borrichia frutescens, Bourreria ovata, Coccoloba diversifolia, Cordia sebestena, Dicliptera assurgens, Eupatorium odoratum, Flaveria linearis, Lantana involucrata, Metopium toxiferum, Morinda royoc, Pithecellobium keyense, Senecio mexicana, Stachytarpheta jamaicensis.* Adults are occasionally seen sipping moisture from wet soil.

STATUS: The Large Orange Sulphur is one of the most abundant and widely distributed butterflies in the Keys. It is also abundant in coastal areas of the southern mainland.

55. ORANGE-BARRED SULPHUR   Pl. 11, Fig. 55
Phoebis philea philea (Johansson)

DESCRIPTION: FW = 35-43 mm. *Phoebis philea* is the largest pierid in the Florida Keys. Males are bright yellow, with an orange patch across the forewing cell and orange along the outer margin of the hindwing above. Females have an outer border of dark spots that coalesce at the apex, a small dark spot in the forewing cell, and a diagonal postmedial line of dark spots that is offset midway along its length. The ground color of females ranges from white to yellow, and most have a reddish-orange border along the outer margin of the hindwings. Males are mostly yellow below, but females are marked with reddish-brown and two white spots at the end of the cell on the hindwing. Individuals that develop during the dry season are more heavily marked with reddish-brown ventrally than those from the wet summer months, especially female adults.

DISTRIBUTION: Big Pine Key, Elliott Key, Key Largo, No Name Key, Plantation Key, Stock Island, Summerland Key.

The mainland subspecies *Phoebis philea philea* is found in southern Florida, Mexico, Central and South America. Other subspecies occur on Cuba and Hispaniola.

NATURAL HISTORY: The Orange-Barred Sulphur is found mostly in urban areas and tropical pinelands near the host plants. The flight is swift and high, but adults frequently visit red or yellow flowers. The eggs are laid singly on the new growth of shrubby or arborescent species of *Cassia* (Fabaceae). *Cassia chapmanii* (= *Cassia bahamensis*) is a larval food plant in the Lower Keys and adults are associated with *Cassia fistula* (an exotic ornamental tree) in the City of Key Largo. The larvae may be green or yellow with a black lateral stripe and numerous small black tubercles. Scott (1986a) mentions that larval color depends upon whether leaves or the yellow flowers of the host are eaten. Bill Seefeldt (pers. comm.) has discovered that larval diet also affects the color of adult females. Those fed only leaves as larvae are white, while those fed *Cassia* flowers are yellow. The bluish-green pupa is strongly flattened laterally and bears a long point on the head. Adults have been reported from every month except March and August in the Keys.

STATUS: This spectacular species became established in Florida some time in the late 1920's (Klots, 1951; Opler and Krizek, 1984). The Orange-Barred Sulphur is locally abundant in southern Florida and the Keys, especially the Lower Keys.

56. CLOUDLESS SULPHUR
Phoebis sennae eubule (Linnaeus)

Pl. 10, Fig. 56

DESCRIPTION: FW = 26-35 mm. The Cloudless Sulphur is a bright lemon-yellow butterfly (Fig. 39). A narrow paler yellow border of androconial scales occurs along the outer margin of the upper forewings of the males. Females have black spots along the outer margins of the wings and a black spot with a pale center at the end of the forewing cell above. The ventral hindwing of females is lightly marked with reddish-brown and has two white spots at the end of the cell. The West Indian subspecies is similar, but the females are whitish instead of yellow.

DISTRIBUTION: Adams Key, Big Pine Key, Elliott Key, Key Largo, Key Vaca, Lignumvitae Key, No Name Key, Plantation Key, Stock Island, Sugarloaf Key, Upper Matecumbe Key, Windley Key.

Phoebis sennae eubule is found throughout the eastern United States, but mostly in southern states. *Phoebis sennae sennae* is the West Indian race found throughout the Bahamas and Antilles.

NATURAL HISTORY: The Cloudless Sulphur occurs primarily in open habitats such as beaches, vacant lots, roadsides, and tropical pinelands. The flight is rapid and often high. We have occasionally seen individuals flying over Biscayne Bay between Elliott Key and the mainland. The pale yellow eggs are laid on the new growth of many species of *Cassia* (Fabaceae). Larvae are usually green (sometimes yellow) with a lemon-yellow lateral stripe, and small dark tubercles (see color photo 32 in Pyle, 1981). Some individuals have patches of dark blue on the sides or in bands along the posterior edge of each segment. Others have little or no dark blue color. The pupa is yellowish-green with a yellow lateral stripe on the abdomen. The pupa is strongly flattened and bears a long point on the head. Adults occur all months of the year in the Keys.

FLOWERS VISITED: *Bidens alba, Lantana involucrata, Stachytarpheta jamaicensis.*

STATUS: *Phoebis sennae eubule* is often sporadic in distribution and abundance in the Keys, but can usually be found during the fall when large numbers of migrating individuals enter south Florida from the north. Several species of *Cassia* grow abundantly in the tropical pinelands of the Lower Keys and probably serve as hosts. H. D. Baggett captured a freshly eclosed female of the West Indian subspecies, *P. s. sennae* on Stock Island, 6 September 1981 (Plate 10).

FAMILY LYCAENIDAE
(Hairstreaks and Blues)

Lycaenids are small, often brightly colored butterflies that occur in most habitats in the Keys. The eyes of the adults are notched toward the bases of the antennae. The forelegs of males, but not females, are often reduced in size. Adults frequently have a fast, erratic flight pattern, making individuals difficult to follow and capture. Males of some species form leks (mating groups) near the tops of trees or shrubs, especially during late afternoon and on cloudy days. These males perch and fly out to investigate other butterflies or circle the perch site looking for females. Perching individuals of both sexes usually orient themselves head downward. The downward position coupled with false face patterns on the hindwings are thought to help deflect predator strikes away from the body (Robbins, 1981). Larvae are slug shaped and have the head partially retracted into the prothorax. The caterpillars feed on the flowers, young fruit, and new growth of many kinds of plants, especially legumes. The larvae are slow moving and cryptically colored, making them very difficult to find. We have found immatures by clipping flowers or fruit from potential hosts and then watching for accumulations of frass in the bottom of the rearing containers. The eggs are flattened and highly sculptured. They are usually brown, white, or bluish-green in color. The compact pupae are attached to a silk pad by hooks at the tip of the abdomen and have a silk girdle about the middle. Lycaenids make up about 16% of the Keys butterfly fauna.

SUBFAMILY EUMAEINAE
(Hairstreaks)

Hairstreaks may be dully or brilliantly colored on the upper sides of the wings. The undersides are often marked with black lines or spots that are highlighted with white. The hindwing usually has one or two pairs of slender tails and one or more small reddish eyespots near the anal angle. When perched, the adults often rub the hindwings together and orient themselves head downward. Wild-caught individuals frequently have the anal angle of the hindwings missing, probably from bird or lizard attacks. Thus, it is presumed that the "false head" pattern around the anal angle of the hindwing acts as a deceptive device to deflect predator attacks away from the more vulnerable true head and body. Males of many species have a small oval patch of androconial (pheromone dispersing) scales midway along the costal margin of the forewing. The larvae often have a small sclerotized plate on the thorax. The most common of the twelve species reported from the Keys are *Strymon columella*, *Strymon martialis*, and *Strymon melinus*.

57. RED-BANDED HAIRSTREAK
Calycopis cecrops (Fabricius)

Pl. 14, Fig. 57

DESCRIPTION: FW = 11-13.5 mm. Males of the Red-Banded Hairstreak are mostly black above, but females have variable amounts of blue on the upper sides, especially on the hindwings. The undersides are gray with a red and white postmedial line. The hindwing has two pairs of thread-like tails. On the ventral side of the hindwing, along the outer margin near the base of the tails, are two eyespots and a small patch of blue. The anal lobe is red above and has a black spot below.

DISTRIBUTION: Big Pine Key, Cudjoe Key, Elliott Key, Key Largo, No Name Key, Plantation Key, Stock Island, Sugarloaf Key, Summerland Key.

Calycopis cecrops occurs throughout Florida and much of the eastern United States.

NATURAL HISTORY: The Red-Banded Hairstreak is found in wooded urban areas, disturbed sites, and tropical hardwood hammocks in the Keys. Adults perch on foliage or the ground, and frequently visit flowers. The brownish eggs are laid singly on dead leaves on the ground and the first-instar larvae seek out food plants after hatching (Opler and Krizek, 1984). The host plants used in the Keys are not known. Mature larvae are brown with darker markings and are densely covered with short hairs. The pupa is light brown with black and dark brown markings and short hairs. Adults have been recorded every month but July in the Keys.

FLOWERS VISITED: *Acacia farnesiana, Bidens alba, Bumelia salicifolia, Flaveria linearis, Lantana involucrata.*

STATUS: The Red-Banded Hairstreak is an abundant butterfly throughout Florida, but is less common in the Keys. We have most frequently encountered this species in the Lower Keys.

58. MAESITES HAIRSTREAK

Pl. 13, Fig. 58

Chlorostrymon maesites (Herrich-Schäffer)

DESCRIPTION: FW = 9.5-11 mm. The Maesites Hairstreak is a small, brilliantly-colored butterfly. Males are iridescent violet above; females are iridescent blue. There is a very short tail followed by a longer tail on the hindwing. The ground color of the ventral wing is yellowish-green. This surface has a narrow black and white postmedial line and a red patch with black spots at the base of the tails. The postmedial line on the underside of the forewing is mostly black.

DISTRIBUTION: Key Largo, Key West, Plantation Key, Stock Island.

Chlorostrymon maesites is also found in the Bahamas, Greater Antilles, and much of the Lesser Antilles (Johnson, 1989).

NATURAL HISTORY: The Maesites Hairstreak flies at the edges of tropical hardwood hammocks. Adults perch on foliage, especially near the tops of the trees (Baggett, 1982) and occasionally visit flowers. The larvae feed on the flowers and young fruit of leguminous trees. Although Carroll (1987, p. 60) listed *C. maesites* as a seed predator of balloon vine, we have examined his specimens and determined them to be *C. simaethis*. On Stock Island, females lay the eggs singly on the flowers of small individuals of *Albizia lebbeck* (H. D. Baggett, pers. comm.). The caterpillars are light green with a pair of red spots on the dorsum of the thorax (Scott, 1986a). Pupae are light brown with small dark spots. Adults have been reported for every month except February and April in the Keys.

FLOWERS VISITED: *Bidens alba, Conocarpus erecta, Eupatorium odoratum.*

STATUS: The Maesites Hairstreak is local in occurrence and usually is quite rare, although adults are occasionally abundant at flowers. This butterfly may easily be overlooked due to its small size, cryptic coloration, and preference for tree tops. *Chlorostrymon maesites* has mostly disappeared from the south Florida mainland.

59. ST. CHRISTOPHER'S HAIRSTREAK
Chlorostrymon simaethis simaethis (Drury)

Pl. 13, Fig. 59

DESCRIPTION: FW = 8.5-13 mm. St. Christopher's hairstreak is similar to its close relative, *Chlorostrymon maesites,* but is larger and has a more conspicuous silvery-white postmedial line beneath. There is only one pair of tails on the hingwing, and the reddish patch on the ventral hindwing extends all the way to the apex. Females are mostly black and grayish-blue above, but males are iridescent violet.

DISTRIBUTION: Elliott Key, Key Largo, Plantation Key.

Chlorostrymon s. simaethis also occurs throughout the Greater and much of the Lesser Antilles (Johnson, 1989). The mainland race is found from southern California to northern Argentina.

NATURAL HISTORY: *Chlorostrymon simaethis* frequents disturbed sites and the edges of hardwood hammocks with an abundance of the larval food plant, balloon vine. The species of balloon vine in the Keys is usually referred to as *Cardiospermum halicacabum* (Sapindaceae), but Scott Carroll (1987 and pers. comm.) believes that *Cardiospermum corindum* is the correct name. Adults perch on the foliage of trees and shrubs, and occasionally visit flowers for nectar. Perching males seem to become especially active late in the afternoon. Females lay the eggs singly near the base of the developing seed pods. After the young larva emerges from the egg, it bores through the thin outer covering of the pod and begins to feed on the developing seeds. Balloon vine pods containing larvae of *C. simaethis* and *Hemiargus thomasi* may be identified by looking for fruit with holes or for the dark frass which can be seen through the thin walls of the pod (Plate 28). Fruit containing larvae are often abscised from the plants, so pods that fall when the plants are shaken, or that are already on the ground, are likely to have caterpillars or show signs of feeding damage. Mature larvae are yellowish green with a light brown head (Plate 27). The larvae leave the pods to pupate. The pupa is brown with darker markings. Adults have been reported every month but April, August, and October in the Keys.

FLOWERS VISITED: *Bidens alba, Eupatorium odoratum.*

STATUS: This elegant little butterfly has only recently become established in southern Florida (Opler and Krizek, 1984), but *Chlorostrymon simaethis* is now locally abundant in the Upper Keys. In southern Dade County, the small fruited balloon vine, *Cardiospermum microcarpum,* is used as a larval host (R. Gillmore, pers. comm.).

60. FULVOUS HAIRSTREAK
Electrostrymon angelia angelia (Hewitson)

Pl. 14, Fig. 60

DESCRIPTION: FW = 8.5-13 mm. The Fulvous Hairstreak is a small brownish butterfly with two pairs of tails on the hindwings. The upper sides are light brown with black borders, especially along the costa of the forewing. Underneath, the hindwing has an orange and black eyespot and a blue patch at the base of the tails. There is also a black and white postmedial line, the white part of which is broken into spots. The sexes are similar.

DISTRIBUTION: Big Pine Key, Key West, Stock Island.

Electrostrymon a. angelia also occurs on Cuba and the Isle of Pines. Other subspecies are found in the Bahamas, Jamaica, and Hispaniola, Puerto Rico, and the Virgin Islands.

NATURAL HISTORY: The Fulvous Hairstreak is usually found in shrubby disturbed sites and urban habitats. Adults perch on the foliage of trees and shrubs and visit flowers. According to H. D. Baggett, the host plant on Stock Island is Brazilian pepper, *Schinus terebinthifolius*

(Anacardiaceae), an invasive shrub of disturbed sites in southern Florida. The brownish larva is very similar to that of *Calycopis cecrops,* but is slightly more patterned with reddish-brown and pairs of small pale spots on the dorsum. The pupa is reddish-brown with black markings similar to those of *C. cecrops.* Adults have been reported for every month but February in the Keys.

FLOWERS VISITED: *Bidens alba, Coccoloba uvifera, Schinus terebinthefolius.*

STATUS: This species was first discovered in Florida by Richard Anderson (1974). The Fulvous Hairstreak has subsequently spread onto the southern mainland where it is locally abundant. This may not have been the only introduction of this butterfly into the state, as Miller (1978) noted that the Strecker collection contains an old specimen which may have been taken in Florida. The Fulvous Hairstreak is most abundant in disturbed areas of the Lower Keys.

61. RUDDY HAIRSTREAK   Pl. 14, Fig. 61
Electrostrymon endymion (Fabricius)

DESCRIPTION: FW = 10-10.5 mm. The Ruddy Hairstreak is smaller than its congener, *Electrostrymon angelia*, and is patterned somewhat differently. Males are orange above with black borders, but females are mostly dark with grayish-blue on the hindwing. The ventral hindwing is grayish with a narrow red and white postmedial line and an orange and black eyespot near the base of the tails.

DISTRIBUTION: The Ruddy Hairstreak ranges from southern Texas to Brazil. One individual has been taken in the Florida Keys recently.

STATUS: The only specimen known from Florida was collected in the vicinity of Grassy Key by M. Salter in February of 1982. This individual is now in the Florida State Collection of Arthropods.

62. ATALA HAIRSTREAK   Pl. 13, Fig. 62
Eumaeus atala florida Röber

DESCRIPTION: FW = 21-24 mm. The Atala is one of Florida's most splendidly colored insects. On the dorsal surface males are black with metallic green on the forewing and have a narrow greenish line along the outer border of the hindwing that is interrupted by the veins. Females are black with a streak of blue along the costal margin of the forewing. Both sexes have a bright red abdomen. The ventral hindwing is black with blue spots and a red patch midway along the inner margin. The Atala is the largest lycaenid in Florida.

DISTRIBUTION: Elliott Key, Key Largo.

Eumaeus atala atala occurs on Cuba, Isle of Pines, Andros, and Great Abaco. Further studies are needed to determine if the Florida population is sufficiently distinct to be called a separate race.

NATURAL HISTORY: The Atala is found in tropical pinelands and hardwood hammocks in close association with the larval food plant, coontie (*Zamia pumila*, Cycadaceae). The adults have a slow fluttering flight pattern. Males perch on the leaves of shrubs and make circular flights around the perch site as do other hairstreaks. Both sexes often visit flowers. The white eggs are laid in clusters on the young growth of coontie. Larvae are bright red with yellow spots (see color plate 29 in Pyle, 1981). Pupae are brown with small dark spots and hang from the substrate by a silk girdle. Droplets of a bitter-tasting liquid are exuded over the cuticle of the pupae. The early stages have been described by a number of authors (Schwarz, 1888; Healy, 1910; Rawson, 1961a; Poley, 1989).

STATUS: The Atala was once abundant in the rimrock areas of the southern mainland, but large-scale harvesting of the host for starch during the late 1800's greatly reduced the number of coontie plants. Urbanization and development of the coastal habitats favored by the Atala also had a large impact. By 1965 the Atala had been reduced to a single known population in Hugh Taylor Birch State Park (Kimball, 1965). After this colony died out, the Atala was feared extirpated from Florida. However, in the late 1970's another colony was found on Virginia Key. Conservationists such as Roger Hammer of Dade County Parks set out potted coontie plants on which females laid eggs. Plants with eggs were then moved to other locations and new colonies were started. The Atala has made a spectacular recovery and is now found in urban and natural areas around Fort Lauderdale and Miami, and has successfully been introduced into Everglades National Park. Some plant nurseries and botanical gardens now consider the Atala a pest species, as the larvae are capable of defoliating *Zamia* species used in landscaping. It is not known whether our current population is of original Florida stock or the result of a new introduction.

There are few records of the Atala from the Keys. Schwarz (1888) stated that it was known to occur on Elliott Key and Key Largo. Small (1913) listed coontie among the plants found in the Keys, but we have not encountered it on any of the islands. The early pioneers probably extirpated coontie (and thereby the butterfly) from the Keys, as it was a readily available source of starch. One of the few modern records of the Atala from the Keys is by Richard Funk (1966), who captured a single male on 5 June 1960 in the City of Key Largo.

63. BARTRAM'S HAIRSTREAK
Pl. 14, Fig. 63

Strymon acis bartrami (Comstock and Huntington)

DESCRIPTION: FW = 10-12.5 mm. Bartram's Hairstreak is dark gray with two pairs of tails on the hindwings. The upper side of the hindwing has a red and black eyespot at the base of the tails. The light gray ventral side is boldly marked with two white spots at the base of the hindwing, a crisp white line near the middle of each wing, and a red patch near the base of the tails. The abdomen of the male is white; the female abdomen is gray.

DISTRIBUTION: Big Pine Key, Key Biscayne, Key Largo.

Bartram's Hairstreak is endemic to southern Florida. Seven other races of *Strymon acis* occur in the Bahamas, Greater Antilles, and northern Lesser Antilles.

NATURAL HISTORY: *Strymon acis bartrami* occurs in close association with its larval host plant, woolly croton (*Croton linearis*, Euphorbiaceae), which grows in the tropical pinelands of the Lower Keys and southern mainland. Adults perch on the flowers and foliage of the host. The eggs, laid singly on the flowers of the host, hatch into pale green larvae that are covered with short hairs (Plate 27). The pupa is greenish with dark markings. Chermock and Chermock (1947) briefly described the immature stages. Adults have been recorded every month except February in the Keys.

FLOWERS VISITED: *Bidens alba, Croton linearis, Lantana involucrata, Serenoa repens.*

STATUS: Bartram's Hairstreak is locally abundant in the pinelands of the Lower Keys. Its range on the mainland is declining due to urban development, but good populations occur in the rimrock areas of Everglades National Park. The few records from the Upper Keys are probably strays from the mainland.

64. MODEST HAIRSTREAK

Pl. 14, Fig. 64

Strymon columella modestus (Maynard)

DESCRIPTION: FW = 9-13 mm. The Modest Hairstreak is a drab little butterfly with only one pair of tails on the hindwing. Males are uniformly dark brown above, with a few black spots at the base of the tails and a black sex patch on the forewing. Females are lighter in color and have grayish-blue on the upper hindwing. The ventral side is light brown, with a red and black eyespot at the base of the tail. *Strymon columella* is closely similar to *Strymon limenia* in appearance, but the anal lobe above is dark brown. The line near the middle of the ventral forewing is curved and is followed by some light wedge-shaped markings.

DISTRIBUTION: Ballast Key, Big Pine Key, Boca Chica Key, Cudjoe Key, Elliott Key, Fleming Island, Geiger Key, Key Largo, Key Vaca, Key West, Lignumvitae Key, Lower Matecumbe Key, Plantation Key, Stock Island, Sugarloaf Key, Summerland Key.

Strymon columella modestus is endemic to southern Florida. Three other subspecies occur in the Greater Antilles and northern Lesser Antilles. *Strymon columella* is also widely distributed in Mexico, Central America, and South America.

NATURAL HISTORY: The Modest Hairstreak flies in weedy disturbed sites and salt marshes. Males perch on low vegetation. Both sexes frequently visit flowers for nectar. The eggs are laid singly on the flowers of bay cedar (*Suriana maritima*, Surianaceae), *Waltheria indica* (Sterculiaceae), and probably weedy malvaceous plants. The caterpillars may be either green, red, or brightly patterned with red and green (Plate 27) closely matching the backgound colors of the host. We reared a parasitic wasp (Braconidae?) from a larva found on *W. indica* flowers on Key Largo. Pupae are brown. Adults may be found all months of the year in the Keys.

FLOWERS VISITED: *Bidens alba, Croton linearis, Flaveria linearis, Lippia nodiflora, Melanthera aspera, Pluchea rosea, Turnera ulmifolia.*

STATUS: The Modest Hairstreak is locally abundant on the southern mainland and throughout the Keys.

65. DISGUISED HAIRSTREAK

Pl. 14, Fig. 65

Strymon limenia (Hewitson)

DESCRIPTION: FW = 12 mm. This drab little hairstreak closely resembles its more common cousin, *Strymon columella*. The Disguised Hairstreak may be identified by the red anal lobe on the upper side of the hindwing. The postmedial band of dark spots on the underside of the forewing is not curved, and the wedge-shaped bands along the outer margin are lacking in *S. limenia*.

DISTRIBUTION: Big Pine Key, Key West, Stock Island.

Strymon limenia is found throughout the Greater Antilles and the Virgin Islands.

NATURAL HISTORY: The Disguised Hairstreak not only looks very similar to *S. columella*, but occurs in the same habitats (salt marshes and weedy areas), often at the same sites (Schwartz, 1989). Nothing is known about the life history. The only specimens from the Keys were taken in April, May, and December.

FLOWERS VISITED: *Bidens alba, Schinus terebinthefolius.*

STATUS: Richard Anderson (1974) first reported *Strymon limenia* from Florida. The Disguised Hairstreak appears to have been temporarily established in the Lower Keys, but none has been taken in more recent times.

66. CUBAN GRAY HAIRSTREAK
Strymon martialis (Herrich-Schäffer)

Pl. 14, Fig. 66

DESCRIPTION: FW = 11.5-15 mm. The Cuban Gray Hairstreak is blue and black above, with two pairs of tails on the hindwing. Females are a lighter blue than males. The ventral pattern is similar to that of *Strymon melinus*, but the white lines are bolder.
DISTRIBUTION: Ballast Key, Big Pine Key, Cudjoe Key, Elliott Key, Key Largo, Key Vaca, Key West, Lignumvitae Key, Stock Island, Sugarloaf Key, Summerland Key.
 Strymon martialis also occurs in the Bahamas and western Greater Antilles.
NATURAL HISTORY: In the Keys, *Strymon martialis* is usually found along shorelines in close association with the larval food plant, bay cedar (*Suriana maritima*, Surianaceae). Stray adults may occasionally be found visiting flowers in vacant lots and other habitats as well. The adults are often found perching on the leaves of bay cedar. The eggs are laid singly on the flowers of the host. Larvae are light green with very short hairs (Plate 27). Pupae are light brown with darker speckles and a small black spot on the dorsum of the abdomen. Adults have been reported for every month but July in the Keys.
FLOWERS VISITED: *Bidens alba, Eupatorium odoratum, Flaveria linearis, Lantana involucrata.*
STATUS: The Cuban Gray Hairstreak is locally abundant throughout the Keys and on the southern mainland. The leaves of *Trema micrantha* (Ulmaceae) are eaten by the larvae on the mainland (Slosson, 1901; H. D. Baggett, pers. comm.).

67. GRAY HAIRSTREAK
Strymon melinus melinus Hübner

Pl. 14, Fig. 67

DESCRIPTION: FW = 11-17 mm. This butterfly is dark gray above and has two pairs of tails on the hindwing. The underside is light gray, with a black and white line across each wing. *Strymon melinus* typically has a reddish-orange and black eyespot at the base of the tails above and below. Occasional specimens from the Keys have pale orange and black eyespots (Plate 14, Fig. 67c). The abdomen of the male is light orange.
DISTRIBUTION: Big Pine Key, Cudjoe Key, Elliott Key, Key Largo, Key Vaca, Key West, Lignumvitae Key, Lower Matecumbe Key, Plantation Key, Stock Island, Summerland Key, Upper Matecumbe Key, Windley Key.
 Strymon m. melinus is found throughout Florida and the eastern United States. Other subspecies occur in western North America, Mexico, and Central and South America.
NATURAL HISTORY: *Strymon melinus* frequents weedy disturbed sites such as vacant lots and roadsides in the Keys. Adults perch on vegetation and visit flowers frequently. Males sometimes congregate on shrubs or trees bordering fields in the late afternoon to await females. Perching males fly out to investigate passing butterflies or to circle the perch area. The bluish-green eggs are laid singly on the flowers and young fruit of bladder mallow, *Herissantia crispa* (Malvaceae), and probably other malvaceous plants such as *Sida* and *Malvastrum* species. Richard Gilmore (pers. comm.) has occasionally reared the larvae from balloon vine (*Cardiospermum halicacabum*, Sapindaceae). The larvae may be whitish (on balloon vine), pink, bright red, or green in color, depending upon the colors of the host. Pupae are light brown with dark markings. Adults occur all months of the year in the Keys.
FLOWERS VISITED: *Bidens alba, Heliotropium angiospermum, Lippia nodiflora, Melanthera*

aspera, Pluchea rosea, Sida hederacea.
STATUS: The Gray Hairstreak is locally abundant throughout the Keys and on the mainland.

68. LIGHT-BANDED HAIRSTREAK
Tmolus azia (Hewitson)

Pl. 13, Fig. 68

DESCRIPTION: FW = 8-9 mm. *Tmolus azia* is the smallest hairstreak in Florida. The upper side of the forewing is mostly black with bluish-white at the base. The upper hindwing is also black and white. There is only one pair of tails on the hindwings. The ventral side is light gray, with a jagged red line near the middle of the wing and a tiny red eyespot at the base of the tail.
DISTRIBUTION: Key Largo, Key West, Plantation Key.
  Tmolus azia is also found on Jamaica and Hispaniola, and is widely distributed in Mexico, Central America, and South America.
NATURAL HISTORY: The Light-Banded Hairstreak is typically found in disturbed sites in close association with the larval host, lead plant (*Leucaena leucocephala*, Fabaceae). The adults perch on the flowers and foliage of this weedy exotic tree. Eggs are laid singly on the flower buds. The larvae are green, red, and white, and have tubercles on the dorsum which bear several long hairs (Plate 27). Pupae are tan with black markings (Plate 28). Adults have been reported for every month but February, March, April, and June.
FLOWERS VISITED: *Eupatorium odoratum, Leucaena leucocephala.*
STATUS: This exotic butterfly has only recently become established in Florida (Opler and Krizek, 1984). It is locally abundant in the Upper Keys and on the southern mainland.

SUBFAMILY POLYOMMATINAE
(Blues)

  As their common name signifies, members of this group of butterflies are often bright blue above. The pigmy blue, however, is mostly brownish. The wings of blue butterflies are rounded and often have eyespots on the hindwings, but usually lack tails. The undersides are often white with black spots. Larvae are frequently green, but some species are marked with red, pink, or white. Many have special glands on the dorsum of the seventh abdominal segment which produce ant-appeasing substances. Ants may tend the larvae, stroking them with their antennae, and will guard them from predators and parasitoids. Of the five species reported from the Keys, all except *Hemiargus ammon* are common butterflies.

69. EASTERN PIGMY BLUE
Brephidium isophthalma pseudofea (Morrison)

Pl. 13, Fig. 69

DESCRIPTION: FW = 6-9 mm. The Eastern Pigmy Blue is one of the smallest butterflies in Florida. Adults are light brown above with a row of small black spots along the outer margin of the hindwing. The wings are banded and spotted with white below. The ventral hindwing bears a row of small black and silver spots along the outer margin. The sexes are similar.
DISTRIBUTION: Big Pine Key, Elliott Key, Geiger Key, Key Largo, Key West, Lignumvitae Key, Plantation Key, Stock Island, Sugarloaf Key, Upper Matecumbe Key.
  There is considerable confusion over the relationships between *B. pseudofea* from the

southeastern U. S., *B. isophthalma* from the Greater Antilles, and *B. exilis* from western North America. We have followed Miller and Brown (1981) in treating *pseudofea* as a subspecies of *B. isophthalma*, but Scott (1986a) considers *pseudofea* and *isophthalma* to be races of *exilis*. *Brephidium i. pseudofea* also occurs in the Bahamas (Riley, 1975; Scott, 1986b). The types are from Key West (Miller and Brown, 1981).

NATURAL HISTORY: The Eastern Pigmy Blue is found in salt marshes that have an abundance of glassworts (*Salicornia bigelovii* and *Salicornia virginica*, Chenopodiaceae) and saltwort (*Batis maritima*, Bataceae), the larval hosts. Adults flutter low to the ground and often perch on vegetation. The eggs are laid singly on the leaves of the hosts. Harvey and Longino (1989) noted that larvae were abundant on host plants adjacent to the nests of an ant, *Tapinoma sessile* (Say), on Sugarloaf Key. The ants tended the larvae, apparently for secretions from a pair of specialized glands on the dorsum of the seventh abdominal segment. They also noted that the pupae stridulate (make squeaking noises) when disturbed. Rawson (1961b) described the immature stages. The head of the larva is black and the body is a uniform green. Pupae are greenish. Adults occur all months of the year in the Keys.

FLOWERS VISITED: *Bidens alba.*

STATUS: This butterfly is often abundant in some salt marshes in the Keys but is absent or only sporadically present in others, even where the larval hosts are common. The limiting factor may be the associated ant, since Harvey and Longino's observations seem to indicate that the immatures had a clumped distribution on plants adjacent to nests of the ant.

70. LUCAS' BLUE
Hemiargus ammon ammon Lucas

Not illustrated.

DESCRIPTION: This species is closely similar to *Hemiargus thomasi;* however, males have a red and black eyespot near the anal angle of the hindwing above. In females of *H. ammon*, this spot is more elongate than in those of *H. thomasi*. A large series of *H. ammon* that we examined in the U. S. National Museum agrees well with Riley's (1975) figure and description, but Jacqueline Miller (pers. comm.) has noted considerable variation in color pattern. It may be neccessary to dissect and examine the genitalia of specimens suspected to be *H. ammon* in order to confirm their identity.

DISTRIBUTION: Cuba, Isle of Pines, in the Bahamas, and the Cayman Islands.

Lucas' Blue has occasionally been reported from the Keys in recent times, but all specimens seen by us or L. D. Miller or J. Y. Miller (Allyn Museum) have turned out to be worn *H. thomasi.*

STATUS: The first report of *H. ammon* from Florida was by Tom Kral (*News of the Lepidopterists' Society*, 1985(2): 29) who took a blue, tentatively identified as this species, on Big Pine Key (5 April 1984). However, the record was of a worn *H. thomasi*. Jacqueline Miller (pers. comm.) notes that the Allyn Museum has no specimens from the Keys. We have not found *H. ammon* in Florida.

71. CERAUNUS BLUE
Hemiargus ceraunus antibubastus Hübner

Pl. 13, Fig. 71

DESCRIPTION: FW = 8-12 mm. Males of the *Hemiargus ceraunus* are blue, above with a narrow black border along the outer margin and white fringes. The dorsal hindwing has a small black eyespot near the anal angle. Females are mostly black above with varying amounts of blue. The undersides are grayish with darker spots, bars, and lines outlined with white (Fig. 43). The ventral hindwing has a pair of eyespots consisting of a black spot surrounded by a narrow orange ring. As in *H. thomasi*, the basal and costal spots on the hindwing are black and conspicuous. John Calhoun (1988) took an aberrant male with smeared black markings on a white ground below on Stock Island (1 September 1982).

DISTRIBUTION: Big Pine Key, Elliott Key, Key Largo, Key Vaca, Key West, Lignumvitae Key, Plantation Key, Stock Island, Sugarloaf Key.

Hemiargus ceraunus antibubastus occurs only in the southeastern United States, and mostly in Florida. Other races are found in the Bahamas, Greater Antilles, and Mexico and Central America.

NATURAL HISTORY: The Ceraunus Blue frequents open disturbed sites and tropical pinelands in the Keys. Adults flutter low to the ground and often perch on vegetation or flowers. The small bluish-white eggs are laid singly on the flowers and buds of leguminous plants. We have reared it from eggs found on the new growth of *Sesbania macrocara* (Fabaceae) on Key West. Larvae vary in color from pale green with a red lateral stripe to dark green with red and pink markings. The head capsule is black or dark brown. The pupa is greenish with dark markings. Adults may be found every month of the year in the Keys.

FLOWERS VISITED: *Bidens alba, Lippia nodiflora.*

STATUS: The Ceraunus Blue is frequently seen in the Lower Keys, but is sporadic in the Upper Keys. On the mainland, it is locally abundant throughout Florida.

72. MIAMI BLUE   Pl. 13, Fig. 72
Hemiargus thomasi bethunebakeri Comstock and Huntington

DESCRIPTION: FW = 8-12.5 mm. The Miami Blue is slightly larger than the similar Ceraunus Blue. Males of *Hemiargus thomasi* are blue above, with a narrow black outer border and white fringes. Females are bright blue dorsally, with black borders and a red and black eyespot near the anal angle of the hindwing. The underside is grayish with darker markings outlined with white and bands of white wedges near the outer margin. The ventral hindwing has two pairs of eyespots, one of which is capped with red. The basal and costal spots on the hindwing are black and conspicuous. John Calhoun (1988) captured an aberrant male with reduced black markings and lengthened white patches on the underside of the wings on Key Largo (14 December 1982).

DISTRIBUTION: Adams Key, Big Pine Key, Elliott Key, Geiger Key, Key Largo, Lignumvitae Key, Old Rhodes Key, Plantation Key, Stock Island, Sugarloaf Key.

The Miami Blue is endemic to Florida. Other races of *Hemiargus thomasi* are found in the Bahamas and the Greater Antilles.

NATURAL HISTORY: The Miami Blue occurs at the edges of tropical hardwood hammocks and occasionally in tropical pinelands. Males often perch on the foliage of shrubs and trees. The flight is swift, especially if disturbed. As in *Chlorostrymon simaethis*, the eggs are laid singly near the base of young pods of balloon vine (*Cardiospermum halicacabum*, Sapindaceae). Newly hatched larva eat through the thin outer wall of the pod and feed on the developing seeds (Plate 28). This species also eats the flower buds of legumes (Klots, 1951), and Frank Rutkowski (1971) observed a female lay an egg just above a lateral bud on snowberry, (*Chiococca alba*, Rubiaceae). The larva is bright green with a black head capsule (unlike *C. simaethis*, which has a tan head). Caterpillars of *H. thomasi* are occasionally tended by ants (*Camponotus* spp.) within the pods of balloon vine. Pupae vary in color from black to brown (Plate 28). Adults may be found every month of the year in the Keys.

FLOWERS VISITED: *Bidens alba, Coreopsis leavenworthi, Heliotropium angio-spermum, Lippia nodiflora, Lantana involucrata, Melanthera aspera, Pithecellobium keyense, Schinus terebinthefolius, Spermacoce* sp.

STATUS: Although populations of the Miami Blue have declined on the southern mainland (Lenczewski, 1980), this pretty little butterfly is still locally common in the Keys.

73. CASSIUS BLUE   Pl. 13, Fig. 73
Leptotes cassius theonus (Lucas)

DESCRIPTION: FW = 7.5-12 mm. Males of *Leptotes cassius* are purplish blue dorsally. Females are white with a blue basal flush and dark borders. The ventral side of the wings is white with brown stripes and spots. The underside of the hindwing has two pairs of eyespots near the anal angle.

DISTRIBUTION: Bahia Honda Key, Big Pine Key, Boca Chica Key, Cudjoe Key, Elliott Key, Geiger Key, Key Biscayne, Key Largo, Key Vaca, Key West, Lignumvitae Key, Long Key, Lower Matecumbe Key, No Name Key, Plantation Key, Ramrod Key, Soldier Key, Stock Island, Sugarloaf Key, Summerland Key, Upper Matecumbe Key, Windley Key.

The Cassius Blue is one of the most ubiquitous of all neotropical butterflies. *Leptotes cassius theonus* is also found throughout the Bahamas and Greater Antilles. Other subspecies are found in the Lesser Antilles and on the mainland of the Americas from Texas to Argentina.

NATURAL HISTORY: The Cassius Blue can be found in many different habitats such as at the edges of tropical hammocks, along beaches, tropical pinelands, and in weedy disturbed sites. The adults commonly fly anywhere from ground level to the top of the forest canopy. The flight pattern is often slow and lazy, but may also be rapid and erratic at times. We once observed an adult caught in the web of a spiny-bellied spider (*Gasteracantha cancriformis*). The eggs are laid singly on the flowers, buds, and young fruit of a variety of plants, especially legumes. We have found larvae on *Galactia striata* flowers and fruit, *Pithecellobium unguis-cati* flowers, *Pithecellobium keyense* buds, *Lysiloma latisiliquum* flowers, and *Piscidia piscipula* flowers. Larvae vary in color from green to red depending on the host (Plate 28). Pupae are greenish with brown markings. Adults occur all months of the year in the Keys.

FLOWERS VISITED: *Alternanthera ramosissima, Bidens alba, Croton linearis, Flaveria linearis, Heliotropium angiospermum, Lantana involucrata, Lysiloma latisiliquum, Melanthera aspera, Morinda royoc, Pithecellobium keyense, Pithecellobium unguis-cati, Schinus terebinthefolius.*

STATUS: The Cassius Blue is one of the most abundant and widely distributed butterflies in the Keys. It also occurs widely throughout peninsular Florida.

FAMILY RIODINIDAE
(Metalmarks)

The Riodinidae are a worldwide group of butterflies, that are especially diverse in the neotropics. This family is closely related to the lycaenids. Many tropical riodinids are brilliantly colored and some have broad tails on the hindwings. The name "metalmark" is derived from the metallic colored spots on the wings of some species. Adults often perch on the undersides of leaves with the wings outstretched. Larvae are more cylindrical than lycaenids. Some are attended by ants. The pupa is attached by hooks to a silk pad at the caudal end, and is supported by a silk girdle around the middle. Only one small and rather plain species occurs in Florida.

74. LITTLE METALMARK   Pl. 14, Fig. 74
Calephelis virginiensis (Guérin-Ménéville)

DESCRIPTION: FW = 8-11.5 mm. The Little Metalmark is a tiny, brownish-orange butterfly with bands, bars, and spots of metallic bluish-gray. The upper and lower surfaces are similarly patterned. Females tend to be slightly larger than males.
DISTRIBUTION: Big Pine Key.
  Calephelis virginiensis occurs throughout mainland Florida and much of the southeastern United States.
NATURAL HISTORY: The Little Metalmark flies low to the ground in wet grassy places near patches of the larval food plants, thistles (*Cirsium* spp., Asteraceae). Adults often perch on vegetation or flowers with the wings outstretched. The larvae are greenish with long white hairs. Pupae are green with small black spots.
STATUS: *Calephelis virginiensis* is locally abundant on the southern mainland. Rutkowski (1971) reported finding a colony on Big Pine Key in rocky pineland adjacent to marsh during August. Although *Cirsium horridulum*, a larval host, grows on Big Pine, no other specimens have been reported from the Keys.

FAMILY LIBYTHEIDAE
(Snout Butterflies)

Snout butterflies are close relatives of the nymphalids, but have very long labial palpi. There are only about a dozen species worldwide. The forelegs of males are greatly reduced, but those of the females are normal. The whitish egg is slightly elongate and ribbed. The larvae lack spines or horns. The pupa is suspended from the caudal end as in the nymphalids. A single species occurs in Florida.

75. BACHMAN'S SNOUT BUTTERFLY
Libytheana bachmanii (Kirtland)

Pl. 20, Fig. 75

DESCRIPTION: FW = 18-22 mm. Bachman's Snout Butterfly may be distinguished from all other Florida butterflies by the very long palpi, which project forward from the head. The upper side of the wings is light orange with dark borders. There are three or four white spots near the apical portion of the forewing. The ventral hindwings are quite variable from uniform gray to bold patterns with light and dark brown patches and striations. The forewings have a distinctive shape due to the strongly produced apex.

DISTRIBUTION: Elliott Key, Key Largo.

Libytheana bachmanii is found throughout mainland Florida and much of the eastern United States.

STATUS: Bachman's Snout Butterfly is rarely encountered in southern Florida, but is locally abundant in the central and northern portions of the state. This species is somewhat migratory (Opler and Krizek, 1984), and stray individuals occasionally turn up in the Upper Keys. The larval hosts, hackberries (*Celtis* spp., Ulmaceae), are not known to grow in the Keys (Little, 1978).

FAMILY NYMPHALIDAE
(Brush-Footed Butterflies)

Nymphalids range in size from small to large butterflies and many species have eyespots or bright colors on the wings. The forelegs are reduced to small brush-like appendages in both sexes. Thus these insects appear to have only four legs. The eggs may be smooth, ribbed, or sculptured, rounded or elongate, and may be white, yellow, or green in color. The larvae are quite varied in form between the several subfamilies, but pupae are always suspended from the caudal end by tiny hooks embedded in a silk pad. Approximately 29% of the butterflies found in the Florida Keys are nymphalids.

SUBFAMILY HELICONIINAE
(Passion Flower Butterflies)

The heliconiines or passion flower butterflies tend to have rather long and narrow forewings and are brightly-colored. This group occurs only in the American tropics. Many species are diversified into quite varied races and are complexly involved in mimicry rings with other butterflies and day-flying moths. The eggs are elongate and ribbed. Larvae usually have a pair of horns on the top of the head and long branching spines on the body. The caterpillars feed exclusively on passionvine plants in the Passifloraceae. Pupae tend to be elongate and resemble dried leaves. Three of the four species recorded from Florida are abundant in the Keys.

76. GULF FRITILLARY
Agraulis vanillae nigrior Michener

Pl. 15, Fig. 76

DESCRIPTION: FW = 31-40 mm. The Gulf Fritillary is a large, orange and black butterfly (Fig. 32) with silvery markings beneath. The forewing cell has three white spots that are ringed with black. This species cannot be confused with any other Florida butterfly. Males are brighter orange and have narrower black markings than females.
DISTRIBUTION: Bahia Honda Key, Big Pine Key, Elliott Key, Key Largo, Key Vaca, Key West, Lignumvitae Key, Lower Matecumbe Key, Old Rhodes Key, Plantation Key, Stock Island, Sugarloaf Key, Summerland Key, Upper Matecumbe Key, Windley Key.

Agraulis vanillae nigrior is found throughout Florida and the southeastern United States. The West Indian subspecies is widely distributed in the Bahamas, Greater Antilles, and northern Lesser Antilles. Other races are found on the mainland from southern California to Argentina. The types of *A. v. nigrior* are from Upper Matecumbe Key (Miller and Brown, 1981).
NATURAL HISTORY: The Gulf Fritillary prefers open weedy sites and is often abundant in urban areas. Adults usually fly low to the ground and frequently visit flowers for nectar. The yellow eggs are laid singly on the tendrils of passion vines (*Passiflora* spp., Passifloraceae), but the caterpillars feed mainly on the young leaves. *Passiflora suberosa* is a host in the Keys. The larvae are orange with a few greenish longitudinal stripes. There is a pair of long black horns on the top of the head, and the body is adorned with long black spines. The pupa is

greenish-brown with a few pinkish-white stripes on the abdomen. Adults occur all months of the year in the Keys.

FLOWERS VISITED: *Bidens alba, Borrichia frutescens, Bougainvillea glabra, Eupatorium odoratum, Heliotropium angiospermum, Lantana camara, Lantana involucrata, Lycium carolinianum, Melanthera aspera, Morinda royoc, Sida acuta, Stachytarpheta jamaicensis, Stylosanthes hamata.*

STATUS: The Gulf Fritillary is locally abundant throughout the Keys and the southern mainland of the United States. Large numbers of these butterflies migrate southward through Florida during the fall (Walker, 1978).

77. BANDED ORANGE
Dryadula phaetusa (Linnaeus)

Pl. 15, Fig. 77

DESCRIPTION: FW = 40.5-43 mm. *Dryadula phaetusa* is bright orange above with broad black stripes. The ventral side has a similar pattern, but the orange ground color is much lighter.
DISTRIBUTION: Mexico, Central America, and South America.
STATUS: Kimball (1965) located several individuals of this species from Key Largo in the Los Angeles County Museum (10 February 1932, Grimshawe). These specimens are probably mislabeled, but it is possible that the Banded Orange could have been temporarily established at that time. There are no recent records of *D. phaetusa* from Florida.

78. JULIA BUTTERFLY
Dryas iulia largo Clench

Pl. 15, Fig. 78

DESCRIPTION: FW = 38-42.5 mm. Males of the Julia are mostly bright orange above with narrow black borders. The forewing has a black bar or two black spots near the end of the cell. The undersides are light brown with dark brown markings. A white and red streak extends along the costal margin from the base of the hindwing. Females are banded with black and light brown on the upper side of the forewing.
DISTRIBUTION: Adams Key, Big Pine Key, Elliott Key, Key Largo, Key Vaca, Lignumvitae Key, No Name Key, Old Rhodes Key, Plantation Key, Stock Island, Sugarloaf Key, Totten Key, Upper Matecumbe Key, Windley Key.

Dryas iulia largo is the endemic south Florida race. The types are from Key Largo (Miller and Brown, 1981). Nine other subspecies are found in the Bahamas, Greater Antilles, and Lesser Antilles. There are also two mainland races, one in Mexico and Central America and the other in South America.

NATURAL HISTORY: The Julia occurs at the edges of tropical hardwood hammocks. Its flight is often swift and high. The yellowish eggs are laid singly on the new growth of passion vines. *Passiflora multiflora* (Passifloraceae), which commonly grows in tropical hammocks, is the most likely host in the Keys, but we have not been able to locate immatures. Adults are occasionally caught in the webs of the golden silk spider (*Nephila clavipes*). The mature larva has a light orange head that is spotted with black. The body is black with white spots along the sides (Plate 29). There is a pair of slender black horns on the top of the head, and the body has long black spines. The pupa is similar to that of *Agraulis vanillae*, but has a few silver spots on the dorsum of the thorax. Adults have been found all months of the year in the Keys.
FLOWERS VISITED: *Bidens alba, Bourreria ovata, Chiococca alba, Coccoloba uvifera,*

Colubrina asiatica, Eupatorium odoratum, Flaveria linearis, Lantana camara, Lantana involucrata, Melanthera aspera, Metopium toxiferum, Morinda royoc, Psychotria nervosa, Stachytarpheta jamaicensis, Suriana maritima, Waltheria indica.
STATUS: The Julia is one of the most abundant butterflies in the Upper Keys, but is only sporadically present in the Lower Keys. It is also locally abundant on the southern mainland.

79. ZEBRA BUTTERFLY   Pl. 15, Fig. 79
Heliconius charitonius tuckeri Comstock and Brown

DESCRIPTION: FW = 27-44 mm. The Zebra is one of the most familar and easily recognized of Florida's butterflies. The long black wings striped with yellow (Fig. 21) distinguish it from all other species. The sexes are similar, but some individuals have a reddish tinge to the yellow forewing stripes.
DISTRIBUTION: Adams Key, Bahia Honda Key, Big Pine Key, Cudjoe Key, Elliott Key, Key Largo, Key Vaca, Lignumvitae Key, Long Key, No Name Key, Old Rhodes Key, Plantation Key, Stock Island, Sugarloaf Key, Summerland Key, Totten Key, Upper Matecumbe Key, Windley Key.

Heliconius charitonius tuckeri is the subspecies found in the southeastern United States, and is limited primarily to Florida. Five other races occur in the Bahamas, Greater Antilles, and northern Lesser Antilles. On the mainland, *H. charitonius* is widely distributed from Mexico into South America.
NATURAL HISTORY: Zebra butterflies occur in wooded habitats, especially along the margins of hardwood hammocks and in urban areas. The adults usually have a slow, fluttering flight pattern. At night, individuals will often roost together on the branches of trees and shrubs. The same roost may be used for several months. The yellowish eggs are laid singly or in small groups on the new growth of passion vines (Passifloraceae) including *Passiflora multiflora* and *Passiflora suberosa* in the Keys. Larvae often are not difficult to locate in patches of the host plant. The caterpillar is white with black spots and long black spines (Plate 29). The pupa has an almost surreal form: it bears thorn-like projections and rows of spines. There is a pair of flatten, leaf-like structures on the head and silver spots on the back. Adults have been found all months of the year in the Keys.
FLOWERS VISITED: *Bidens alba, Coccoloba diversifolia, Dicliptera assurgens, Eupatorium odoratum, Heliotropium angiospermum, Lantana involucrata, Lantana ovatifolia, Metopium toxiferum, Morinda royoc, Stachytarpheta jamaicensis.*
STATUS: Although the Zebra Butterfly is commonly found throughout the Keys, it never seems to achieve the abundance of the mainland populations.

SUBFAMILY NYMPHALINAE
(Brush-Footed Butterflies)

The Nymphalinae is the largest subfamily of brush-footed butterflies. This group has a worldwide distribution. Adults vary from small to large butterflies. In most species the cell of the hindwing is open or weakly closed. Many nymphalids are patterned with bright colors and eyespots. Some are attracted to fermenting fruit or fresh animal droppings. Eggs are usually slightly elongate and sculptured. The larvae often have branching spines on the body and horns on the head. The pupa is somewhat elongate and angular. The White Peacock, Florida Purple

Wing, Black Mangrove Buckeye, Cuban Crescent, and Phaon Crescent are some of the more common nymphalines found in the Keys. Twenty-one species belonging to this group have been recorded from our area.

80. CUBAN PEACOCK
Anartia chrysopelea Hübner

Pl. 16, Fig. 80

DESCRIPTION: FW = 18.5-21 mm. The Cuban Peacock looks quite different from its relative, the White Peacock (*Anartia jatrophae*). This smallish nymphalid is black with a white bar across the forewing and a white patch near the middle of the hindwing. The outer margins of the wings are bounded by a broken red line. There is a small red eyespot with a black pupil near the anal angle of the forewing and a similar one on the hindwing. The hindwing also has a short tail. The sexes are similar.

DISTRIBUTION: Big Pine Key, Key West.

The Cuban Peacock also occurs on Cuba, Isle of Pines, and Jamaica.

STATUS: A few specimens of this mostly Cuban butterfly were taken in the Keys during the early 1970's. Richard Anderson (1974) collected a fresh male in Key West on 22 February 1973 and noted another record from Big Pine Key taken in 1972. Bennett and Knudson (1976) found six fresh specimens on Big Pine Key on 24 and 25 April 1973. There have been no other reports of this species from Florida.

81. WHITE PEACOCK
Anartia jatrophae guantanamo Munroe

Pl. 16, Fig. 81

DESCRIPTION: FW = 19-30 mm. The White Peacock is a medium-sized, whitish butterfly with brown and orange bands on the wings (Plate 29). There is one black eyespot near the middle of the forewing and two on the hindwing. The hindwing also has a short tail. The sexes are similar.

DISTRIBUTION: Big Pine Key, Elliott Key, Key Biscayne, Key Largo, Key Vaca, Lignumvitae Key, Plantation Key, Stock Island, Sugarloaf Key.

Anartia jatrophae guantanamo is the race found in Florida, the Bahamas, and Cuba. Other races occur elsewhere in the Greater Antilles, the Lesser Antilles, and Mexico, Central America, and South America.

NATURAL HISTORY: The White Peacock prefers open disturbed sites, tropical pinelands, and occasionally beaches. Adults fly low to the ground and often perch on vegetation or visit flowers. This species is most numerous around patches of *Lippia nodiflora* (Verbenaceae). Another food plant, *Bacopa monnieri* (Scrophulariaceae), is sparingly present in freshwater marshes in the Keys and may also be used. The larva is black with small red and white spots on the body. The head has a pair of long horns, and the body is covered with branching spines. The pupa is pale green with a small black dot in the middle of the wing case and others on the dorsum of the abdomen. Adults occur all months of the year in the Keys.

FLOWERS VISITED: *Bidens alba, Borrichia frutescens, Lippia nodiflora, Melanthera aspera.*

STATUS: The White Peacock is a common butterfly on the southern mainland. In the Keys, *Anartia jatrophae* is sporadic in distribution and abundance, but may be numerous at times. This species has migratory tendencies.

82. EIGHTY-EIGHT BUTTERFLY
Diaethria clymena (Cramer)

Pl. 20, Fig. 82

DESCRIPTION: FW = 21-22 mm. *Diaethria clymena* is black above, with an iridescent green band on the forewing and an iridescent blue line along the outer margin of the hindwing. The ventral side of the forewing is mostly uniform bright red, with some black and white lines near the apex. The hindwing is patterned with black and white lines below. Those near the middle form the number "88". The costal margin of the ventral hindwing is also bright red.
STATUS: There are two old records of this South American butterfly from Key West (Kimball, 1965) which may be based on mislabeled specimens. Klots (1951, p. 279) listed a record from the southern mainland which he believed to be valid. No other specimens have been reported from Florida.

83. CUBAN CRESCENT
Eresia frisia frisia (Poey)

Pl. 17, Fig. 83

DESCRIPTION: FW = 14-20 mm. The Cuban Crescent is a small brownish-orange and black butterfly. The outer margin of the forewing is slightly concave. The forewings are marked with a distinctive black pattern which breaks the ground color into spots. These spots are bright brownish-orange in males and yellowish in females. The underside of the hindwing is yellowish-brown with darker bands and spots. Two other similar butterflies, *Phyciodes tharos* and *Phyciodes phaon*, also occur in the Keys.
DISTRIBUTION: Adams Key, Elliott Key, Key Largo, Key West, Lignumvitae Key, Lower Matecumbe Key, Old Rhodes Key, Plantation Key, Sands Key, Stock Island, Upper Matecumbe Key.
   Eresia frisia frisia is the West Indian race found in south Florida, the Bahamas, and the Greater Antilles. Other subspecies occur in Mexico, Central America, and South America.
NATURAL HISTORY: The Cuban Crescent flies low to the ground in open areas such as beaches, hammock edges, and vacant lots that have an abundance of *Dicliptera assurgens* (Acanthaceae), the larval host plant. Eggs are laid in clusters on the leaves of the host. The caterpillars feed gregariously during the early instars. The mature larva is variegated brown and white, with darker stripes. The head is light orange with black markings. The body is covered with branching spines (Plate 29). The spines on the prothorax are orange, those along the sides are tan, and the spines on the dorsum are blackish. Pupae are light brown. Chermock and Chermock (1947) described the immature stages in detail. Adults have been reported from every month but February in the Keys.
FLOWERS VISITED: *Bidens alba, Borrichia frutescens, Eustoma exaltatum, Melanthera aspera, Tournefortia volubilis.*
STATUS: The Cuban Crescent is locally abundant in the Upper Keys. It is uncommon in the Lower Keys and on the southern mainland.

84. DINGY PURPLE WING
Eunica monima (Stoll)

Pl. 20, Fig. 84

DESCRIPTION: FW = 20-21 mm. The Dingy Purple Wing is dark iridescent violet with black borders above. The forewing has three whitish spots near the middle and two others near the apex. The ventral hindwing is purplish-brown with several small eyespots. The sexes are similar.

DISTRIBUTION: Big Pine Key, Key Largo, Key West, Stock Island, Upper Matecumbe Key.

This species is widely distributed in southern Florida, the Bahamas, Greater Antilles, and on the mainland from Mexico to northern South America.

NATURAL HISTORY: Adults of the Dingy Purple Wing frequent the canopy of tropical hardwood hammocks. Adults perch on leaves and chase each other around perch sites in the canopy. They are attracted to rotting fruit and have been collected in bait traps. The larvae live communally in a silken web spun about the leaves of gumbo limbo, (*Bursera simaruba*, Burseraceae), a common tree of tropical hammocks in south Florida. The larva is brownish with a yellow lateral stripe. The head is orange and black. The body is covered with tiny tubercles and there are several rows of conical spines along the sides. Larger spines occur on the dorsum of the eighth abdominal segment. The pupa is green, with a ridge on the dorsum of the thorax and two projections on the head. The adults have been reported from May, July, August, October, November, and December in the Keys.

STATUS: Although Kimball (1965) listed only a few records of *E. monima* from south Florida, this species is now well established. The Dingy Purple Wing appeared in numbers on Key Largo in the early 1970's (H. D. Baggett, pers. comm.), and in hammocks near avocado groves around Florida City and Homestead on the mainland. The Keys populations have since declined, but *E. monima* is still locally abundant in southern Dade County. This butterfly has migratory tendencies (Jenkins, 1990).

85. FLORIDA PURPLE WING

Pl. 20, Fig. 85

Eunica tatila tatilista Kaye

DESCRIPTION: FW = 21-29 mm. The Florida Purple Wing is a larger and more brightly colored butterfly than its relative, *Eunica monima*. The upper side of the male is iridescent violet; females are iridescent blue. The forewings are spotted with white. The underside of the hindwing varies from a uniform grayish to patterns with dark bands and eyespots (Fig. 23). Occasional individuals have a light streak from the base of the hindwing to the outer margin below, and others have a pale apical patch (Fig. 52). The apical portion of the outer margin of the forewing is notched.

DISTRIBUTION: Adams Key, Big Pine Key, Elliott Key, Key Largo, Lignumvitae Key, Long Key, Lower Matecumbe Key, Old Rhodes Key, Plantation Key, Totten Key, Upper Matecumbe Key, Windley Key.

The West Indian race, *E. tatila tatilista*, occurs in southern Florida, the Bahamas, and the Greater Antilles. Other subspecies of *E. tatila* are found in Mexico, Central America, and South America.

NATURAL HISTORY: The Florida Purple Wing flies in the shade of tropical hardwood hammocks, and along trails and hammock edges. The adults perch on leaves, branches, and tree trunks, and make short flights. The brilliant upper sides flash in the sunlight, but the butterfly seems to disappear when perching. Adults rarely visit flowers and although they are reported to visit rotting fruit (Opler and Krizek, 1984), we have not taken them in traps baited with fermenting apples, bananas, and molasses. On a few occasions we have observed males basking in the sun on rocky trails with wings outstretched. The eggs are laid singly on the leaves of crabwood (*Gymnanthes lucida,* Euphorbiaceae). Larvae are brownish-orange with greenish stripes. The head has a long pair of horns. There are also spines on the body. The pupa is light green. Adults have been reported from every month in the Keys.

Fig. 52. The ventral surfaces of four adult specimens of *Eunica tatila tatilista*, showing the variation in pattern on the forewing apex and hindwing. All were taken on 22-23 March 1987 on North Key Largo (upper left, male; lower left, female) or Elliott Key (upper right, male; lower right, female).

FLOWERS VISITED: *Eupatorium odoratum*, and on a few occasions, adults have been observed probing the withered flowers of *Bidens alba*.

STATUS: The Florida Purple Wing is locally abundant in the hammocks of the Upper Keys. It is less common in the Lower Keys and on the southern mainland. This species undergoes boom and bust population cycles and has migratory tendencies (Jenkins, 1990).

86. VARIEGATED FRITILLARY Pl. 16, Fig. 86
Euptoieta claudia (Cramer)

DESCRIPTION: FW = 23-31 mm. The Variegated Fritillary is light orange, with a yellowish medial band and black markings. The forewing cell has a conspicuous yellowish spot. The underside of the hindwing is complexly patterned with white and brown. The sexes are similar.

DISTRIBUTION: Big Pine Key, Key Largo, Key West, Sugarloaf Key.

Euptoieta claudia is also found in the Bahamas, Greater Antilles, and in North, Central, and South America.

NATURAL HISTORY: Adults of the Variegated Fritillary fly low to the ground in open areas. The eggs are laid singly on the new growth of plants in the Violaceae and Passifloraceae. Larvae are orange with white stripes and bluish-black spines (see color photo 20 in Pyle, 1981). The spines on the prothorax are especially long and are clubbed at the tip. The pupa is marked with black, yellow, and golden spots. Adults have been recorded during March, May, August, and October in the Keys.

STATUS: The Variegated Fritillary is sporadic in distribution and abundance in southern Florida. The few specimens taken in the Keys are probably strays from the mainland.

87. HAITIAN CRACKER

Pl. 19, Fig. 87

Hamadryas amphichloe diasia (Fruhstorfer)

DESCRIPTION: FW = 31-35.5 mm. The Haitian Cracker is a handsome, tropical butterfly. The upper sides are cryptically colored bluish-gray, with dark markings and white spots. There is a short, thick, reddish bar across the forewing cell. The undersides are white with black markings. The hindwing has a row of small eyespots. Males have a white flush on the forewings.

DISTRIBUTION: Key Largo, Plantation Key.

Hamadryas amphichloe diasia occurs in southern Florida and the Greater Antilles. Other races are found in Mexico, Central America, and South America.

NATURAL HISTORY: Adults of the Haitian Cracker perch on tree trunks with the wings outspread against the bark. They make short flights to investigate passing butterflies or to move to new perches. When disturbed, males of many species of *Hamadryas* make clicking sounds as they fly, and are thus commonly known as "crackers". The source of this sound has been controversial, but Daniel Otero (1990) has experimentally shown that the wing veins at the end of the forewing cell are responsible. The larvae probably feed on vines in the genus *Dalechampia* (Euphorbiaceae) (Scott 1986a). Adults have been seen in July and October in the Keys.

STATUS: A few specimens have been observed in the Upper Keys (Jenkins, 1983; Kruer, 1988, *Southern Lepidopterists' News*, 11:21) and on the southern mainland recently.

88. COMMON BUCKEYE

Pl. 18, Fig. 88

Junonia coenia coenia (Hübner)

DESCRIPTION: FW = 18-27.5 mm. *Junonia coenia* is one of three similar buckeye butterflies that occur in the Keys. All three species have one small and one large eyespot on the upper side of the forewing, and two large eyespots on the hindwing. The forewing cell has two reddish-orange bars, and there is a pale band from the costa to the outer margin of the wing. Males have a slightly more concave outer margin of the forewing than females. The Common Buckeye may be identified by the white forewing band, which nearly encloses the larger eyespot, and the great disparity in the size of the eyespots on the hindwing.; the upper spot is twice as large as the lower one. In the summer or wet season phenotype, the underside of the hindwing is light brown with a pale reddish streak and faint eyespots. The dry season form is a uniform reddish-brown beneath. Schwartz (1987) has misidentified this species as *Junonia evarete*.

DISTRIBUTION: Big Pine Key, Big Torch Key, Cudjoe Key, Elliott Key, Key Largo, Key West, Stock Island, Sugarloaf Key, Summerland Key.

The Common Buckeye occurs throughout Florida, most of the United States, Mexico, the Bahamas, and Cuba.

NATURAL HISTORY: The Common Buckeye flies in open weedy habitats and tropical pinelands. Adults have a swift flight low to the ground. Males defend small territories, perching on the ground or low vegetation within them and frequently fly out to investigate passing butterflies. Eggs are laid singly on the leaves of plants in the Scrophulariaceae in southern

Florida. *Agalinus* spp. and *Buchnera floridana* are the most likely hosts in the Keys. The larva is variegated black and pale yellow, and has branching spines (see color photo 23 in Pyle, 1981). The head is black and orange with a pair of very short horns on the top. There are also orange spots along the sides of the body. The pupa may be cream-colored or grayish with pink spots and markings. Adults have been recorded every month except November in the Keys.

FLOWERS VISITED: *Bidens alba, Eupatorium coelestinum, Stachytarpheta jamaicensis.*

STATUS: This butterfly is locally common on the southern mainland, but is sporadic in distribution and abundance in the Upper Keys. It may be abundant at times, especially during the fall when great numbers of individuals migrate southward through Florida (Walker, 1978). *Junonia coenia* seems to be more consistently found in the pinelands of the Lower Keys where potential host plants are available.

89. BLACK MANGROVE BUCKEYE
Junonia evarete (Cramer)

Pl. 18, Fig. 89

DESCRIPTION: FW = 26-31 mm. *Junonia evarete* is readily distinguished from other buckeye butterflies by its larger size, the pale orange forewing band, and the size of the eyespots on the upper side of the hindwing. The upper spot is only slightly larger or is the same size as the lower spot. The underside of the hindwing resembles the wet season phenotype of *J. coenia*: light brown with a pale reddish streak and faint eyespots. There seems to be little seasonal variation, except for darkening of the reddish streak on the underside of the hindwing in occasional individuals from the dry season (Plate 18, Fig. 89d). Schwartz (1987) has misidentified this species as *Junonia coenia*.

DISTRIBUTION: Adams Key, Big Pine Key, Boca Chica Key, Elliott Key, Geiger Key, Key Largo, Key Vaca, Key West, Lignumvitae Key, Lower Matecumbe Key, No Name Key, Plantation Key, Stock Island, Sugarloaf Key, Summerland Key, Upper Matecumbe Key, Windley Key.

Junonia evarete also occurs in the Bahamas, Greater Antilles, and Lesser Antilles. Its distribution on the mainland has been confused with that of other similar buckeyes, but it probably coincides with the range of the larval host.

NATURAL HISTORY: *Junonia evarete* frequents the edges of mangroves, salt marshes, and occasionally turns up in weedlots. Males defend small territories and often perch on bare patches of soil within the territory. The eggs are laid singly on the new growth of small black mangroves, (*Avicennia germinans*, Avicenniaceae). The larva is mostly black with spines on the body. The bases of the mid-dorsal spines are iridescent turquoise (Turner and Parnell, 1985). The pupa is dark brown or gray with black markings. Adults occur all months of the year in the Keys.

FLOWERS VISITED: *Bidens alba, Eupatorium coelestinum, Flaveria linearis, Heliotropium angiospermum, Lantana involucrata, Pithecellobium keyense, Pluchea rosea, Senecio mexicana.*

STATUS: The Black Mangrove Buckeye is locally abundant throughout the Keys and coastal areas of the Florida peninsula.

90. CARIBBEAN BUCKEYE
Junonia genoveva (Stoll)

Pl. 18, Fig. 90

DESCRIPTION: FW = 23-28 mm. *Junonia genoveva* has a pinkish-white forewing band that does not extend downward along the inner edge of the larger forewing eyespot. The eyespots on the upper side of the hindwing are relatively small and nearly equal in size. The underside of the hindwing has a prominent reddish band and well-defined eyespots. There is little seasonal variation, except that dry season individuals are somewhat more contrastingly patterned below.

DISTRIBUTION: Big Pine Key (?), Key Largo, Plantation Key.

The Caribbean Buckeye also occurs in the Bahamas and the Greater Antilles.

NATURAL HISTORY: *Junonia genoveva* is found in weedy open habitats in the vicinity of urban areas. Like other buckeyes, males perch on the ground or low vegetation and defend small territories. Such individuals tend to be extremely wary and difficult to approach. The eggs are laid singly on the leaves of plants in the Verbenaceae such as *Stachytarpheta jamaicensis*. The larva is similar to that of *J. evarete*, but the bases of the mid-dorsal spines are iridescent purple (Turner and Parnell, 1985). Adults have been recorded during January, February, September, October, November, and December in the Keys.

STATUS: The taxonomic status of *Junonia evarete* and *Junonia genoveva* has been much confused in the past. These taxa were often treated as seasonal forms of a single species. When *J. genoveva* was discovered in abundance in south Florida, the nomenclature was so confused that the two were simply referred to as "species A" and "species B" in newsletter reports. Turner and Parnell (1985) investigated the biology of these taxa, showed that the two were distinct species, and verified the nomenclature. *Junonia genoveva* seems to have only recently become established in Florida. Thomas E. Pliske took one on Key Largo, 16 August 1961 (John Calhoun, pers. comm.). During 1978, members of the Southern Lepidopterists' Society discovered large numbers of *J. genoveva* in weedlots in the City of Key Largo (H. D. Baggett, pers. comm.). The Caribbean Buckeye was also found in abundance on the southern mainland at the Florida Institute of Food and Agricultural Sciences in Homestead at that time. This species is still present in the Keys, but not in the numbers seen in 1978. The only population that we have located occurs in a large weedy field in the City of Key Largo where only a few individuals have been seen per visit. On 6 December 1987, males of all three buckeye species were present and interacting at this site!

91. FLORIDA VICEROY
Limenitis archippus floridensis (Strecker)

Pl. 19, Fig. 91

DESCRIPTION: FW = 34-42 mm. The Florida Viceroy is a medium-sized, brownish-orange butterfly that superficially resembles the Queen butterfly. The outer margins of the wings are bordered with black bands bearing small white spots. The wing veins are also outlined with black. The forewing has a white and black diagonal line near the end of the cell. There is also a black line near the middle of the hindwing. Males and females are similar.

DISTRIBUTION: Elliott Key, Key Largo.

Limenitis archippus floridensis is limited to Florida. *Limenitis archippus* occurs as several other races throughout much of North America.

NATURAL HISTORY: The Florida Viceroy is usually found in the vicinity of freshwater wetlands having an abundance of willows (*Salix* spp., Salicaceae), the larval host. Males perch on the foliage of trees and shrubs and make short flights. Viceroys rarely visit flowers, but are readily attracted to fermenting fruit and are easily captured in bait traps. The eggs are laid singly on the new growth of willows. *Salix caroliniana* is the host plant in south Florida. Mature larvae are olive-green with a pinkish-white saddle and lateral line. There is a pair of long tubercles on the dorsum of the prothorax and small tubercles elsewhere on the body. The pupa is brown with pinkish-white markings and a rounded flange on the dorsum of the abdomen. The few adults from the Keys were seen during May and August.

STATUS: The Florida Viceroy is locally abundant in southern Florida, but only a few stray specimens have been taken in the Keys. Little (1978) lists the larval food plant (*Salix caroliniana*) as occurring in the Keys, but it is not common.

92. MANY-BANDED DAGGER WING   Pl. 19, Fig. 92
Marpesia chiron (Fabricius)

DESCRIPTION: FW = 29 mm. The wings of *Marpesia chiron* are striped with dark and light brown above. The forewing has three white spots near the apex. Ventrally, the basal half of the wings is striped with light blue, brown, and white. The outer half is dark brown with bluish markings. Like all dagger wings, the hindwings have a pair of long tails. The sexes are similar in appearance.

STATUS: Richard Boscoe took one specimen on Big Pine Key, 7 November 1985, that was visiting *Lantana* flowers (*News of the Lepidopterists' Society*, 1986 (2):34). This tropical butterfly is found in Cuba, Jamaica, Hispaniola, and on the mainland from Mexico into South America.

93. CUBAN DAGGER WING   Pl. 19, Fig. 93
Marpesia eleuchea eleuchea Hübner

DESCRIPTION: FW = 27-31 mm. The Cuban Dagger Wing is similar in appearance to *Marpesia petreus*. The wings above are light brownish-orange with dark lines and there is a pair of long tails on the hindwings. *Marpesia eleuchea*, however, is smaller than *M. petreus*. The tip of the forewing is also less produced, and the medial line is bent inward at the forewing cell. The wings (and body) are light brown below, with darker lines and faint eyespots. There is a small white spot midway along the costal margin of the hindwing. The sexes are similar.

STATUS: Richard Anderson (1974) captured a male of this species as it visited the flowers of Brazilian pepper (*Schinus terebinthifolius*) on Sugarloaf Key, 14 October 1973. No other specimens have been reported from the Keys. This butterfly is found in several races in the Bahamas and the Greater Antilles.

94. RUDDY DAGGER WING   Pl. 19, Fig. 94
Marpesia petreus petreus (Cramer)

DESCRIPTION: FW = 34-42 mm. The Ruddy Dagger Wing is brownish-orange with dark brown borders and lines above. The hindwing has a long tail, and the anal lobe also bears a short tail. The ventral surface is light brown with a purplish sheen and a dark brown stripe (resembling the midrib of a dead leaf) near the middle of each wing. Unlike *Marpesia eleuchea*, the body is white below, contrasting sharply with the ground color of the hindwings. Females are similar to males, but have a slightly duller ground color and darker markings.

DISTRIBUTION: Cudjoe Key (?), Elliott Key, Key Biscayne, Key Largo, Lignumvitae Key, Old Rhodes Key, Plantation Key, Stock Island, Sugarloaf Key, Upper Matecumbe Key.

   Marpesia petreus petreus has also been recorded from Puerto Rico and is widely distributed

in tropical North, Central, and South America. Another race occurs in the Lesser Antilles.
NATURAL HISTORY: The Ruddy Dagger Wing flies near the edges of tropical hardwood hammocks. The adults perch on the foliage of trees and shrubs, and visit flowers readily. The eggs are laid singly on the new growth of figs. Strangler fig (*Ficus aurea*, Moraceae; Fig. 22) is the main host on the mainland, but short-leaved fig (*Ficus citrifolia*) is also eaten. Both of these trees occur in the Keys. The mature larva is gaudily-colored orange and white with bluish-black markings on the sides. The head is orange with two black lines and an extremely long pair of curved black horns on the top. There is also a long bluish-black spine on the dorsum of abdominal segments two, four, six, and eight. The pupa is yellowish-green with two black spines on the head and others on the dorsum of the abdomen (Plate 29). Adults have been recorded every month except March, April, and December in the Keys.
FLOWERS VISITED: *Coccoloba uvifera, Schinus terebinthefolius.*
STATUS: The Ruddy Dagger Wing usually occurs in low abundance in tropical hammocks throughout the Keys. It is much more common on the southern mainland.

95. PHAON CRESCENT

Pl. 17, Fig. 95

Phyciodes phaon (W. H. Edwards)

DESCRIPTION: FW = 11.5-16 mm. *Phyciodes phaon* is one of three crescent butterflies that occur in the Keys. The upper sides of the wings are brownish-orange with dark borders and lines. The Phaon Crescent may be distinguished by the yellowish band across the middle of the forewings (readily seen on the ventral side). The ground color of the ventral hindwing is whitish in the summer or wet season form, and brownish in the winter form. The sexes are similar, but females tend to be larger and more brightly patterned.
DISTRIBUTION: Big Pine Key, Elliott Key, Key Largo, Key West, Lignumvitae Key, Plantation Key, Stock Island, Sugarloaf Key, Upper Matecumbe Key.

The Phaon Crescent is also found in Cuba, the Cayman Islands, and from the southeastern United States into Central America.
NATURAL HISTORY: *Phyciodes phaon* occurs in weedy disturbed sites, usually in close association with its larval host, carpetweed (*Lippia nodiflora*, Verbenaceae). Adults fly low to the ground and frequently perch on vegetation or flowers. The whitish eggs are laid in clusters on the leaves of carpetweed. The larvae feed gregariously while young, but become solitary in the later instars. The mature caterpillar is tan with black stripes. The head is also tan and black. The body is covered with branching spines. Pupae are light brown. Adults occur all months of the year in the Keys.
FLOWERS VISITED: *Bidens alba, Lippia nodiflora.*
STATUS: The Phaon Crescent is locally abundant in weedy areas of the Upper Keys and the mainland. This butterfly is less common in the Lower Keys.

96. PEARL CRESCENT

Pl. 17, Fig. 96

Phyciodes tharos tharos (Drury)

DESCRIPTION: FW = 14-17 mm. The Pearl Crescent is brownish-orange above, with black borders and lines. The underside of the hindwing is yellowish, with light brown lines and a brown patch along the outer margin. *Phyciodes tharos* has bands of color on the forewings, rather than the spots typical of *Eresia frisia*, and lacks the yellowish medial band of *Phyciodes* *phaon.* Males are brighter and have wider black borders than females. The winter form is contrastingly patterned with brown and white on the underside of the hindwing.

DISTRIBUTION: Big Pine Key, Elliott Key, Key Largo, Key Vaca, Lower Matecumbe Key, Plantation Key, Stock Island.

The Pearl Crescent is found throughout much of the United States and Mexico, and occasionally strays to the Bahamas. The typical race is found in the eastern part of the range.

NATURAL HISTORY: The Pearl Crescent occurs in a variety of habitats such as tropical pinelands, weedy sites, and the edges of hardwood hammocks. How strange it seems to find this mostly temperate butterfly flitting about the tropical vegetation of the Keys! The flight is often swift and low to the ground, but adults frequently perch on vegetation and visit flowers. The pale yellow eggs are laid in clusters on the leaves of *Aster* species (Asteraceae), but the specific host used in the Keys has not been determined. The larva is black with white lateral stripes. The head is mostly black, and the body is covered with branching spines. Pupae are light brown. Adults have been recorded every month of the year in the Keys.

FLOWERS VISITED: *Bidens alba, Borrichia frutescens, Lippia nodiflora.*

STATUS: The Pearl Crescent is regularly present in the tropical pinelands of the Lower Keys, where breeding populations seem to be established. This butterfly is spordically present in the Upper Keys, however. *Phyciodes tharos* is widely distributed and locally abundant throughout Florida.

97. MALACHITE BUTTERFLY   Pl. 19, Fig. 97
Siproeta stelenes biplagiata (Fruhstorfer)

DESCRIPTION: FW = 38-46 mm. The Malachite is the only Florida butterfly with green patches on the wings. The green color varies between individuals from yellowish- to bluish-green. The upper sides are dark brown with green patches and spots, including two in the forewing cell. There is a reddish spot near the anal angle of the hindwing. The ventral side is light brown and orange with the same pattern of green. The hindwing has a short tail. The sexes are similar.

DISTRIBUTION: Adams Key, Big Pine Key, Elliott Key, Key Largo, Key West, Lignumvitae Key, Plantation Key, Stock Island, Summerland Key.

The typical race of *Siproeta stelenes* from the eastern Greater Antilles has only one green spot in the forewing cell. Florida specimens have two such spots, as do the Cuban and mainland populations. The Cuban population has been named *insularis* (Holland), but there do not seem to be any consistant differences between it and mainland *S. stelenes biplagiata*. The Malachite occurs widely in Mexico, Central America, and South America, but Cuban and Floridian populations are isolated and disjunct from this gene pool.

NATURAL HISTORY: The Malachite is found in shrubby disturbed sites and tropical hardwood hammocks. In southern Dade County, this species breeds in shady avocado and citrus groves adjacent to hardwood forest. Adults often visit flowers. The eggs are laid singly on the leaves of green shrimp plant (*Blechum brownei*, Acanthaceae). The caterpillars feed on the leaves of the host. The larva is velvety black, with two rows of reddish-orange spines on the dorsum and blackish spines along the sides. The head has a pair of long blackish spines on the top. The pupa is green with small black spots and pale orange spines (Plate 29). The black cremaster is attached to a relatively long pad of silk. Adults have been recorded for every month but August and September in the Keys.

FLOWERS VISITED: *Flaveria linearis.*

STATUS: The Malachite has changed in abundance in recent times. Kimball (1965) listed only a few specimens from Florida, but this handsome butterfly is now locally abundant near patches of the host plant in the southern part of the state. The Malachite is sporadically present in the Keys, but may occasionally be fairly common.

98. RED ADMIRAL

Pl. 16, Fig. 98

Vanessa atalanta rubria (Fruhstorfer)

DESCRIPTION: FW = 23-28 mm. The Red Admiral is very dark brown above, with an orangish-red band across the forewing and a reddish border along the outer margin of the hindwing. The forewing has some white spots near the apex. The underside of the hindwing is blackish. Males and females are similar.

DISTRIBUTION: Big Pine Key, Elliott Key, Key Largo, Key Vaca, Key West, Stock Island.

Vanessa atalanta rubria occurs throughout much of North America, southward into the highlands of Central America. This species is also found occasionally in the Greater Antilles. The typical race occurs in Europe and temperate parts of Asia. This butterfly has also been introduced into Hawaii and New Zealand (Opler and Krizek, 1984).

NATURAL HISTORY: The Red Admiral may occasionally be found along beaches and at the edges of mangroves and hardwood hammocks in the Keys. Adults have a rapid flight, but often perch on the foliage of trees and shrubs or on the ground. Males defend small territories and fly out to investigate other butterflies. Both sexes are attracted to fermenting fruit. Plants in the Urticaceae are the larval hosts, but it is not known if this species breeds in the Keys. The greenish eggs are laid singly on the leaves of the host. The larva lives in a nest of leaves and silk, or in a single folded leaf. The mature caterpillar is variable in color. Some individuals are black with small white spots, others are mostly pale brown. There is a white lateral stripe, and the body is covered with branching spines. The head is black. Pupae are brown with gold spots. Adults have been taken during January, February, March, May, and October.

FLOWERS VISITED: *Cardiospermum halacacabum, Senecio mexicana.*

STATUS: The Red Admiral is abundant throughout Florida, but is sporadically present in the Keys.

99. PAINTED LADY BUTTERFLY

Pl. 16, Fig. 99

Vanessa cardui (Linnaeus)

DESCRIPTION: FW = 29-31 mm. The Painted Lady is a medium-sized, pinkish-orange butterfly with black markings. There are some white spots near the apex of the forewing, and the hindwing has a row of small eyespots along the outer margin. The underside of the hindwing is variegated with white and shades of brown, and has several small eyespots. The sexes are similar.

DISTRIBUTION: Big Pine Key, Key West, Lignumvitae Key, Stock Island, Sugarloaf Key.

Vanessa cardui is also found in the Bahamas, Greater Antilles, Lesser Antilles, and throughout much of North America, Central America, Europe, Asia, and Africa.

NATURAL HISTORY: The Painted Lady is occasionally encountered in tropical pinelands and at the edges of mangroves and hardwood hammocks. Adults perch on foliage and visit flowers for nectar. The flight is rapid. The larvae live singly in a web on the leaves of thistles, *Cirsium* species (Asteraceae). *Cirsium horridulum* grows in the pinelands of the Lower Keys and may potentially be used as a host. The mature caterpillar varies in color from black to pale brown and has branching spines. The pupa also varies from dull gray to lusterous green with gold spots. Adults have been found during April, September, October, November, and December in the Keys.

STATUS: *Vanessa cardui* is not a permanent resident of Florida, but may be locally numerous on occasion, especially during the fall when individuals migrate southward through the state. The Painted Lady is sporadic in the Keys. Most records are from the Lower Keys.

100. AMERICAN PAINTED LADY   Pl. 16, Fig. 100
Vanessa virginiensis (Drury)

DESCRIPTION: FW = 23-32 mm. Like *Vanessa cardui*, the American Painted Lady is orange with dark markings on the wings above. The ground color, however, is darker on the upper side and more reddish on the underside of the forewing. *Vanessa virginiensis* is easily distinguished by the two relatively large eyespots on the underside of the hindwing. The sexes are similar.

DISTRIBUTION: Elliott Key, Key Largo, Sugarloaf Key.

Vanessa virginiensis occurs throughout Florida and much of North America into the highlands of Central America and northern South America. It also occurs in the Greater Antilles, and we have encountered breeding populations in the mountains of Hispaniola.

NATURAL HISTORY: The American Painted Lady may turn up in many different habitats in the Keys. We have found individuals along beaches and at the edges of salt marshes and tropical hammocks. Adults perch on the ground or foliage and sometimes visit flowers. The flight is rapid. Eggs are laid singly on the leaves and flowers of *Gnaphalium* species (Asteraceae), but this species probably does not breed in the Keys. The caterpillar is handsomely banded with yellow and black. There are two rows of white spots on the dorsum, and the body is armed with branching spines. The head is black. Pupae vary from gray to lusterous green. Adults have been found in May, June, and October in the Keys.

FLOWERS VISITED: *Avicennia germinans, Borrichia frutescens.*

STATUS: The American Painted Lady is sporadic in distribution and abundance in southern Florida. The few records from the Keys are probably strays from the mainland.

SUBFAMILY CHARAXINAE
(Leaf Wing Butterflies)

This tropical group is poorly represented in Florida. One species inhabits the northern part of the state, and the Florida Leaf Wing is found in the tropical pinelands of the southeastern coast and Keys. Adult charaxines are often brightly colored above, but mimic dead leaves below. Although flowers are rarely visited, the adults may feed at fermenting fruit, fresh droppings, or urine. The larvae lack spines but have small knobs on the head. The pupa is somewhat similar to that of the danaines in shape.

101. FLORIDA LEAF WING

Pl. 20, Fig. 101

Anaea troglodyta floridalis **Johnson and Comstock**

DESCRIPTION: FW = 34-38 mm. The Florida Leaf Wing is mostly reddish-orange above, with a dark spot in the forewing cell, a dark postmedial line, and dark borders. The hindwing has a short tail. The undersides are grayish with dark striations. There are a few small dark spots near the base of the tails. Females tend to be larger and have darker markings above than males.

DISTRIBUTION: Big Pine Key.

Anaea troglodyta floridalis occurs only in south Florida. Six other races of *A. troglodyta* are found in the Greater Antilles and northern Lesser Antilles. Another subspecies also occurs in Mexico and Central America.

NATURAL HISTORY: The Florida Leaf Wing flies in open tropical pinelands near patches of the larval host plant. Adults perch on the foliage of trees and shrubs and make short flights if disturbed. This butterfly may be protected from predators by foul tasting chemicals. Rutkowski (1971) observed an adult become entangled in the web of an unidentified spider, which immediately tasted and then discarded the butterfly. Eggs are laid singly on the leaves of woolly croton, *Croton linearis* (Euphorbiaceae). The larvae eat the leaves and live exposed on the plant. The last instar caterpillar is green with a yellow lateral stripe curved upward to a pair of dark spots on the dorsum of the second abdominal segment (Plate 29). The dorsum of the last two abdominal segments also has some dark patches. The body is covered with small whitish tubercles, giving it a granular appearance. The head is light green and lacks horns, but is covered with numerous small, whitish protuberances. There are several larger orange protuberances on the top and sides of the head, and a pair of black ones on top. The pupa is pale green, with a light yellow transverse ridge on the dorsum of the abdomen and yellow around the margins of the wing cases. Adults have been reported from every month of the year in the Keys. Dale H. Habeck and M. K. Hennessey (pers. comm.) found eggs of the Florida Leaf Wing all months of the year as well.

FLOWERS VISITED: *Serenoa repens* (Habeck and Hennessey, pers. comm.); rotting grapefruit (Schwartz 1987). Lenczewski (1980) remarked that adults often sip water from the edges of mud puddles in Everglades National Park.

STATUS: The Florida Leaf Wing is locally abundant in the tropical pinelands of Big Pine Key. This species has lost habitat on the mainland due to urban development, but is abundant in the rimrock areas of Everglades National Park.

SUBFAMILY SATYRINAE
(Satyrs and Wood Nymphs)

Wood nymph butterflies are typically of medium size, dull coloration, and are usually adorned with eyespots on the wings. Several of the wing veins are swollen at the base. Adults tend to fly low to the ground and are frequently attracted to fermenting fruit. The eggs may be round to slightly elongate, and are smooth or sculptured. The larva has a bifurcate anal plate and often a pair of short horns on the head. Grasses are the usual hosts. Pupae are angular and vary from green to brown. Only two satyrines occur in southern Florida, neither of which are resident in the Keys.

102. CAROLINA SATYR
Hermeuptychia sosybius (Fabricius)

Pl. 20, Fig. 102

DESCRIPTION: FW = 16-19 mm. The Carolina Satyr is a small, plainly marked butterfly. The upper side is a uniform dark brown. The ventral surface is light brown with two darker lines across the middle of the wings. The forewing usually has a small eyespot near the apex below. There is a row of eyespots near the outer margin of the ventral hindwing consisting of two relatively large spots and one or more smaller ones. The sexes are similar.

DISTRIBUTION: Key Largo.

Hermeuptychia sosybius is found throughout Florida and the southeastern United States. This taxon is part of the *Hermeuptyphia hermes* (Fabricius) species complex which is widely distributed in North, Central, and South America.

NATURAL HISTORY: The Carolina Satyr inhabits shaded grassy areas. Adults have a bouncing flight low to the ground. This drab little butterfly is easily attracted to rotting fruit but rarely visits flowers. The round, pale green eggs are laid singly on low-growing grasses. The caterpillar is light green with a row of tiny white spots along the side. Pupae are green with brown spots and striations.

STATUS: A colony of the Carolina Satyr was at one time established in a trash dump on northern Key Largo (H. D. Baggett, pers. comm.) near what is now called Mahogany Hammock. Small patches of St. Augustine grass, a larval host plant, grow at this site. The grass, however, was clearly introduced with lawn trash. The butterfly no longer seems to be present. There are no other records of *Hermeuptychia sosybius* from the Keys. The Carolina Satyr is abundant on the southern mainland.

103. GEORGIA SATYR
Neonympha areolata areolata (J. E. Smith)

Pl. 20, Fig. 103

DESCRIPTION: FW = 16-18 mm. The Georgia Satyr is plain brown above, but below the wings are prettily marked with orange lines. The ventral hindwing also has a row of well-developed, teardrop-shaped eyespots. Males and females are similar in appearance.

DISTRIBUTION: Big Pine Key, Key Largo, Lignumvitae Key.

The Georgia Satyr occurs in the southeastern United States. A disjunct population in New Jersey has been described as a separate race.

NATURAL HISTORY: The Georgia Satyr is found in open wet prairies with an abundance of grasses and sedges. The adults fly low to the ground, within the cover of the vegetation. The green-colored larvae feed on the leaves of sedges. Adults have been taken in September in the Keys.

STATUS: Although locally abundant in wet prairies on the southern mainland, the Georgia Satyr is rare in the Keys. Stray individuals have been taken in both the Upper and Lower Keys. Leroy Koehn (pers. comm.) reported taking one on Key Largo as it flew across from the mainland on the Card Sound Bridge.

SUBFAMILY DANAINAE
(Milkweed Butterflies)

Many milkweed butterflies feed as larvae on members of the Asclepiadaceae (milkweeds) and gain protection from vertebrate predators by using poisonous compounds taken from the plants for their own defense. The adults tend to be contrastingly patterned, large butterflies with slow, fluttering flight behavior. The eggs are elongate and ribbed. Larvae are usually brightly colored and have several pairs of fleshy filaments on the body. The pupae are compact and often are adorned with gold spots. The Queen butterfly is the only resident member of the group in the Keys, but Monarchs may also be locally common during the fall.

104. SOLDIER BUTTERFLY
Pl. 21, Fig. 104
Danaus eresimus tethys Forbes

DESCRIPTION: FW = 30-44.5 mm. The Soldier has a yellowish-brown ground color above. The outer borders are black with two rows of small white spots. The forewing has larger white spots near the end of the cell and in a postmedial line. The ventral hindwing is light brown with the veins outlined in black. There is also a characteristic postmedial band of faint spots on the hindwing below. Males have a conspicuous scent pouch on the upperside of the hindwing.
DISTRIBUTION: Elliott Key, Key Largo, Lower Matecumbe Key, Upper Matecumbe Key.
   Danaus eresimus tethys is found in south Florida and the Greater Antilles. Other races occur widely on the mainland from Mexico into South America.
NATURAL HISTORY: The Soldier frequents shrubby disturbed sites in south Florida. Adults have a lazy flight pattern and frequently visit flowers for nectar. The yellowish eggs are laid singly on the young growth of white vine, *Sarcostemma clausum* (Asclepidaceae). The larva is gray with transverse yellow and black stripes and a broad white lateral stripe. The head is white with narrow black stripes. There are pairs of fleshy filaments on the dorsum of the second thoracic, second abdominal, and eighth abdominal segments. The pupa is green with golden spots. Adults have been found in May, June, and November in the Keys.
FLOWERS VISITED: *Bidens alba.*
STATUS: Kimball (1965) listed few records of this species from Florida; however, the Soldier is now locally abundant in the southern part of the state. Although the larval host plant grows abundantly at the edges of salt marshes and disturbed sites throughout the Keys, only a few stray individuals have been reported from the Upper Keys.

105. QUEEN BUTTERFLY
Pl. 21, Fig. 105
Danaus gilippus berenice (Godart)

DESCRIPTION: FW = 37-43 mm. The Queen butterfly is similar to *Danaus eresimus*, but has a much darker ground color and lacks the row of faint spots on the underside of the hindwing characteristic of the Soldier. Males have black scent pouches on the upper sides of the hindwings.
DISTRIBUTION: Big Pine Key, Elliott Key, Key Largo, Key Vaca, Key West, Lignumvitae Key, Old Rhodes Key, Plantation Key, Stock Island, Sugarloaf Key (?), Summerland Key, Upper Matecumbe Key.

Danaus gilippus berenice is found in the southeastern United States (primarily Florida), the Bahamas, Cuba, and the Cayman Islands. Two other endemic races occur on Jamaica and Hispaniola-Puerto Rico. Other subspecies are found on the mainland from the southwestern United States southward into South America.

NATURAL HISTORY: The Queen occurs most often in open habitats such as salt marshes and tropical pinelands. Adults fly slowly and frequently visit flowers. The eggs are laid singly on the new growth of white vine (*Sarcostemma clausum*). Other plants in the milkweed family (Asclepiadaceae) such as *Asclepias* spp. and *Cynanchum* spp. may also be used in the Keys. The larva is transversely striped with yellow, black, and white (see color photo 33 in Pyle, 1981). There are three pairs of black fleshy filaments as in *D. eresimus*. The head is white with black stripes. Pupae are green with small golden spots. Adults have been found every month of the year in the Keys.

FLOWERS VISITED: *Bidens alba, Borrichia arborescens, Flaveria linearis, Morinda royoc, Sesuvium portulacastrum, Solanum blodgettii.*

STATUS: Although locally abundant on the southern mainland, the Queen is variably present in the Keys. On Elliott Key, the Queen is a temporary colonizer; it is sometimes abundant, but more typically is uncommon or absent.

106. MONARCH BUTTERFLY
Danaus plexippus plexippus (Linnaeus)

Pl. 21, Fig. 106

DESCRIPTION: FW = 45-53 mm. The Monarch is easily distinguished by its large size, orange ground color, and black borders and wing veins. The apical spots on the dorsal forewing are mostly light orange in the typical race, and white in the West Indian subspecies, *Danaus plexippus megalippe* (Hübner). Males have black scent pouches on the hindwings.

DISTRIBUTION: Adams Key, Big Pine Key, Craig Key, Elliott Key, Key Largo, Key Vaca, Key West, Lignumvitae Key, No Name Key, Stock Island, Sugarloaf Key.

The Monarch occurs in much of North, Central, and South America. This majestic butterfly has also become established on certain islands in the Pacific such as Hawaii, in Australia and New Zealand, India, and other parts of the Old World (Scott, 1986a). Stray individuals of the West Indian race, *Danaus plexippus megalippe*, have been taken on Key West and Key Largo.

NATURAL HISTORY: Monarchs frequent open habitats, including urban areas, disturbed sites, beaches, and tropical pinelands. Adults fly slowly, often gliding, and visit flowers for nectar. The eggs are laid on the new growth of milkweeds, *Asclepias* spp. (Asclepidaceae). It is not known if the Monarch breeds in the Keys, but *Asclepias viridis* grows on Big Pine Key and *Asclepias curassavica* is sometimes found in disturbed sites. The caterpillar is transversely striped with yellow, black, and white. There are only two pairs of black fleshy filaments, one pair on the second thoracic and the other on the eighth abdominal segments. The pupa is pale green with golden spots (see color photo 35 in Pyle, 1981). South Florida populations of the Monarch do not migrate, but elsewhere in the state, this butterfly is usually only seasonally present during the spring and fall. Monarchs have been recorded in the Keys in January, March, August, September, October, November, and December.

FLOWERS VISITED: *Bourreria ovata, Lantana involucrata, Pithecellobium keyense, Senecio mexicana.* Several individuals were observed drinking dew from the grass early in the morning on Elliott Key, 24 October 1987.

STATUS: The Monarch may be abundant in the Keys during the fall when migrating adults fly southward through Florida enroute to overwintering sites in Mexico (Fig. 53).   At other times, strays from the resident populations on the mainland or rare individuals of race *megalippe* turn up in the Keys.

Fig. 53. Monarch migration to overwintering sites (after Urquhart, 1976).

CHECK LIST OF THE BUTTERFLIES OF THE FLORIDA KEYS

HESPERIIDAE

Subfamily PYRGINAE (Broad-Winged Skippers)

_____ 1. *Epargyreus zestos zestos* (Geyer) - Zestos Skipper
_____ 2. *Ephyriades brunnea floridensis* Bell and Comstock - Florida Dusky Wing
_____ 3. *Erynnis zarucco* (Lucas) - Zarucco Dusky Wing
_____ 4. *Gorgythion begga pyralinus* (Möschler) - Variegated Skipper
_____ 5. *Phocides pigmalion okeechobee* (Worthington) - Mangrove Skipper
_____ 6. *Polygonus leo savigny* (Latreille) - Hammock Skipper
_____ 7. *Pyrgus oileus oileus* (Linnaeus) - Tropical Checkered Skipper
_____ 8. *Staphylus hayhurstii* (W. H. Edwards) - Southern Sooty Wing
_____ 9. *Urbanus dorantes dorantes* (Stoll) - Dorantes Skipper
_____10. *Urbanus proteus proteus* (Linnaeus) - Long-Tailed Skipper

Subfamily HESPERIINAE (Grass Skippers)

_____11. *Asbolis capucinus* (Lucas) - Monk Skipper
_____12. *Atalopedes campestris huron* (W. H. Edwards) - Field Skipper
_____13. *Calpodes ethlius* (Stoll) - Canna Skipper
_____14. *Copaeodes minima* (W. H. Edwards) - Southern Skipperling
_____15. *Cymaenes tripunctus tripunctus* (Herrich-Schäffer) - Three Spot Skipper
_____16. *Euphyes arpa* (Boisduval and Leconte) - Palmetto Skipper
_____17. *Euphyes pilatka pilatka* (W. H. Edwards) - Sawgrass Skipper
_____   *Euphyes pilatka klotsi* Miller, Harvey, Miller - Klots' Sawgrass Skipper
_____18. *Hesperia meskei* (W. H. Edwards) - Rockland Grass Skipper
_____19. *Hylephila phyleus phyleus* (Drury) - Fiery Skipper
_____20. *Lerema accius accius* (J. E. Smith) - Clouded Skipper
_____21. *Lerodea eufala* (W. H. Edwards) - Eufala Skipper
_____22. *Nastra neamathla* (Skinner and Williams) - Neamathla Skipper
_____23. *Nyctelius nyctelius nyctelius* (Latreille) - Nyctelius Skipper
_____24. *Oligoria maculata* (W. H. Edwards) - Twin Spot Skipper
_____25. *Panoquina ocola ocola* (W. H. Edwards) - Ocola Skipper
_____26. *Panoquina panoquin* (Scudder) - Salt Marsh Skipper
_____27. *Panoquina panoquinoides panoquinoides* (Skinner) - Obscure Skipper
_____28. *Polites vibex vibex* (Geyer) - Whirlabout
_____29. *Wallengrenia otho* (J. E. Smith) - Broken Dash

PAPILIONIDAE

Subfamily PAPILIONINAE (Swallowtails)

_____30. *Battus polydamas lucayus* Rothschild and Jordan - Polydamas Swallowtail
_____31. *Eurytides celadon* Lucas - Cuban Kite Swallowtail
_____32. *Eurytides marcellus floridensis* (Holland) - Zebra Swallowtail
_____33. *Papilio andraemon bonhotei* Sharpe - Bahama Swallowtail
_____34. *Papilio aristodemus ponceanus* Schaus - Schaus Swallowtail
_____35. *Papilio cresphontes* Cramer - Giant Swallowtail
_____36. *Papilio palamedes* Drury - Palamedes Swallowtail
_____37. *Papilio polyxenes asterius* Stoll - Eastern Black Swallowtail

PIERIDAE

Subfamily PIERINAE (Whites)

_____38. *Appias drusilla neumoegenii* (Skinner) - Florida White
_____39. *Ascia monuste phileta* (Fabricius) - Great Southern White
_____ *Ascia monuste evonima* (Boisduval) - Caribbean White
_____40. *Pieris rapae* (Linnaeus) - European Cabbage Butterfly
_____41. *Pontia protodice* (Boisduval and Leconte) - Checkered White

Subfamily COLIADINAE (Sulphurs)

_____42. *Anteos maerula* (Fabricius) - Giant Brimstone
_____43. *Aphrissa orbis orbis* (Poey) - Orbed Sulphur
_____44. *Aphrissa statira floridensis* (Neumoegen) - Statira Sulphur
_____45. *Colias eurytheme* Boisduval - Orange Sulphur
_____46. *Eurema boisduvaliana* (Felder and Felder) - Boisduval's Sulphur
_____47. *Eurema daira daira* (Godart) - Barred Sulphur
_____ *Eurema daira palmira* (Poey) - Caribbean Barred Sulphur
_____48. *Eurema dina helios* M. Bates - Bush Sulphur
_____49. *Eurema lisa lisa* Boisduval and Leconte - Little Sulphur
_____50. *Eurema nicippe* (Cramer) - Sleepy Orange
_____51. *Eurema nise nise* (Cramer) - Jamaican Sulphur
_____52. *Kricogonia lyside* (Godart) - Guayacan Sulphur
_____53. *Nathalis iole* Boisduval - Dainty Sulphur
_____54. *Phoebis agarithe maxima* (Neumoegen) - Large Orange Sulphur
_____55. *Phoebis philea philea* (Johansson) - Orange-Barred Sulphur
_____56. *Phoebis sennae eubule* (Linnaeus) - Cloudless Sulphur
_____ *Phoebis sennae sennae* (Linnaeus) - Caribbean Cloudless Sulphur

LYCAENIDAE

Subfamily EUMAEINAE (Hairstreaks)

_____57. *Calycopis cecrops* (Fabricius) - Red-Banded Hairstreak
_____58. *Chlorostrymon maesites* (Herrich-Schäffer) - Maesites Hairstreak
_____59. *Chlorostrymon simaethis simaethis* (Drury) - St. Christopher's Hairstreak
_____60. *Electrostrymon angelia angelia* (Hewitson) - Fulvous Hairstreak
_____61. *Electrostrymon endymion* (Fabricius) - Ruddy Hairstreak
_____62. *Eumaeus atala florida* Röber - Atala Hairstreak
_____63. *Strymon acis bartrami* (Comstock and Huntington) - Bartram's Hairstreak
_____64. *Strymon columella modestus* (Maynard) - Modest Hairstreak
_____65. *Strymon limenia* (Hewitson) - Disguised Hairstreak
_____66. *Strymon martialis* (Herrich-Schäffer) - Cuban Gray Hairstreak
_____67. *Strymon melinus melinus* Hübner - Gray Hairstreak
_____68. *Tmolus azia* (Hewitson) - Light-Banded Hairstreak

Subfamily POLYOMMATINAE (Blues)

_____69. *Brephidium isophthalma pseudofea* (Morrison) - Eastern Pigmy Blue
_____70. *Hemiargus ammon ammon* Lucas - Lucas' Blue
_____71. *Hemiargus ceraunus antibubastus* Hübner - Ceraunus Blue
_____72. *Hemiargus thomasi bethunebakeri* Comstock and Huntington - Miami Blue
_____73. *Leptotes cassius theonus* (Lucas) - Cassius Blue

RIODINIDAE

Subfamily RIODININAE (Metalmarks)

_____74. *Calephelis virginiensis* (Guérin-Ménéville) - Little Metalmark

LIBYTHEIDAE

(Snout Butterflies)

_____75. *Libytheana bachmanii* (Kirtland) - Bachman's Snout Butterfly

NYMPHALIDAE

Subfamily HELICONIINAE (Passion Flower Butterflies)

_____76. *Agraulis vanillae nigrior* Michener - Gulf Fritillary

_____77. *Dryadula phaetusa* (Linnaeus) - Banded Orange
_____78. *Dryas iulia largo* Clench - Julia Butterfly
_____79. *Heliconius charitonius tuckeri* Comstock and Brown - Zebra Butterfly

Subfamily NYMPHALINAE (Brush-Footed Butterflies)

_____80. *Anartia chrysopelea* Hübner - Cuban Peacock
_____81. *Anartia jatrophae guantanamo* Munroe - White Peacock
_____82. *Diaethria clymena* (Cramer) - Eighty-Eight Butterfly
_____83. *Eresia frisia frisia* (Poey) - Cuban Cresent
_____84. *Eunica monima* (Stoll) - Dingy Purple Wing
_____85. *Eunica tatila tatilista* Kaye - Florida Purple Wing
_____86. *Euptoieta claudia* (Cramer) - Variegated Fritillary
_____87. *Hamadryas amphichloe diasia* (Fruhstorfer) - Haitian Cracker
_____88. *Junonia coenia coenia* (Hübner) - Common Buckeye
_____89. *Junonia evarete* (Cramer) - Black Mangrove Buckeye
_____90. *Junonia genoveva* (Stoll) - Caribbean Buckeye
_____91. *Limenitis archippus floridensis* (Strecker) - Florida Viceroy
_____92. *Marpesia chiron* (Fabricius) - Many-Banded Dagger Wing
_____93. *Marpesia eleuchea eleuchea* Hübner - Cuban Dagger Wing
_____94. *Marpesia petreus petreus* (Cramer) - Ruddy Dagger Wing
_____95. *Phyciodes phaon* (W. H. Edwards) - Phaon Crescent
_____96. *Phyciodes tharos tharos* (Drury) - Pearl Crescent
_____97. *Siproeta stelenes biplagiata* (Fruhstorfer) - Malachite Butterfly
_____98. *Vanessa atalanta rubria* (Fruhstorfer) - Red Admiral
_____99. *Vanessa cardui* (Linnaeus) - Painted Lady Butterfly
_____100. *Vanessa virginiensis* (Drury) - American Painted Lady

Subfamily CHARAXINAE (Leaf Wing Butterflies)

_____101. *Anaea troglodyta floridalis* Johnson and Comstock - Florida Leaf Wing

Subfamily SATYRINAE (Satyrs and Wood Nymphs)

_____102. *Hermeuptychia sosybius* (Fabricius) - Carolina Satyr
_____103. *Neonympha areolata areolata* (J. E. Smith) - Georgia Satyr

Subfamily DANAINAE (Milkweed Butterflies)

_____104. *Danaus eresimus tethys* Forbe - Soldier Butterfly
_____105. *Danaus gilippus berenice* (Godart) - Queen Butterfly
_____106. *Danaus plexippus plexippus* (Linnaeus) - Monarch Butterfly
_____ *Danaus plexippus megalippe* Hübner - Caribbean Monarch Butterfly

LITERATURE CITED

Ackerman, B.
1957. *The Florida Keys.* Florida Department of Agriculture, Tallahassee, Florida. 58 pp.

Alexander, T. R.
1953. Plant succession on Key Largo, Florida involving *Pinus caribaea* and *Quercus virginiana*. *Quarterly Journal of the Florida Academy of Sciences*, 16: 133-138.
1967. A tropical hammock on the Miami (Florida) limestone - A twenty-five-year study. *Ecology*, 48: 863-867.
1968. Effect of Hurrican Betsy on the southeastern everglades. *Quarterly Journal of the Florida Academy of Sciences*, 30: 10-24.

Alvarez, L. W., W. Alvarez, F. A. Savo, and H. V. Michel
1980. Extraterrestrial cause for the Cretaceous-Tertiary extinction. *Science*, 208: 1095-1108.

Anderson, R. A.
1974. Three new United States records (Lycaenidae and Nymphalidae) and other unusual captures from the Lower Florida Keys. *Journal of the Lepidopterists' Society*, 28: 354-358.

Baggett, H. D.
1982. Lepidoptera. Pp. 72-81. *In* R. Franz (ed.), *The Rare and Endangered Biota of Florida*. Volume 6. Invertebrates. University Presses of Florida, Gainesville. 131 pp.

Bates, M.
1934. Notes on some tropical Florida butterflies (Lepid.: Rhopalocera). *Entomological News*, 45: 166-169.

Bell, E. L., and W. P. Comstock
1948. A new genus and some new species and subspecies of American Hesperiidae (Lepidoptera; Rhopalocera). *American Museum Novitates*, No. 1379: 23 pp.

Bennett, R., and E. C. Knudson
1976. Additional new butterfly records from Florida. *Journal of the Lepidopterists' Society,* 30: 234- 235.

Brown, C. H.
1976. A colony of *Papilio aristodemus ponceanus* (Lepidoptera: Papilionidae) in the upper Florida Keys. *Journal of the Georgia Entomological Society*, 11: 117-118.

Brown, F. M.
1978. The origins of the West Indian butterfly fauna. Pp. 5-30. *In* F. B. Gill (ed.). *Zoogeography in the Caribbean*. Academy of Natural Sciences Philadelphia, Special Publication 13. 128 pp.

Brown, F. M., and B. Heineman
1972. *Jamaica and Its Butterflies*. E. W. Classey, London. 478 pp.

Brown, L. N.
1973a. Populations of a new swallowtail butterfly found in the Florida Keys. *Florida Naturalist,* April 1973: 25.

1973b. Populations of *Papilio andraemon bonhotei* Sharpe and *Papilio aristodemus ponceanus* Schaus (Papilionidae) in Biscayne National Monument, Florida. *Journal of the Lepidopterists' Society,* 27(2): 136-140.
1974. Haven for rare butterflies. *National Parks and Conservation Magazine,* July 1974: 10-13.

Butler, J. F., and H. A. Denmark
1990. Tick (Acari: Ixodidae) vectors of Lyme Disease organisms (*Borrelia burgdorferi*) in Florida. Florida Department of Agriculture and Consumer Services Entomology Circular 326. 6 pp.

Calhoun, J. V.
1988. Aberrant Polyommatinae (Lycaenidae) from Ohio and Florida. *Journal of Research on the Lepidoptera*, 26: 264-266.
1989. Observations of *Eurema nise* in Florida. *Southern Lepidopterist's News*, 11: 35-36.

Calhoun, J. V., and R. A. Anderson
1991. A review of the status of *Eurema daira palmira* (Poey) (Pieridae) in Florida, including additional records from the lower Florida Keys. *Journal of the Lepidopterists' Society*, 45: 58-62.

Carey, B.
1986. Biscayne National Park. Pp. 46-73. *In* J. V. Murfin, D. Young, J. Norton, and A. Sanghri (eds.). *The Sierra Club Guides to the National Parks of the East and Middle West*. Stewart, Tabori and Chang, New York. 395 pp.

Carroll, S. P.
1987. Contrasts in reproductive ecology between temperate and tropical populations of *Jadera haematoloma*, a mate-guarding hemipteran (Rhopalidae). *Annals of the Entomological Society of America*, 81: 54-63.

Chermock, R. L.
1946. Migration in *Ascia monuste phileta* (Lepidoptera, Pieridae). *Entomological News*, 57: 144-146.

Chermock, R. L., and O. D. Chermock
1947. Notes on the life histories of three Floridian butterflies. *Canadian Entomologist*, 79: 142-144.

Clench, H. K.
1970. New or unusual butterfly records from Florida. *Journal of the Lepidopterists' Society,* 24: 240- 244.

Clench, H. K., and K. A. Bjorndal
1980. Butterflies of Great and Little Inagua, Bahamas. *Annals of Carnegie Museum*, 49: 1-30.

Correll, D. S., and H. B. Correll
1982. *Flora of the Bahama Archipelago (including the Turks and Caicos Islands)*. A. R. Gantner Verlag, Vaduz, Liechtenstein. 1692 pp.

Dickson, J. D., III, R. O. Woodbury, and T. R. Alexander
1953. Check list of the flora of Big Pine Key, Florida and surrounding keys. *Quarterly Journal of the Florida Academy of Sciences*, 16: 181-197.

Dyar, H. G.
1897. Life-history of *Erycides amyntas* Fab. *Entomological News*, 8: 182-183.

Emmel, T. C., and G. T. Austin
1990. The tropical rain forest butterfly fauna of Rondonia, Brazil: species diversity and conservation. *Tropical Lepidoptera*, 1: 1-12.

Emmel, T. C., and J. B. Heppner
1992. Papilionidae. *In* J. B. Heppner (ed.), *Atlas of North American Lepidoptera*, 5(95): 1-33. Gainesville: Assoc. Trop. Lepid.

Emmel, T. C., and M. C. Minno
1988. *Habitat requirements and status of the endemic Schaus Swallowtail in the Florida Keys.* Final Report. Florida Game and Fresh Water Fish Commission, Division of Nongame Wildlife, Tallahassee, Florida. 202 pp.

Fairbridge, R. W.
1984. The Holocene sea-level record in south Florida. Pp. 427-435. *In* P. J. Geason (ed.). *Environments of South Florida: Present and Past.* II. Miami Geological Society, Coral Gables, Florida. 552 pp.

Funk, R. S.
1966. Record of *Eumaeus atala* (Lycaenidae) from the Florida Keys. *Journal of the Lepidopterists' Society*, 20: 216.

Gentry, R. E.
1974. Early families of Upper Matecumbe. *Tequesta*, 34: 57-63.

Gerberg, E. J., and R. H. Arnett, Jr.
1989. *Florida Butterflies.* Natural Science Publications. Baltimore, Maryland. 90 pp.

Gilbert, L. E.
1984. The biology of butterfly communities. Pp. 1-54. *In* R. I. Vane-Wright and P. A. Ackery (eds.). *The Biology of Butterflies.* Academic Press, London. 429 pp.

Harlen, P. W.
1979. Aerial photographic interpretation of the historical changes in northern Biscayne Bay, Florida. *University of Miami, Sea Grant Technical Bulletin No. 40.* 23 pp.

Harvey, D. J., and J. Longino
1989. Myrmecophily and larval food plants of *Brephidium isophthalma pseudofea* (Lycaenidae) in the Florida Keys. *Journal of the Lepidopterists' Society,* 43: 332-333.

Hathway, T. R.
[Undated]. *Key Largo, Island home.* The Key Largo Foundation, Coral Gables, Florida. 94 pp.

Healy, J. L.
1910. The larva of *Eumaeus atala. Entomological News,* 21: 179-180.

Heppner, J. B.
1975. The bean leaf roller, *Urbanus proteus* and the related *Urbanus dorantes* in Florida (Lepidoptera: Hesperiidae). *Journal of the Georgia Entomological Society,* 10: 328-332.
1992. Classification of the Lepidoptera, with keys to families of the world. *Tropical Lepidoptera,* 3 (Suppl. 3): [in press].

Hildebrand, A. R., and W. V. Boynton
1991. Cretaceous ground zero. *Natural History,* June (1991): 46-53.

Hodges, R. W., T. Dominick, D. R. Davis, D. C. Ferguson, J. G. Franclemont, E. G. Munroe, and J. A. Powell (eds.)
1983. *Check list of the Lepidoptera of America north of Mexico, including Greenland.* E. W. Classey, Faringdon, England, and the Wedge Entomological Research Foundation, Washington, D. C. xxiv + 284 pp.

Hoffmeister, J. E., and H. G. Multer
1968. Geology and origin of the Florida Keys. *Bulletin of the Geological Society of America,* 79: 1487-1502.

Howard, R. A.
1950. Vegetation of the Bimini Island group, Bahamas, B. W. I. *Ecological Monographs,* 20: 319-349.

Howe, W. H.
1975. *The Butterflies of North America.* Doubleday, Garden City, New York. 633 pp.

Jenkins, D. W.
1983. Neotropical Nymphalidae I. Revision of *Hamadryas. Bulletin of the Allyn Museum,* No. 81. 146 pp.
1990. Neotropical Nymphalidae VIII. Revision of *Eunica. Bulletin of the Allyn Museum,* No. 131. 177 pp.

Johnson, K.
1989. Revision of *Chlorostrymon* Clench and description of two new austral neotropical species (Lycaenidae). *Journal of the Lepidopterists' Society,* 43: 120-146.

Kimball, C. P.
1965. The Lepidoptera of Florida. An Annotated Checklist. Florida Department of Agriculture, Division of Plant Industry, Gainesville. *Arthropods of Florida and Neighboring Land Areas,* 1: 1-363.

Klots, A. B.
1951. *A Field Guide to the Butterflies of North America, east of the Great Plains.* Houghton-Mifflin, Boston. 349 pp.

Lamas, G.
1983. How many butterfly species in your backyard? *News of the Lepidopterists' Society,* July/Aug (1983): 53-55.

Lawrence, P. O.
1972. The Jamaican 'Orange Dog', *Papilio andraemon* (Lepidoptera: Papilionidae). *Florida Entomologist,* 55: 243-246.

Lazell, J. D., Jr.
1989. *Wildlife of the Florida Keys: A Natural History.* Island Press, Washington, D. C. 254 pp.

Lenczewski, B.
1980. *Butterflies of Everglades National Park.* National

Park Service, South Florida Research Center, Homestead, Florida. Report T-588. 110 pp.

Leston, D., D. S. Smith, and B. Lenczewski
1982. Habitat, diversity, and immigration in a tropical island fauna: the butterflies of Lignumvitae Key, Florida. *Journal of the Lepidopterists' Society*, 36: 241-255.

Little, E. L.
1978. *Atlas of United States Trees. Volume 5. Florida.* U. S. Department of Agriculture Miscellaneous Publication No. 1362. vi + 283 pp.

Long, R. W.
1984. Origin of the vascular flora of southern Florida. Pp. 118-126. *In* P. J. Gleason (ed.). *Environments of South Florida. Present and Past. II.* Miami Geological Society, Coral Gables. 552 pp.

Long, R. W., and O. Lakela
1971. *A Flora of Tropical Florida.* University of Miami Press, Coral Gables. 962 pp.

Loope, L. L.
1980. *Phenology of flowering and fruiting in plant communities of Everglades National Park and Biscayne National Monument, Florida.* U. S. National Park Service, South Florida Research Center, Homestead, Florida. Report T-593. 50 pp.

MacArthur, R. H., and E. O. Wilson
1963. An equilibrium theory of insular zoogeography. *Evolution*, 17: 373-387.
1967. *The Theory of Island Biogeography.* Princeton University Press, Princeton, New Jersey. 203 pp.

McGuire, W. H.
1982. New oviposition and larval hostplant records for North American *Hesperia* (Rhopalocera: Hesperiidae). *Bulletin of the Allyn Museum*, 72: 6 pp.

Miller, L. D.
1978. *Electrostrymon angelia angelia* (Lycaenidae): The oldest Florida record? *Journal of the Lepidopterists' Society,* 32: 139-140.

Miller, L. D., and F. M. Brown
1981. A catalogue/checklist of the butterflies of America north of Mexico. *Memoir of the Lepidopterists' Society*, No. 2. 280 pp.

Miller, L. D., D. J. Harvey, and J. Y. Miller
1985. Notes on the genus *Euphyes* with description of a new subspecies (Lepidoptera: Hesperiidae). *Florida Entomologist*, 68: 323-335.

Miller, L. D., and J. Y. Miller
1989. The biogeography of West Indian butterflies (Lepidoptera: Papilionoidea, Hesperioidea): a vicariance model. Pp. 229-262. *In* C. A. Woods (ed.). *Biogeography of the West Indies. Past, Present, and Future.* Sandhill Crane Press, Gainesville, Florida. 878 pp.

National Oceanic and Atmospheric Administration
1988. *Climatological Data Annual Summary, Florida.* 92(13): 32 pp.

Niedhauk, C. A.
1969. Pioneering on Elliott Key, 1934-1935. *Tequesta*, 29: 27-44.
1973. *Charlotte's Story. Parts of an Undated Florida Key Diary, 1934-1935.* Published by the author, Islamorada, Florida. 205 pp.

Opler, P. A., and G. O. Krizek
1984. *Butterflies East of the Great Plains: an Illustrated Natural History.* The Johns Hopkins University Press, Baltimore. 294 pp. + 54 pls.

Otero, L. D.
1990. The stridulatory organ in *Hamadryas* (Nymphalidae): preliminary observations. *Journal of the Lepidopterists' Society,* 44: 285-288.

Peck, S. B., and H. F. Howden
1985. Biogeography of scavenging scarab beetles in the Florida Keys: post-Pleistocene land-bridge islands. *Canadian Journal of Zoology*, 63: 2730-2737.

Perfit, M. R., and E. E. Williams
1989. Geological contraints [sic] and biological retrodictions [sic]in the evolution of the Caribbean Sea and its islands. Pp. 47-102. *In* C. A. Woods (ed.). *Biogeography of the West Indies. Past, Present, and Future.* Sandhill Crane Press. Gainesville, Florida. 878 pp.

Poley, R.
1989. Florida's rare atala butterfly. *Florida Wildlife*, 43: 23-26.

Pyle, R. M.
1981. *The Audubon Society Field Guide to North American Butterflies.* Alfred A. Knopf, New York. 916 pp.

Ray, A. A. (ed.)
1982. *SAS User's Guide: Statistics.* SAS Institute, Inc., Cary, North Carolina. 584 pp.

Rawson, G. W.
1961a. The recent rediscovery of *Eumaeus atala* (Lycaenidae) in southern Florida. *Journal of the Lepidopterists' Society*, 15: 237-244.
1961b. The early stages of *Brephidium pseudofea* (Morrison) (Lepidoptera, Lycaenidae). *Journal of the New York Entomological Society*, 69: 88-91.

Richards, P. W.
1952. *The Tropical Rain Forest: An Ecological Study.* Cambridge University Press, Cambridge, U.K. 450 pp.

Riley, N. D.
1975. *A Field Guide to the Butterflies of the West Indies.* William Collins Sons and Co., London. 224 pp. + 24 pls.

Robbins, R. K.
1981. The "falsehead" hypothesis: predation and wing pattern variation of lycaenid butterflies. *American Naturalist*, 18: 770-775.

Rosen, D. E.
1976. A vicariance model of Caribbean biogeography. *Systematic Zoology*, 24: 431-464.

Rutkowski, F.
1971. Notes on some South Florida Lepidoptera. *Journal of the Lepidopterists' Society,* 25: 137-139.

Schwartz, A.
1987. The butterflies of the Lower Florida Keys. *Milwaukee Public Museum Contribution in Biology and Geology,* No. 73. 34 pp.
1989. *The Butterflies of Hispaniola.* University of Florida Press, Gainesville. 580 pp.

Schwarz, E. A.
1888. Notes on *Eumaeus atala. Insect Life,* 1: 37-40.

Scott, J. A.
[1971].A list of Antillean butterflies. *Journal of Research on the Lepidoptera,* 9: 249-256 (1970).
1972. Biogeography of Antillean butterflies. *Biotropica,* 4: 32-45.
1986a. *The Butterflies of North America.* Stanford University Press, Stanford, California. 583 pp.
1986b. Distribution of Caribbean butterflies. *Papilio* (new series), 3: 1-26.

Shields, O., and S. K. Dvorak
1979. Butterfly distribution and continental drift between the Americas, the Caribbean and Africa. *Journal of Natural History,* 13: 221-250.

Slosson, A. T.
1901. A successful failure. *Entomological News,* 12: 200-203, 236-239.

Small, J. K.
1913. *Flora of the Florida Keys.* Published by the author, New York. 162 pp.

Smith, D. S., D. Leston, and B. Lenczewski
1982. Variation in *Eurema daira* (Lepidoptera: Pieridae) and the status of *palmira* in southern Florida. *Bulletin of the Allyn Museum,* No. 70. 8 pp.

Snyder, J. R., A. Herndon, and W. B. Robertson, Jr.
1990. *South Florida Rockland.* Pp. 230-277. *In* R. L. Meyers and J. J. Ewel (eds.). *Ecosytems of Florida.* University of Central Florida Press, Orlando. 765 pp.

Tebeau, C. W.
1971. *A History of Florida.* University of Miami Press, Coral Gables, Florida. 502 pp.

Tomlinson, P. B.
1980. *The Biology of Trees Native to Tropical Florida.* M. M. Cabot Foundation, Harvard University, Cambridge, Mass. 480 pp.

Turner, T. W., and J. R. Parnell
1985. The identification of two species of *Junonia* Hübner (Lepidoptera: Nymphalidae): *J. evarete* and *J. genoveva* in Jamaica. *Journal of Research on the Lepidoptera,* 24: 142-153.

Urquhart, F. A.
1976. Found at last: the monarch's winter home. *National Geographic,* 150(2): 160-173.

Visher, S. S.
1925. Tropical cyclones from an ecological viewpoint. *Ecology,* 6: 117-122.

Walker, T. J.
1978. Migration and re-migration of butterflies through north peninsular Florida: quantification with Malaise traps. *Journal of the Lepidopterists' Society,* 32: 178-190.

White, W. A.
1970. The geomorphology of the Florida peninsula. *Florida Department of Natural Resources, Bureau of Geology, Tallahassee, Florida. Geological Bulletin* No. 51. 164 pp.

Williams, E. E.
1989. Old problems and new opportunities in West Indian biogeography. Pp. 1-46. *In* C. A. Woods (ed.). *Biogeography of the West Indies. Past, Present, and Future.* Sandhill Crane Press. Gainesville, Florida. 878 pp.

Wood, D. A.
1990. *Official lists of endangered and potentially endangered fauna and flora in Florida.* Florida Game and Fresh Water Fish Commission, Tallahassee, Florida. 23 pp.

Wunderlin, R. P.
1982. *Guide to the Vascular Plants of Central Florida.* University Presses of Florida, Gainesville. 472 pp.

GLOSSARY

ALLELE - one form of a gene.

ANDROCONIA - specialized scales that aid in the dissemination of pheromones.

APICULUS - the tapering portion of the antennal club in skipper butterflies.

CAUDAL - toward the posterior end.

COSTA - the anterior margin of the forewings and hindwings.

COSTAL FOLD - a narrow flap covering a patch of androconial scales along the anterior margin of the forewings of some male skipper butterflies.

DICOTYLEDON - member of the class of flowering plants characterized by the presence of two seed leaves.

DORSAL - the upper surface.

ENDEMIC - restricted to a particular locality or region.

FALCATE - sickle shaped.

GENITALIA - the reproductive organs.

GROUND COLOR - the color occupying most of the wing.

INSTAR - one of the several larval stages.

INTROGRESSION - the transfer of genes from one taxon to another by natural hybridization.

LEGUME - a member of the bean family (Fabaceae).

MONOCOTYLEDON - member of the class of flowering plants characterized by the presence of one seed leaf.

NEOTROPICAL - tropical areas of the Americas.

OSMETERIUM - the eversible, fleshy organ on the prothorax of swallowtail caterpillars that emits defensive chemicals.

PALPUS - three-segmented structure projecting in front of the face of adult moths and butterflies.

PHEROMONE - a chemical released by one individual that elicits a behavioral response in others of the same species, especially for mating.

PROTHORAX - the first of the three segments of the thorax, lying directly behind the head.

RACE - a geographically distinct form of a species.

SCLEROTIZED - hardened.

STIGMA - a patch of androconial scales located in the middle of the forewing of some male skipper butterflies.

SUBSPECIES - a race or geographical variant of a species.

TAXON - a scientifically recognized grouping of organisms.

TUBERCLE - a protuberance or projection on a larva or pupa.

TYPE SPECIMENS - the specimens examined and used to formally describe a particular taxon.

UNIVOLTINE - having a single generation each year.

VENTRAL - the underside.

Index to Butterfly Species